BERNADETT KECZER

Grab 'Em by the Bitcoins

Bitcoin, Blockchain, and the War for the Control of Society

To the Brave.

Contents

1

Interesting Times

E very generation has its own set of challenges to face and if you were suddenly transported into any historical era, you would probably find that the people of the day experienced their present as the most challenging of all times. However, independently of our self-centeredness, we can safely say that the beginning of the twenty-first century is a very important turning point on an evolutionary scale, and not just for our generation, when our knowledge base is increasing at an exponential rate. We are currently living the beginning of the most important societal transformation in human history, which makes the industrial revolution look like a change in fashion from one year to the next.

The rate of our technological evolution has been exponentially accelerating, so much so that the majority of people cannot keep up with it in understanding. The general population is definitely lagging behind our scientists and innovators, most people do not even understand how our basic household appliances work. And now, all of a sudden, we are being bombarded with headlines talking about artificial intelligence, nanotechnology, the possibility of the total connectedness of all appliances to a mass cloud computing system, robots for personal and household use, the future of robot workers, life extension via gene modification, and other things that twenty years ago would have sounded right out of science fiction.

There is a group of people who are striving to achieve physical immortality and they think it will be possible by merging with machines or downloading their minds into computers. And they really mean it. Not the normal conversation topic for people over fifty. It seems as if we had been plunged into another level of reality where technological possibilities are opening up which could radically widen the horizon of the human experience.

But the real catalyst of a possible complete overhaul of what we think of the economy, governance and society as a whole has been Bitcoin, an ingenious cryptocurrency which first appeared on the world stage in October 2008 in a whitepaper that proposed a peer-to-peer decentralized electronic cash, just at the right moment when the global financial crisis was causing worldwide turmoil and when people started to realize the inherent flaws in the financial system.

Bitcoin introduced a new technology called blockchain which can revolutionize how we do things in many areas of life. Blockchain technology promises to eliminate the need of a central organization to deal with any kind of transactions, including payments, contracts, and other forms of information exchange. Bitcoin could potentially be a valid substitute for the current corrupted and corruptible fiat currencies that are prone to inflation and are major tools of control over the lives of the many by the few.

Similarly to what happened during the beginning stages of the first industrial revolution, there are relatively few people today who can grasp the real potential of this technological evolution and the impact it may have not only on the economy and the concept of money, but also on the entire structure and functioning of our society.

The aim of this book is to give you a good understanding of what Bitcoin, cryptocurrencies, and the blockchain are, and what implications their appearance could have on you personally and on our world at large.

Even though Bitcoin and the blockchain technology have been appearing more and more often in the mass media in the past few years, we are not yet at the point of mass adoption. At the end of 2017 the market capitalization of Bitcoin and cryptocurrencies in general have reached an all time high due to the break-neck speed rise in the price of Bitcoin on cryptocurrency exchanges, which reached its all time maximum of nearly $20,000 on

December 18, 2017.

The mass media added to the hype and many people who were new to cryptocurrencies invested in Bitcoin in the hope of making a quick buck. The highest market capitalization of Bitcoin (on December 19, 2017) reached $320 billion, while the highest global market capitalization of the entire market, including all the available cryptocurrencies, was $828 billion in early January 2018.

When prices fell back quickly in a couple of days, Bitcoin and cryptocurrencies in general received a wave of negative media coverage. The thousands of people who jumped on the crypto bandwagon at the highest prices without any knowledge suffered a quick and devastating loss. The market has not recovered since December 2017 (and only started to reach $10,000 price levels again in June 2019), and the market capitalization of Bitcoin fell to a little over $110 billion, while the global market cap was hovering around $220 billion. By the time of writing this book the capitalization of Bitcoin has further shrunk down to $90 billion, while the global market capitalization decreased to $180 billion. Due to the June 2019 price increase when Bitcoin went above $10,000 again, the market capitalization of Bitcoin reached $228 billion and the total market capitalization of the crypto market grew to $370 billion.

Compared to these figures, Apple, Inc. reached its all time high of market capitalization in 2018 with $1.12 trillion. Over four times more than the entire cryptocurrency market. The global gold market's worth is $8 trillion. While these market capitalization figures exclude over-the-counter investment figures, it is clear that cryptocurrencies are just at the beginning of their journey, and interest for them is on the rise.

To date, Bitcoin has not had the easiest road toward mass adoption. Billionaires and important personalities in the global financial world have been bashing Bitcoin, talking about the Bitcoin bubble that was inevitably going to burst sooner than later, comparing Bitcoin to tulips (which is inherently a wrong comparison, taking into account that Bitcoin has a finite supply by design, as there can only be 21 million bitcoins, while tulips can propagate and propagate *ad infinitum*). Others made seemingly ludicrous claims, showing how certain they were that the value of Bitcoin would rise much more. John McAffee predicted that by 2020 the price of Bitcoin will reach $1 million.

After the big fall of the crypto market many people who bought into Bitcoin at peak prices abandoned and sold their coins at a substantial loss. A little later some of the same global players who earlier were bashing Bitcoin "changed their minds" and announced that they were now interested in investing in Bitcoin. Many of the big names, including George Soros, the Rockefellers, and the Rothschilds started to show "support" for, and invested in, Bitcoin.

Also, major banks, corporations, and various governments have been actively investigating how they could best implement the blockchain technology for their own interests, and many of them are already using blockchain. They also have been investing in cryptocurrency exchanges and blockchain development.

Even though the money invested in Bitcoin a little while ago was fifty times less than that in gold (which has a current global value of 8 trillion dollars)[1], in the past couple of years there has been a clear trend of exponential growth. While at the beginning of 2015 there were 3.1 million bitcoin wallets, this number increased to more than 25 million, and probably closer to 30 million, but many suggest that the usable wallets may hover around 25 million[2]. The velocity of adoption have been definitely increasing, but if we compare the 25 million Bitcoin wallets to the approximately 7.5 billion people in the world, that is still only around 0.33 percent of the global population. Not counting children and the elderly, that would leave us with approximately 1% of the worldwide adult population.

However, we get a more precise picture if we look at specifically the most "advanced" countries where new technologies are usually first introduced. Based on who conducts the surveys, in the United States between 5% and 16% of the grownup population owns Bitcoin, and even though this seems like a big enough number, Bitcoin is still in an "early adopters" phase.

There is a natural curve in the adoption of any kind of new technology with five distinct phases. Some people say that we are still in the *early adopters* phase of the adoption curve with Bitcoin, while others think that we are already beyond that and it is too late to enter to invest in Bitcoin.

In February 2019 a data scientist issued a report according to which Bitcoin has reached global penetration. He also found that while North America and Europe had started adoption earlier, they have been overtaken lately by South American and African countries due to various local economical and political reasons.[3]

In the first phase an invention appears out of nowhere and is only adopted by people who are immersed in innovation, those who are heavily technologically oriented. In the case of Bitcoin it would be computer geeks and programmers interested in cryptography. Not surprisingly, it is called the *innovator phase,* which lasts until the adoption reaches 2.5% of the population. The second, *early adopters* phase is when "visionaries" step in who do not necessarily have the sufficient technical knowledge but understand enough to be able to envision the future potential of the technology. Until 16% of the population adopts Bitcoin, according to the adoption curve, we are still in the early adopters phase.

Early adopters are followed by the *early majority* during the third phase, which means a level of adoption between 16% and 34% of the population. These people are only willing to adopt Bitcoin when they can clearly see that adopting it has more advantages to them personally than not doing it. For such an obvious comparative advantage Bitcoin has to be something that they actually need (in other words, it has to provide some service, or have some characteristics that make it desirable for the user), and at the same time, it cannot be too difficult to understand. It has to be practical, easy to use and easy to access, with special emphasis on a clear proof that it actually works as it is supposed to.

Some people say that due to these conditions necessary for early majority adoption, there is actually a gap between the early adopters and the early majority phases where developments are made to prepare the technology for mass adoption. However, there have already been rumors of the "imminent worldwide mass adoption" of Bitcoin, so probably we are getting quite close to the early majority stage.

Once the adoption rate reaches over 34%, we enter the *late majority* phase when those who do not really like technology and are very conservative in their habits adopt the technology, having seen the obvious positive effects it has in the life of the population who have been already using Bitcoin. Finally, the last 16% are the *laggards* who will only adopt the technology when they have no other choice.

The blockchain technology is being studied, further developed and adopted at a steadily growing rate, although according to a January 2019 article published by Maven 11 Capital, a European blockchain technology investment firm, in the broader adoption of blockchain technology we are just getting to the end of the innovator phase.[4] There are hundreds of new cryptocurrencies, tokens, blockchain based applications and projects available and their number is growing every day. We are still in a technological "Wild West" with high volatility and uncertainty, where a huge dose of idealism, enthusiasm and honest efforts to create a better technology and worthwhile applications of it mingles with sheer profit steered actions on behalf of not only corporations, banks and institutions, but also individuals who are only into cryptos for the money.

The only thing we can be certain of at this stage is that blockchain will become more and more prominent in the coming years, so it is important that we understand how it works and what its adoption and use could mean for us personally and society as a whole.

If you want to understand in which direction our economy and our society are going, so that you can position yourself to have a better chance at adapting to the changes already in motion and those to come, read on. Be ahead of trends before they hit the phase of majority adoption, learn the basics and educate yourself to be able to make the right decisions for your future and for the future of your family and your community.

This book will not only introduce you to the world of Bitcoin along with a few other important cryptocurrencies and the blockchain, but will also provide a broader context, a framework to better understand the possibilities and challenges this unprecedented technological evolution brings. But above all, hopefully it will trigger your critical thinking, a skill we as a society seem to have forgotten in the new millenium.

But now let's turn the page. Our story starts on a tiny little planet called Earth...

2

Bitcoin out of the Blue?

I f we want to understand the real importance and potential impact of Bitcoin as well as the revolutionary blockchain technology it introduced, we need to take a step back and observe the environment, the situation in which it was developed. Obviously, Bitcoin did not appear in a vacuum, independently of what came before it.

According to the statement of its mysterious inventor who called himself Satoshi Nakamoto (whoever he, she or they may be), Bitcoin was created with the intention to be a possible solution to the problems and shortcomings of the current economic system which is flawed *by design*. This system is based on the monopoly of a few to create money; whereas only central banks and governments have the right to issue currencies, and what we use to exchange goods and services is not "real money" but *fiat currencies*.

Fiat currencies are created out of nothing, just by printing more bank notes or by keying in digits into bank accounts, without any real value, as they do not have to be backed by anything that would provide a relatively constant value like for example precious metals have.

The economy we know, and suffer from, is ruled by recurring cycles of growth and collapse caused by the systemic faults in the kind of money we use. At this moment the global economy is still using the US dollar as its reserve currency, however, that is in the process of changing and there is a currency war going on for world domination between the US and China.

The problem with the dollar is that since August 16, 1971 it has been decoupled from gold, thanks to Nixon. Before that banks had to possess a certain amount of gold to back the money they issued. This made it difficult for them to just issue more bank notes whenever they wanted to, because in order to do so they had to have accumulated more gold to back the new supply.

After decoupling the dollar from the gold standard, creating more money became easier. The Federal Reserve Bank only had to print bank notes without having to acquire more gold, thus directly causing the inflation which lead to the extreme loss of purchasing value of the people.

The dollar has since been tied to the fluctuation of the price of oil, which resulted in the many wars of the past decades up to the present. The dollar is said to only have retained 2% of its value compared to that in 1913, and some estimate this percentage to be even lower. Even if we accept the 4.08% figure published by the Bureau of Labor Statistics, that is still an extreme loss of value.

Although many economists and decision makers like to make claims that there is nothing we can do because this is just the way the economy works, that everything happens because this is how the "powers of the market" are moving, this notion is completely false.

It appears that those in power are perfectly aware of the flaws of the money system, of its recurring boom and bust cycles; but instead of trying to create a better system, they act as if nothing else would be possible. If you take a look at what is being taught and discussed versus what is not taught or talked about publicly, it becomes clear that "this is how things are and there is nothing we can do" is one of the basic tenets of education and political discourse.

The system acts as if all its decision makers were blind, deaf and unable to think outside the box, and this "there-is-nothing-else-we-can-do" attitude is propagated on purpose everywhere to make people believe it is so.

There seems to be a high probability that the system was designed to be flawed on purpose, because not only its managers do not encourage the discovery of alternatives, but if you tried to create your own alternative money and managed to succeed in making your local economy thrive, the narrative has always been that you are undermining the state and the security of the people.

During the 2008 financial crisis it became clear that things would never come back to the ways they had always been and that our economy and society are declining fast. We are running in close-ranked lines toward the proverbial cliff like dumbed down lemmings zombified by our cell phones and daily distractions as if everything was fine and dandy.

Fiat money as we know it is based on debt and what keeps our economy alive is the constant creation of more debt which is necessary to get the funding for people, companies and countries to repay the interests that banking institutions, shielded by the law, put on their loans.

The entire economy is parasitic in nature, and just like any good parasite, it camouflages its intentions and makes its hosts (people, companies, and countries alike) crave what it needs to survive and thrive. And what it needs is that we go on with the mindless consumption culture, and that we keep placing profit above everything else.

This parasitic economy leeches the last drops of our time and energy and stifles our creativity. When the parasite becomes too big and the host too weak, the process ends with the death of the host. That's one heck of a sunny horizon for humanity, folks, unless we do something about it.

Bitcoin appeared in such a perilous situation while we were happily sliding, gaining velocity down the slope. But before we take a look at Bitcoin itself and its potential for positive change in the economy and the entire structure of society, we need to introduce a few basic assumptions that may be painful to assume.

You may not like to hear some or any of them, however, they are important to consider, even if just as a remote possibility. Warning, it's time to put on your outside-the-box thinking hat for the next couple of pages. Eat some chocolate if you need to. You may be glad later you did.

3

What They Did Not Teach You About the Economy and Society

The following is a non-comprehensive list of some inconvenient truths about the world we live in. Perhaps you will feel offended by some of these assumptions and think they are stupid "conspiracy theories", or that I am paranoid and you should throw this book into a corner. There could be some preinstalled beliefs and programs ready to jump in to "save your sanity" and cry out loud that all this is bullshit.

I had to warn you that this may happen because such is the nature of the trance we have been living in; mostly unknowingly.

Please do not let your emotions taint your understanding when you read this list. Step back and consider everything you know about the world, everything you have observed up until now and, in light of all your experiences, let these assumptions sink in. You do not have to believe them, what's more, I ask you *not to believe* them, but to step out of your standard frame of thinking and ask what if these assumptions were true. Would that explain better your personal situation as well as that of the world?

We are put into schools and told how to behave, how to draw and walk between the lines. We are conditioned to choose the "correct answers" from a few pre-existing options instead of being creative to find new, better or more exciting solutions. We are forced to memorize things presented as facts instead of learning to research, observe, discover and analyze things independently.

We are penalized for making mistakes, and trained to obey without questions, or else we will be punished, and are definitely taught to not think for ourselves. And unfortunately, thinking, just like any bodily function, can atrophy if we don't practice it regularly.

You may not agree with some or any of the below assumptions, but it is important that you consider them. Biting your nails yet? Grab those chocolates and let's see the list.

(a) You are not a free individual

You may think or believe that you are, but just take a look at your life. Really step back. Are you controlled to behave in certain ways and to avoid doing certain things or else there will be unwanted consequences? Do you have to pay for being able to meet your basic needs for shelter, food, water and safety (in other words, are you penalized for having been born on Earth)?

Do you have to spend a large chunk of your life doing something you may not like to do and doing it again five times a week at a designated time and place, repeating it for 35-40 years of your life? People have to work eight, and in many cases more, hours a day to be able to cover their basic needs, to pay for a place to live and to be able to eat.

The majority of workers receive just enough money to pay for their basic needs and to be able to put gas into their cars to get back to work the next week. We have to pay not only for shelter, but also for water, when over two thirds of the surface of our planet is covered in water. It is a freaking water planet, water is more than abundant, so why do we have to pay for it? Yes, that water needs to be treated, sanitized, piping and waste water management systems need to be installed, and the entire functioning of the water utilities must be managed. But don't we pay enough taxes for at least the water to be provided for free?

We must pay taxes, and not just a symbolic amount. Income tax is actually a huge chunk which, depending on the country you live in, can get up to as high as 61% of your total income (that is Sweden, by the way). That is insane.

But that's not all. You are also taxed after any goods or services you buy, and this is called value added tax (VAT) which could be as high as 27% percent (the winner here is Hungary, but the typical VAT rate worldwide is 10-20%). And then you must pay to be able to use your car, keep your property year after year, get married or divorced, build a house, and so on and so forth.

"If confiscating 100 percent of your economic output constitutes slavery, at which point does it cease to be slavery? 80 percent? 50 percent? 39.6 percent?"[5]

Wouldn't the state be able to pay something as basic for human life as water from all the taxes it collects? It turns out that they have more important things to do, like paying billions for weaponry and for maintaining an unfortunately overactive military. Also, there is the occasional cost of bailing out failed banks and such. My bad.

You may think, well, we have to contribute to society so that it can function, otherwise there would only be chaos. Yes, sure, but have you thought of why you have to comply with a system that you did not choose?

They say that in the West we live in democracies. Were you actually asked even once after you reached legal adulthood whether you like the system, whether you agree to be a part of it or if we should come up with something better? It is understandable that they would not let children vote about their own future, but what about adults?

Did you decide to live in this type of society or were you born into it? Do you have the chance to opt out, and if you did, would nothing detrimental happen to you? Don't you think it is logical to ask why wouldn't each and every one of us have the right to choose in what kind of society we want to live?

What if you could choose between actually being taxed and paying social security, which would let you reap the benefits of the central system, and only paying for the services you or your family personally use? With the technology we have today such a system would be ridiculously easy to implement. If it is technically possible, why nobody does it?

We are told it is what it is, no way out, you do what you must do, you are a cog in the machine. Interestingly, the English language gives us a clue about what actually happens to us according to those who had set up the system, created its language and its laws. I wouldn't say it is coincidental.

Those who deal with the distinction between natural law (i. e. the moral compass that guides us internally, something that comes from within and directs life according to the ethos of doing no harm) versus man-made law (which is just a set of complicated conditions placed on everybody else by the few for their own benefit, while they want to make us believe that these laws our there to protect us) know that human beings are treated as subjects to maritime law.

The legal system treats human beings as mere goods or assets owned by the system (just think of the expression "human resources"). If you do not believe it, research the significance of your birth certificate.

In the English language which is probably not coincidentally the most widespread language today, when you appear as a living being, when you are born, you go through *birth*. Interestingly, the area allotted for a ship in a port or harbor is called exactly the same, although with a slight twist in spelling to hide this connection. The ship arrives at the port and it is berthed, and you, the human spirit/soul are "*berthed*", unloaded from the sea of spiritual existence onto the banks of reality/solidity into your physical body. Which means (according to "them") that once the cargo is offloaded, once you get out of your mother's womb, you have been "shipped" and the system owns you.

Consequently, we do not really own anything, and what we think to be our properties are not ours, but belong to those who "own us". Isn't that the definition of slavery?

And the most ingenious system of slavery is in which the bars of our cage are created and maintained by our very minds. They are made up of our belief that we are free and of thoughts that limit our vision about who and what we are and what life is about. The rabbit hole of our being "berthed" into the system is deep indeed.

(b) The system is not set up to benefit everyday people but only a small minority (the 1%)

Think of the cultural lies we are fed. On the surface everything that governments and their numerous specialized agencies do is meant to benefit the entire population of their countries. Politicians promise whatever people want to hear to get into power, everyone knows that.

If you ever worked for a corporation, you may be familiar with the notion which many companies like to propagate among their workers that their company is like a big, happy family. Repeating slogans like "we are working for everybody, for the benefit of all". They feed workers this lie, but many times do not even bother to make the cover decent enough.

They may circulate the yearly profitability report where they celebrate how many percents of extra profit the company made over what was budgeted, and assure all employees that the company could not have achieved this stellar result without them. Then the next day they may tell you that, due to budget restraints, this year there will be no bonus for simple workers like you, and what's more, they will have to lay people off. Meanwhile those in the management still receive their flashy bonuses.

Of course, everyone with more than two brain cells is capable of seeing through this game of lies, but not everyone registers it consciously. It is too hard to be confronted with the fact that you have been fed lies on a systemic level, and either you conform and act as if you believed them, or you will find yourself on your own, thrown out of the system.

The average company culture is based on pure lies and manipulations. You know that. It is the way of capitalism. People come up with laws and regulations that make it easier for them to abuse others monetarily and otherwise. That is our society today.

Inequality has already reached shocking levels both worldwide and also within individual countries. Less then 2% of the United States owns over 60% of the wealth of the nation, and 60% of the goods and services of the entire world are consumed by the United States which constitutes roughly 3% of the world population.

The balance is seriously skewed. Proponents of neoliberalism argue that globalization reduces poverty, however, what we are seeing is that the gap actually has been widening since globalization started to gain traction. One may think then that communism or socialism could be the solution, similarly to how a left-right political divide is emphasized on purpose as the default mode of politics. To date, there hasn't been any successful practical implementation of either, which could be a convincing sign that we should start searching for the solution elsewhere.

(c) We are made to believe that humans are inherently bad

We are brainwashed since day one at school, through what we absorb from our family environment, from the media, books, films, from the discourses of politicians and governments to believe that we need this system of control as a framework for human life because people are inherently evil.

This notion that we need to be controlled by some external authority, or else people would commit bad things and everybody would cheat, rob and hurt others is reinforced in people again and again until most of us believe it.

Also, as the vast majority of people are actually inherently good, you are led to believe that *you* of course wouldn't do anything bad, but the world is filled with bad people, and if you and your family are not bad people (and normal people do not think that they or their families are evil), then the bad guys must be people of some other group, from other neighborhoods, other political views, other countries, other races, or other religions.

Instead of maintaining healthy and beautiful traditions, national/ethnic roots and identities which would provide a healthy sense of belonging, we are encouraged to engage in "us against them" style group thinking by various means. A good example is how schools promote competitive sports events. The absolutely ridiculous hype around football, soccer, and the likes aimed at the adult population, which tries to pull people into a divisive and competitive mindset, also belongs into this category.

Your team competes with another team, and there must be a winner and a loser. It seems harmless enough, or is it? What does this actually translate into in "real life"? Well, into the notion that *competing* is the way of life, that there are no win-win situations generally, that either you win or you lose.

Instead of cooperation, competition is touted as the only way there is. Cooperative sports or games are seldom played or encouraged.

When they talk about cooperation, what they usually really mean is that the people have to sacrifice their time or money, and the company or the state will gobble it up. We know that the system is corrupt, but we are brainwashed that there is no other way but the way things have always been and currently are.

On top of that, we are also made to believe that we live in a democracy, where each individual has a voice. Seriously? How does choosing between a couple of corrupt parties every four years equal having a say in what will happen in your life? Can you decide if you want your tax money to fund wars and the military, or instead to provide safe technologies, renewable energy and affordable, pesticide-free food for everyone? Can you decide if you want to fund any church or any kind of measures and programs instituted by the state? Nope.

You are given a circus where you have the choice to choose between people who will ultimately, to a greater or lesser degree, play into the same corrupt system. And the narrative we are fed is that otherwise all hell would break loose because we, the people, are inherently bad, evil, and immoral by nature. Which is, of course, a complete lie.

All this wouldn't be possible if the collective consciousness of humanity weren't so riddled with fear. But fear is pervasive, it's everywhere, and we are constantly bombarded with information designed to keep us in a state of fear, where we are more inclined to give up our sovereignty to the state or any conceived authority in exchange for the illusion of safety.

(d) We live in an artificial system that is parasitic

By artificial here I mean that if we did not have civilization, if there were only plants and animals plus naturally existing humans on the planet, the system would work synergistically, as natural systems do. Such systems recycle, they never do only one function at the same time, they are interconnected and the energy in them keeps moving around in a balanced way so that the overall energy of the system is never depleted. That is how life on Earth should be for us too.

In contrast to that, it is easy to see that we, humans living in today's society have finite energy and finite time to live and we are corralled into a system where we are mostly taken advantage of and discarded when we are no longer "productive" or "useful".

They call it "survival of the fittest", incessantly quoting Darwin. If you ever watched nature channels on television, you could notice that they somehow always manage the show the most gory and horrifying scenes, portraying nature as cruel and dangerous, and life as a constant struggle for survival.

Of course, there is an inherent balance in nature, and microorganisms, plants, and animals are all part of a closed food chain. But that does not mean that we humans, who are supposedly more evolved than animals, should base our existence on the level of sheer survival instinct.

They make us believe that it is "natural" to act according to the Darwinian law of the "survival of the fittest" and that it is a "dog-eat-dog" world. Basically, we are indoctrinated to think that we humans have no other choice but to behave as beasts without any morality.

Where is *cooperation* in this world view? Where are love and compassion, empathy and community? I hope you see how distorted and far from our true nature the presently popularized world view is.

It was E. J. Schumacher in the 1970's who emphasized how great a problem the adoption of the Darwinian view regarding human life and human society meant. According to him, this evolutionist view is used to validate and legitimize the total lack of morality in the behavior and deeds of both the individual and the system as a whole. This logic says that compassion, empathy, and a sense of belonging to a community are characteristics of the losers and the weak, while winners must follow the path of the mercantilist law of "genetic excellence".[6]

Schumacher believed that all the important theories of the modern age emphasized the animalistic in humans, instead of the spiritual. The fact that in order to keep the debt machine going, our society is based on the cult and necessity of mindless consumption instead of the cultivation of our virtues, creativity, healthy relationships, and a constant thriving to better ourselves, our relationships, and the environment indicates that Schumacher was right.

The very fact that we are being used and abused, coaxed and robbed of our precious time and energy on a constant basis, and upon threat of punishment if we do not comply, makes us act selfishly. In a selfish system it is a logical self-preserving reaction to act selfishly because if you don't, you are to lose very soon.

But are we not supposed to be further along the line of evolution? Are we not beings with ethics and morals dictated by our very spirits, without the need to be told what is good and what is wrong? Causing pain and suffering is not good, everyone knows that, so until we do not cause pain and suffering to others, including nature, we should be free to do as we please.

Are we really such an intelligent species if we still have to slave away for forty years of our lives in so called "jobs" before we are allowed to do whatever we want, or rather whatever we are still capable of doing due to old age, sickness and limited finances?

Just to have a point of comparison, you may find it interesting that the seemingly so busy ants, these epitomes of diligence and hard work do not have what we could call a strong work ethic. Actually, only 10% of an ant colony are working at any time, the rest are just lounging about in their underground city, having fun and doing ant things, living their life.

Would you say that humans are more intelligent than ants? If yes, why couldn't we reach this level of efficiency, not to mention, transcend it? We certainly could, if it weren't for a minor obstacle: the current system that is parasitizing us.

(e) Large amounts of the money taken from us in the form of all types of taxes are used to feed the war machine

It is also used to pit groups and nations against each other to cause suffering and maintain a constant level of stress, fear, and desperation, to create and feed terrorism which is then "fought" by the governments.

Of course, it is not the governments proper that are behind all this, but the "deep state", the organizations that control the system from the shadows. If you want to know more about what Ole Dammegard calls the circus of terror, I suggest you search for his books or his interviews where he dismantles the official narrative of certain terror events.

It is a vicious money extracting system. First they search for enemies. If there are no viable enemies, well, they create one. The important thing is to keep some conflict going at all times, to keep people in a constant state of fear and generate a "need" for weapons and military intervention. These past years those who are ready to tell the truth have been labeled terrorists by the terrorists themselves. How ironic.

They sell weapons to both sides of a conflict, and pit the sides against each other even more. Once a conflict gets to the warring level, an international call is made to "do something to stop it". "Upon the will of the people" who have been primed by the media, they decide to allocate further tax money, and many times troops, to solve the crisis that they either created or at least exacerbated.

Money is siphoned off of countries on both sides of the conflict, as well as from the people of those countries who step in to "reset the order" and "create peace".

The military industrial complex is huge and they are not your friends. As they say, wars are fought by the poor people for causes invented by the rich people. This may be a very uncomfortable assumption to ponder, in part because of the following assumption.

(f) We are taught to put the wealthy and powerful on a pedestal

We are so used to putting people who "made it", who "reached the top" on a pedestal that it can blur our vision at times which makes us more susceptible to accepting whatever comes from those people at the top.

There is nothing inherently wrong with wealth and abundance. The issue is the hierarchical, top-down structure of our societies, and the fact confirmed by various psychological studies that the more psychopathic a person is, the more chances and the stronger motivation he has to get to the top.

Psychopaths are born, not raised. It is not like having narcissistic personality traits that mostly come from childhood experiences. The narcissistic person still has a capacity to feel emotions. Psychopathy, however, is a genetic problem which makes the person unable to feel emotions, so in a way they are not really human. A psychopath does not care how much his actions may hurt others because he is unable to feel empathy.

Now think about this. If having psychopathic traits is an advantage to get to a higher leading position, what does that say about our society?

Their lack of empathy and emotions mean that these leaders often do not take into consideration the repercussions their decisions could have on a huge number of people. They are unable to place themselves into the situation of another person. This problem with their genetic-psychological makeup is often accompanied by their many times scornful opinion of ordinary people.

So in case you thought otherwise, the majority of top leaders, despite what they want you to believe, do not care about you; they see people as mindless sheep or "useless eaters". According to Mark Passio, those in the Church of Satan even call ordinary people "the dead".

This majority often includes political leaders, especially the ones at the very top. Of course, there are normal people in leading positions too, but those who have these traits are more predisposed and more motivated to reach the top, often at any cost.

These people are not like the rest of humanity, but they managed to con us into believing that the human being is inherently bad. They made us believe that we are like them. But that is not true. The tendency of common people to give more weight to the words and opinions of the wealthy and authority figures (due to indoctrination) often results in the majority blindly accepting decisions and opinions that go against the interest of common people, and also in ordinary people adopting the psychopathic behaviors of the admired "top guys" because they believe that is the way to success.

(g) Everything is hidden in plain sight

Let's call those who came up with this system of controlling the entire human population by controlling our minds *the controllers.* They are the visible oligarchy and the ones above them, and they think they have a god-given right to rule or whatever they tell themselves.

The controllers of this system will not tell you clearly, explicitly what they are really doing. However, they believe that in order for them to be able to stay in the game and avoid bad karma, they must tell us in some way what they plan to do.

Everything we need to know to find out what is really going on is out there, many times hidden in plain sight, but we cannot see it because we are trained to not see and not think outside of the box.

Why would they give up their control? It is only logical that they want to keep us in the dark. What they do is they tell us what they are up to covertly, putting it into symbolic messages, for example in music videos, in movies, or they put it out there via the use of symbols. If we do not comprehend what they exactly mean, or if we do not understand what pieces of, for example, a movie are there "for reasons of disclosure" on their part, that is not their problem.

If that's the case, they can argue that we have been notified and if we say or do nothing to oppose their plans, they got our tacit consent. According to their twisted logic, even if they tell something in a movie as fiction, they still "told us", so it is our fault if we did not get the message. Which according to their thinking gives them free rein to do whatever they want.

They told you, you did not object, so now the blame is on you. You should have figured out that a particular movie was not "just entertainment", how silly of you. It is a twisted logic, but that is what they work with, consistently. Similarly to how not knowing the law does not exempt anybody from being subject to it.

(h) The controllers think long term

The controllers of this system of parasitism are very good at playing chess. They do not just react to the needs and demands of the public as the common man would think and as it may seem from the actions and trends played out by their pawns, the politicians, major corporations etc.

We are lulled into believing that everything happens relatively randomly, as if the actions of key players in the system were mere consequences of what the population of a country wants or needs.

But in fact, they think for a much longer time frame ahead, taking more than the next three or four steps into consideration, so we often cannot see what their end goal really is with anything that is going on.

The average person, who has not practiced critical thinking and who does not care about the world at large and just wants to live a peaceful life, to be able to pay the bills and be happy, probably does not see that everything around him is nothing but lies and manipulations.

In comparison, the average "truther" or "conspiracy theorist" who thinks he understands what is going on and prides himself on being able to see the manipulation, often only grasps one single step beyond what is visible at any given moment. But to be able to see truly behind the scenes, to have a glimpse of the true intentions of the controllers, you have to think way ahead.

You have to step out of the "us versus them" dualistic thinking and see the sequence of events as a chess game, which is not about the individual figures or groups pitted against each other on the chess board, but about the invisible hand that moves the pieces.

(i) Problem, reaction, solution

The basic tool of operation of the controllers is to hide behind artificially generated problems so that people themselves rise and request a solution to those problems. This "beauty" of the art of manipulation is called "problem, reaction, solution".

Instead of introducing something that they know people would not like and would oppose, for example more of the police state (and this is hard to fathom, I know), they generate a problem to which they know that people will react with fear and in that fearful or shocked state will request a solution.

The controllers can then give them the solution requested by the people, and it will seem that they are implementing those measures not because they wanted to introduce them in the first place, but because the people demanded it to happen.

Let's imagine for example a peaceful political manifestation taking place against any measure of the government. If people feel safe to participate in political manifestations because those tend to be peaceful, it is more likely that many people will participate in such manifestations. Now let's imagine that for whatever reason (and what could those reasons be?) the controllers did not want people to feel safe to participate in manifestations in order to reduce the potential positive impact manifestations could make. They can have their own people infiltrate the manifesting crowd.

Those infiltrating elements could then start to act violently, maybe even attacking the police. These violent acts "of the crowd" would give the police a legal reason to jump into action which would likely escalate the violence. In such a situation the police would be entitled to use force against the crowd which is no longer peaceful because the infiltrating elements are behaving violently as part of the crowd.

The above is not a perfect example though, because it is not the people who demand the police to use force against the crowd, but the violent acts of the infiltrating individuals provide a legally acceptable reason for the police to "restore the order".

The following example may be better. Imagine that you want to keep the population of your country in a constant state of fear so that it is the people who "demand" you to spend more on security (maybe by pumping more money to your friends at the military industrial complex, or perhaps by militarizing the police so that dissenters to your power could be taken care of as early as possible), but obviously, you cannot do it overtly. People would not agree with you and could protest to stop you from implementing this fantastic idea of yours.

You cannot just go ahead and start repeating "we need more security". You could maybe ride the already existing animosity between the people of two neighboring countries. For historical reasons there could be enmity between your country and its neighbors. If so, you are in luck. The only thing you have to do is use any aggression or crime perpetrated by some individuals of the other nation against some individuals of your nation. Maybe the aggression was motivated by hatred toward your people, but anyway, it was not a generalized hatred acted out by the entire population of the neighboring country.

However, you can pick this case up and inundate all the news channels with it, pushing onto your people the notion that the nation living next to yours hates your people and they are attacking people of your country. Because the case is all over the media, now politicians must manifest their opinions about the issue and they can start generating and strengthening the atmosphere of animosity and panic.

You generalize things and keep repeating the same message, using carefully crafted repeated phrases to incite fear until it sticks. Pushing this repeated message creates a state of constant fear which makes people more vulnerable and more predisposed to accept any kind of decisions that promise to make their situation "safer".

Basically, the goal of the controllers is to get the population into a state of fight or flight response where reason is thrown out the window. Once this state is achieved by pumping the fear narrative out for long enough, now your politicians can come up with a suggestion to somehow reinforce security in, and outside of, the country. Voilà, your end goal is achieved and it is "not your fault".

(j) "Divide and conquer" is king

The tactic of "divide and conquer" never goes out of fashion because it always works. It's a definite keeper in the world dominator's tool kit. This tactic is so effective because we have been groomed since early childhood to look at the world as a place of fierce competition (which again, goes back to the Darwinian view).

We were taught that we must fight to survive. Besides, each of us acquired a distinct cultural identity that also clashes constantly with other cultural identities. Unless we make an effort to free ourselves from the collective programming, on a psychological level we remain influenced by the belief systems of not only our families, but our nationalities, religions and other affiliations.

The truth is that we have been kept children psychologically on purpose, and so few of us manage to grow up and develop into fully responsible adults in the spiritual and psychological sense of the word.

The arrested psychological development of the population benefits the controllers because the psychology of children is such that they do not take responsibility for their thoughts and actions, nor do they need or like to do so. It is so much easier to blame others for our misfortune and for all the bad things happening to us personally and in the world at large. Blaming an entire group instead of another individual is even easier because now we can project onto an abstract group instead of somebody we know. It takes the personal out of the equation.

The avoidance of taking responsibility is usually coupled with an unconscious self-blame when the child blames herself for everything negative that happens in her life. As the logic of the child concludes that she must be bad or evil, or otherwise everything would be fine around her, she pushes this sense of self-blame into her subconscious. This is a fertile soil for the need to search for somebody or something outside of her to blame for everything bad that happens.

The controllers direct our attention to where they want to by providing us with political and cultural dramas where the public is polarized between two opposite sides, while what they really want to get away with goes unnoticed.

In plain terms, they throw a bone at two dogs so that the dogs start fighting for the bone and do not notice that the controllers are there to rob the house the dogs were meant to protect.

(k) Concentration of power is the main cause of our problems

So many problems have been plaguing humanity for thousands of years and we never seemed to be able to solve most of them. This is all because of the concentration of power.

The centralization of power is rooted in a centrally controlled money system which is based on debt, as well as on the lack of access to renewable or free energy in a closed system. The concentration of power over society means that it is a parasitic system which sucks out resources from the people and from the planet in order to perpetuate itself to keep the controllers in power. We don't have to go further than to remember the famous quote from Amschel Rothschild who said "Give me control of a nation's money supply, and I care not who makes its laws."

It is clear that we need to do something to change the current political system, and the way society is organized. We need to find a way that allows people to self-govern their communities without being oppressed and abused by those who had grabbed, and have been maintaining, the financial control of the planet. However, to be able to do that, we have to cut their source of power, which is their monopoly to create money and to use their already existing corrupted wealth to further enslave humanity.

As long as our species operates in the current financial system, the economy must keep growing and growing to be able to pay back the debt which is the motor of the economy. You have to remember that the controllers are so few in numbers compared to the masses of the entire human race.

They can only retain their control over us if they make us create and maintain our own prison. The way they do it is by making us believe that what we have now is the only viable system, and no questioning it is supported, or even allowed, by the system.

But the fact is that there *are* alternatives which have been studied, however, you do not hear or read about them in the mainstream media, nor do you learn about them in school. Why? It does not benefit the controllers. Those sheep gotta keep thinking inside the box, remember?

(I) The controllers know well how the human psyche and the mind work

The controllers have amassed an incredibly thorough body of knowledge about human psychology over the decades and centuries, and are well versed in the art of manipulation. They have set up extensive research programs to study human psychology and the art of influencing. Think of the Tavistock Institute for example, or of the entire psychological movement of behaviorism.

Why is it so important that the controllers know how the human psyche works? Because they know how to push our buttons, how to manipulate us in subtle ways that make it more difficult to uncover their manipulations. They know what our weak spots are by design (or by being shaped and molded in a certain way by our childhood environment and the control grid of society).

Knowledge is power and they like to work under the cover of darkness. Once you are told how a magic trick is done, the feelings of awe are gone and you see clearly what is going on. Something similar happens when you become aware of their ways of operation.

It opens your eyes. You start to see when the controllers hijack certain organically occurring movements, be those political movements or spiritual awakening, as in the case of the hijacking of the hippie movement to change its focus from love, freedom and community to libertarianism, ungroundedness by the introduction of hard drugs, escape into la la land and sexual promiscuity. A beautiful organic movement fueled by the need of a generation to live differently and create a better world has been turned into a dead end. And that is not the only time such a hijacking happened.

(m) We are emotional and not rational beings

This may be difficult to accept, especially for men, but we are emotional rather than rational beings. Even though we like to think the opposite, we make decisions not based on logic but by how we feel about things.

This conclusion comes from the Max Planck Institute for Human Cognitive and Brain Sciences based on their experiment to study how decisions are made.

What they found was quite shocking: even though we believe that we consider various options rationally before we decide and that the decisions we make our based on reasoning and logic, it turns out that up to ten seconds before we consciously become aware of our decisions, the signal of the decision made can already be picked up from the brain.[7]

It seems that the subconscious mind makes the decisions which are picked up by our conscious mind (at which moment we think that we actually came to a decision as a result of our process of considering the options based on logic).

What this means for us as members of a species living in a controlled system is that we can be more easily manipulated via our unconscious and subconscious than we like to believe. Those who know how to exploit this peculiarity of the human mind have the upper hand when it comes to achieving their goals in terms of manipulation.

(n) We are controlled and limited by the language we use

Language is an artificial construct and acts as a filter through which we see and understand reality. Inuit people for example have over fifty words for various types of snow. This obviously means that they learn to differentiate between fifty states/qualities of one phenomenon that other languages treat to only one word. The language is a fingerprint of the way a people sees the world.

Because we speak different languages, we see and understand reality through different filters. However, there is more to language than you may think.

The controllers like to use symbolic language and double or hidden meaning. To understand the double or hidden meaning of words and expressions, think of the common meaning of the word. Obviously, not all words have hidden meanings but many do. The "surface meaning" of a word is what is generally understood by it in everyday communication. The hidden meaning of the word may only be seen by those who think outside of the mind control box.

Let's see an example for such a double meaning, in this case of a Spanish language expression. While I was driving on the freeway in Spain a couple of years ago, I came across an electronic message sign that was installed above the lanes. It was there to alert drivers to road conditions and accidents, but also displayed ongoing traffic control campaigns which the traffic police was executing that day.

As I was driving my car, the following message appeared on the electronic message sign: "operación zero lesionados". This means "operation zero injured people" in English. To the everyday person this expression has one very clear meaning: it is a statement that there is an active police campaign with more frequent traffic control with the aim to prevent accidents and consequently injuries on the roads.

However, the reality might just be a bit different. If what really mattered most to the authorities was saving lives and having no traffic accidents instead of reaching traffic fine quotas, the first thing they should have done by now is to prohibit the use of metals for manufacturing the chassis of vehicles, and instead make the use of carbon fiber for chassis obligatory. The carbon fiber chassis could prevent the majority of deaths and injuries on the road due to accidents, especially collisions. Apart from this, there could be other technical ways to achieve better road security.

If we think of this, there is traffic patrol on the roads, however, a large proportion of the traffic police income is generated by fining drivers. Should you see a sign alerting you about a new operation called "zero injured people", you may want to think about the hidden goal of income generation. Think of how soldiers before a battle may be told to take no prisoners which is just another way of saying "leave zero injured people behind". If you leave no prisoners it is because you were ordered to kill everyone. And in terms of fining drivers, well, the possible hidden meaning then could be something like this: "we are on a mission to catch as many people as possible doing something illegal in traffic and fine the heck out of them; with this campaign we will catch everybody and make their wallets bleed to death".

You may think that one has to have a convoluted, paranoid mind to come up with such a distorted second meaning. Maybe. Maybe this was not the best example. But remember, the controllers are psychopaths, and their actions may be convoluted too.

We can observe the use of double meaning of certain words and expressions in wider societal narratives also, in governance, in political campaigns, in the repeated phrases of the media. People will hear only what they want, and what their programming will allow them, to hear.

There are many more things we could mention as part of this list of basic assumptions, but I think all this is enough to demonstrate that thinking outside the box is not only beneficial to be able to better understand what life on Earth means for human beings, but it is a requirement for our survival.

We are controlled and brainwashed to think in certain ways that benefit the controllers by making it possible for the system to continue unchanged. If you find it hard to believe the above assumptions, I can only recommend one thing. Search your heart, search your soul. Hell, search Google!

4

In Debt We Trust

The divide between the rich and the poor has grown at a breakneck speed over the past decades and the widening of this gap keeps accelerating. If we want to examine what the cause of such polarization of wealth and opportunities may be, we can argue that it is all the result of an unfortunate chain of bad political and economic decisions or suboptimal management of the resources of the countries.

There are also those who would vehemently blame the poor for their own impoverishment. According to their reasoning poor people lack initiatives, they are getting more inactive and dependent on welfare doled out by the state, which actually deprives them of possibilities and any bargaining power when it comes to taking advantage of opportunities, or standing up for a decent living wage.

However, as we have seen earlier, we have to look at the root cause and not the symptoms. If you step back and examine the situation from afar, it becomes more obvious. The real reason for the growing inequality is not the way political powers are managing our society, nor is it a question of wrongly chosen or incorrectly applied governmental policies, as the controllers would like to make us believe.

They would like people to think that life would be much better should this or that political party or wing get into power. But the thing is, left or right and any combination of any parties are just playing on a seesaw, but nothing essential ever changes. Sure, there are some things, some improvements that are executed to keep the façade of the system, to maintain the appearance that things are changing for the better and that political parties have a real say in how things evolve.

The widening gap between the rich and the poor, as well as the accelerating deterioration of our relationships, our health, the biodiversity of nature, and actually any major problem you can think of that affects humanity and Earth are all symptoms of the same systemic issue. But let's just keep to the question of the economy for now.

This societal division is ingrained into the very system we are all subject to. It comes from the facts that we are ruled by a bunch of people who are only motivated by their self-interest and who couldn't care less about humanity and, as a direct consequence of this, our carefully thought-out monetary system is based on debt.

Consider what an astronomical leap we have seen in the past 150 years in terms of technological development. Getting from steam powered machines to the use of nuclear power, plasma technology and artificial intelligence in such a short time is a very significant development in technology. Why could this happen? If this was an organic development we can assume that humans are really a talented bunch when it comes to technology.

But then take a look at our monetary systems and the way our economies and societies have been functioning (and this includes not only capitalistic but socialist and communist systems too throughout history).

Have the basic principles of what money is and how it should be used changed for the better? Have we seen a radical betterment in the quality of life in the world? Can we say that our lives are easier, more peaceful, more in harmony with others and nature as a whole system? Have we reached new heights of cultural development, a general rise in our intellectual but also emotional, psychological, artistic and cognitive capabilities?

I do not mean whether there are now some people who have enhanced capabilities compared to the average of say 150 years ago. A true evolutionary step forward would be if we as a race, meaning the grand average of all people, would exhibit significant positive developments in all aspects of life.

Does it really make sense that all this talent, all this brain power that has been able to move us from the industrial age into the age of artificial intelligence, robotics, nano and plasma technology in such a short time, has been unable to make any meaningful positive adjustments to one of the most basic aspects that define how our society is structured?

Has nobody been able to improve the characteristics and use of money or invent a better, more just way to operate the economy that does not imply sacrificing anything on the altar of profit? This, ladies and gentlemen, smells like a big, fat hoax.

Someone must have been purposefully working to prevent any manner of positive change to other aspects of our lives, including our money system and the basic concept of what money is. Could this be the hidden hand of the controllers, or just an unfortunate case of centuries-long continued bad luck? Could it be that only those aspects have seen an accelerated evolution that contribute to the enslavement of our race as a whole? You tell me.

We have not really heard much about "fiat money" until the world financial crisis of 2007, when it became painfully apparent just how much our economy is based on something so inherently flawed.

The majority of people never learn much about money as a basic concept, we do not learn in school how it is created, and for obvious reasons we are not taught who really controls money and why it is such an effective tool for mass control. We do not learn that inequality is embedded into the system even more than we may think it is.

Banks create new money arbitrarily, just by typing the digits into their accounts, or printing a new batch of bank notes in case of central banks. They then lend out this new money created out of thin air, and the borrower has to repay not only the amount borrowed but the interest on it as well. The problem is that the amount of the interest was not created.

For example, if the bank created 100 dollars and it lends it to you with a 10% interest rate, in the moment you borrowed the 100 dollars, the total supply of money in the economy increased by 100 dollars. However, now you would have to pay back 110 dollars, that is the 100 dollars plus an interest of 10 dollars. To be able to pay back the interest, you will have to get those 10 dollars from somebody else.

The problem with this is that if all the money put into circulation was once created by the banks lending it out for interest, in any given moment the total supply of money in existence is smaller than the total amount owed by everybody to the banks. Because of the interests they all have to pay.

It is no wonder that the practice of charging interest for lending out money was frowned upon both by the Bible and the Koran. Usury, remember? And it just happens to be at the very core of all the issues which we have been struggling with for hundreds of years.

So, the only way for you to pay back the interest is to get the money from somebody else. In this system in order for the debt of some people, companies, or governments to be paid back, there must be others (people, companies, or governments) who cannot pay back their debt, and go bankrupt.

The other way to obtain the money to pay the interest could be to take out another loan, but this second loan will also have to be paid back with interests. With this system there will never be a time when all the debt is paid back. And we may not even realize how big a negative impact this practice has on our economy and society.

We are never told that the interest on borrowed money is the biggest cost we as an economy have to pay. Margrit Kennedy and Stephanie Ehrenschwendner in their excellent book, *Occupy Money: Creating an Economy Where Everybody Wins*[8] wrote that according to data collected in Germany in 2006, 40% of the total spendings of German households were paid as interests borne in the prices of goods and services. What does it mean?

Well, if the banks didn't charge interest for the loans they give (i.e. if money was treated like a public utility and issued free of charge, just like water, sunshine and air should be free, as they do not belong to any entity, corporation or person, and they are essential for life), Germans could save 40% more of their money. The percentages may slightly vary from country to country due to differences in taxation, but the order of magnitude for any Western country seems just about right.

If this figure is not surprising enough, you are in for another treat. We said earlier that the use of interest on money is the direct cause of the widening gap between the rich and the poor, but Kennedy and Ehrenschwendner revealed something even more shocking. It turns out that because the interest is concealed in the prices of all goods and services, 80% of the German population pay twice as much interest as they receive. This means that 80% of the population have no money to lend out to others and they cannot receive interest for it, but instead they spend more paying for goods and services, so they are paying interest included in the price of those goods and services too.[9]

Ten percent of German people, who are more well off, receive a little more interest than they pay, and the highest earning 10% have enough money to invest and receive interest for their investments. People in this top 10% receive more interest than they pay. Their interest surplus comes directly from what the less lucky 80% pay out.[10] So in case you thought everything is all right with the monetary system, you may want to think twice.

Bernard Lietaer[11] believes that all our economic and related societal problems originate from the characteristics of the official currencies we use. According to him, to have a well functioning, healthy economy, money should fulfill only two functions: it should serve (1) as a *medium of exchange* which is more effective and more practical than bartering, and (2) as a *unit of account* to compare the prices of products. The problem is that currently any official currencies have two further functions which are responsible for all our economic troubles.

Official currencies today also serve (3) as *a store of value*, so if you put your money into the bank, it will give you an interest, and (4) as a *tool of speculation*, which can be easily observed in the activity of the stock exchanges and financial markets where traders make money by buying and selling currencies (among a plethora of other financial products) and in doing so they influence the economies of the issuing countries.

The store of value and tool of speculation functions of currencies cause problems because when people expect that the future will bring greater uncertainty, they will save up more of their money and will spend less, reducing their direct consumption of goods and services in the present. So at the first sign of a recession everybody will save more and spend less, which will automatically increase the recession and this behavior becomes a self-fulfilling prophecy.

In contrast, when the economy is on the booming side of the cycle, people tend to spend more and save up less because everything, including the unpredictable future seems brighter during an economic boom. This increased spending will push the economic growth into an inflationary period.

As people's economic behavior is highly emotional, we are mostly doomed to follow these boom and bust cycles in our personal economic behavior, unless we have an exceptional control over our emotions. And with this we are back again at the question whether humans are rational beings or are ultimately driven by emotions.

If we could eliminate the store of value function of a currency so that the currency would only function as a medium of exchange and a unit of account, it would automatically reduce the fluctuation between booms and recessions. We could probably have one type of money to store value if we absolutely had to, and another type to be used for everyday purchases which would not have a store of value function.

The tool of speculation function negatively affects the stability of the economy too, because it undermines the unit of account function of money as speculation makes exchange rates fluctuate continuously. In a healthy and just economy probably there should not be any speculation with currencies or anything that is tied to the survival and wellbeing of people, but that is another question.

This mess with the four functions of which two are causing problems for everybody, except for the controllers, has everything to do with the fact that we do not differentiate between money and currency. These two concepts are blurred together in the minds of the majority of people which makes it easier for the system to carry on with the debt-scam right under our noses.

Both currency and money can serve as a medium of exchange, a unit of account, they are portable, durable, divisible and fungible, so it is easy to get confused about which one is which. What we think of as money in day-today life is in fact currency: it is just a promise to pay to the bearer of that bank note x amount of money. It is traditionally printed on paper which lacks intrinsic value. Is it really worth spending 40 plus hours a week so that you can collect a few grams of watermarked paper?

Money, in contrast, maintains its purchasing power and has intrinsic value like gold and silver do. The intrinsic value of precious metals lies in their rarity, in the fact that their supply is limited, so there is no chance that somebody will all of a sudden dump hundreds of tons of gold or silver onto the market and have them devalued because of the inflation of the supply. When the US dollar was decoupled from gold in 1971, it lost its intrinsic value and ceased to be a true money in the store of value sense of the world.

The global issue is that central banks can, unlike in the case of gold, at any time flood the economy with tons of newly printed paper (excuse me, bank notes), which automatically reduces the purchasing power of everybody who holds any amount of that currency, either in the form of bank notes or as digits sitting on their bank accounts.

The real value is created by people who produce goods and provide services, so if the money supply is augmented artificially while the total production of goods and services remains the same, the result will be the devaluation of the purchasing power of the currency that you obtained by selling your goods and services.

"Let there be money" is more or less how we could translate "fiat money". It means that the central banks do not actually create any value, nor do they issue new money based on the increase of supply of something that has intrinsic value (and, consequently, neither do they create a true store of value) when they issue new money. Instead of adding new supply of something that has intrinsic value, they just say: "I will now create this new batch of paper notes because I want to, and it will work as money".

They know well that by printing more money they are leeching wealth out of the population (because with each new fiat money creation you lose purchasing power, as the value of the currency you worked for is decreasing while the production of products and services stay the same).

In theory, everybody could create their own currency (or money in colloquial language) because it is just a way to facilitate economic exchange and keeping tabs easily.

Money creation has always been monopolized by the state, central banks and banks (as far as our modern history goes back). Until its decoupling from the gold standard the US dollar was backed by a certain amount of gold, which kept the value of the dollar relatively stable and served as a storage of value. Since then, central banks did not have to possess a stipulated amount of gold to back the new amount of money they wanted to issue. This translated into giving central banks free rein to pump out as much newly minted and printed money (i.e. currency) as they needed to keep the cycle of debt going and ever expanding.

When you deposit money (currency, technically) into your bank account, you would expect that it will be sitting there idly, waiting for you to spend it. This would be logical, right? After all, it is *your* money. Well, the truth is that banks now only have to keep a certain amount of your deposit available in actual bank notes, should you decide to take all your money out of the bank.

The logic behind this is that, unless a major financial crisis hits, only a small percentage of their customers are likely to withdraw all the money they have on their bank accounts at any given moment, so this seems like a smart thing to do because the bank can then use the larger part of your deposit to make money from your money without your conscious consent.

The minimum percentage that banks must have in their vaults as compared to the total amount on bank accounts is called the cash reserve ratio. Each country has its own regulations, with the majority of them having their cash reserve ratio between 0% and 17% (with a few exemptions that have 20-45% reserve ratios and some countries where no reserve ratio is stipulated). In the United States this figure is 10%, but for example in Canada, the United Kingdom, Australia, New Zealand and Hong Kong it is 0%.[12]

So if you live in the United States and deposited 100 dollars into your bank account, the bank is only obliged to have 10 dollars in their vault for the "unlikely event" of you wanting to take your money out of the bank in cash. The bank can lend out the remaining 90% to people who need loans. So they take your 100 dollar bill and enter the amount of 100 dollars into your account. Then they can lend out 90 dollars to John Doe who just requested a loan of 90 dollars.

This scheme works very well for the bank because they will not give John Doe the money in cash, but will only type in some digits on his account instead. As if by magic, 90 dollars will instantly appear on his account that he will have to pay back to the bank, as well as the stipulated interest they request from him in exchange for lending him your money.

According to regulations, once those 90 dollars appear on John Doe's account, the bank has to deposit in its vault only 10 %, i.e. 9 dollars from it and can lend out the remaining 81 dollars from the account of the unsuspecting John to a third client, while John will have to pay back the principle (90 dollars) plus the stipulated interest on this loan. Isn't it such a fair, win-win situation, folks?

The insidious interest is the evil tool the controllers used to create a chicken that keeps laying (even though ever smaller) golden eggs. Good for the banks (and we must remember, the majority of banks are not owned by the states; they are private enterprises), bad for all the other participants of the economy.

As we discussed earlier, inflating the amount of money in circulation causes a general increase of the prices of all products, which means that with each injection of a new supply of printed bank notes (which they nowadays like to call "quantitative easing") the currency loses its purchasing value. That is why the dollar has lost virtually all its original purchasing power compared to that of 1913.

Banks lend you the money which cost them nothing (they literally just make it up) and now you have to spend time and energy to pay it back with interest. A clear case falling under the definition of usury as discussed in the Bible.

In a debt based system if banks stopped lending out money of their clients, it would put a serious brake on the economy. People and enterprises would not be able to finance their operations, consequently, they could not pay back their debts. There would be more bankruptcies, more lay-offs, and more burden on the administration to pay unemployment subsidies etc. As a consequence, the government would need to take out even more loans to be able to finance the operations of the country, indebting its people more in the process.

For the economy to stay in motion it is necessary that the debts people and companies owe to the banks plus the interests on those amounts are paid back consistently, and that is only possible if the banks keep lending and lending and thereby keep creating more debt to be repaid. They are milking the population for profit directly (by requesting an interest on loans), while at the same time, as a consequence of their continued money lending practices, the purchasing power of the population decreases. This means that there will inevitably be those who will be unable to keep paying their mortgages or whose businesses will go bankrupt. More power to the banks!

This ties in neatly with Bernard Lietaer's observation regarding what actually is needed for something to be considered as money. He says that money does not have to be backed by anything intrinsically valuable to serve as a medium of exchange (which would be the most important function money should have). In fact, "the magic of money is bestowed on something as soon as a community can agree to use it as a medium of exchange. Our money and monetary system are, therefore, *not de facto realities* like air or water, but are *choices*, like social contracts or business agreements."[13] It is good to remember this when we think about the future of money and what role cryptocurrencies will pay in it.

If you think that the controllers are hiding the characteristics of this usurious money system from us, you are mistaken. It is actually in our faces, but we cannot see it all that easily because we are indoctrinated to always think inside the box, and that actually there is nothing outside the box, so we do not even try to venture there most of the time.

Then there are the complicated processes in operation which may see clumsy, convoluted and ineffective, as if the legislators were unable to come up with a more intelligent and straightforward solution for controlling the flow of money within an economy. This, coupled with the artificially overcomplicated language the media and "experts" use to discuss everything related to the economy puts up a mental barrier in most people. But things are actually not as complicated as they seem.

The Federal Reserve System which is comprised of twelve Federal Reserve Banks based in the twelve federal reserve districts is the central bank of the United States. However, it actually happens to be a privately owned corporation, even though on their website they state that *"the Federal Reserve System is not 'owned' by anyone. Although parts of the Federal Reserve System share some characteristics with private-sector entities, the Federal Reserve was established to serve the public interest."*[14] Well, if they say so...

However, if we visit for example the official website of the St. Louise Federal Reserve Bank, we find the following statement under the title *"Who Owns Reserve Banks?"*:

"The Federal Reserve Banks are not a part of the federal government, but they exist because of an act of Congress. *Their purpose is to serve the public. So is the Fed* private or public?

The answer is both. *While the Board of Governors is an independent government agency, the Federal Reserve Banks are set up like private corporations. Member banks hold stock in the Federal Reserve Banks and earn dividends. Holding this stock does not carry with it the control and financial interest given to holders of common stock in for-profit organizations. The stock may not be sold or pledged as collateral for loans. Member banks also appoint six of the nine members of each Bank's board of directors."* [15]

It is very interesting that while the website of the Federal Reserve System tries to convince readers that they are not privately owned, the Federal Reserve Bank of St. Louise, one of the twelve Federal Reserve Banks that make up the Federal Reserve System confirms that the Fed *is* private and public, meaning it has a public function but its owners are private entities. Interesting. Especially if we believe that "the single most profitable business in the US, by SEC code, is the central bank, the Federal Reserve."[16]

The curious thing is that they do not state who the owners of the Federal Reserve Banks are. Why would they not want to do that? Several people list different financial entities as supposed owners of the Fed, either mentioning the London branch of the Rothschild banking family as the ones who are behind the Fed through various of their financial institutions, or some well-known banks, but they are not officially confirmed either.

After extensive research into this theme, Thomas D. Schauf wrote an article titled *The Federal Reserve Bank is Privately Owned*[17], which provides a list of the owners of the twelve Federal Reserve Banks. According to him, the owners of the Fed are the following: Rothschild Bank of London, Warburg Bank of Hamburg, Rothschild Bank of Berlin, Lehman Brothers of New York, Lazard Brothers of Paris, Kuhn Loeb Bank of New York, Israel Moses Seif Banks of Italy, Goldman, Sachs of New York, Warburg Bank of Amsterdam, Chase Manhattan Bank of New York.

It also seems that the Constitution of the United States stipulates that only Congress has the power to create money and regulate its value. Instead, it is the Fed that creates money and regulates its value. According to Schauf the Federal Reserve System collects billions of dollars in interest and distributes the profits to its shareholders.

Another blatant, though lesser known example is the case of the Central Bank of Europe (CBE) which was established to function as a central bank of the European Union. It was set up by the member states of the EU, and the member states provided deposits to its central pool from which countries can request loans as needed. All this sounds pretty reasonable, right? There is one problem though.

The logical way for the Central Bank of Europe would be to give a loan to the central bank of the state which requested it. Also, as the CBE was set up by member states, it should not apply any interest whatsoever. It would be enough if the member state borrowing the loan would pay the money it received back on schedule.

Instead, the reality is that if a member state requests a loan, the CBE does not lend it to the central bank of the requesting country, but to commercial banks which operate in that state.

It is worth repeating. The central financial institution which was funded with 100% state-owned money lends the money initially provided by those states to private corporations, private banks operating in the member states. These private banks then go about their normal business and shamelessly lend the money to the government, requesting the government to pay back not only the principle (the total amount of what the state borrowed from the bank), but interests as well.

Excuse me! How can this be a legally accepted practice? What this means is that private corporations use the money of the European Union (which belongs to the population of the member states) to make good, private profit at the expense of entire countries. This is ridiculous, evil and insane, and it really makes one think to what extent countries belong to their population and to what extent they are really owned by corporate entities.

The case of changed constitutions in Europe is another disturbing example of who and what really enjoys priority in the world today. After the financial world crisis of 2007-2008 many of the European countries fell into severe recession, especially Portugal, Italy, Greece, and Spain, and their public debts were reaching perilous heights. You may remember how it all ended for Greece; with their failing banks bailed out with tax money against the will of its people. The country has been going through a very difficult period ever since and today it is technically bankrupt.

Germany suggested the capping of budget deficit for the member states of the EU and incorporated this cap into its constitution in 2011. Other countries followed its example. The Spanish government for example made unconstitutional changes to its national constitution, without calling for a referendum they included the cap to the budget deficit (which they determined to be conveniently applied from 2020 onward, by when the decision makers responsible for it personally would not be affected as politicians).

Shockingly, the Spanish constitution now says that the repayment of the public debt must be prioritized as opposed to the functions of the various public institutions like health care, education, public roads, unemployment subsidies, or retirement pensions. Of course, the changes to the constitution were made without consulting the citizens. A country hijacked by the banking system and its corrupt politicians.

This may remind you of the similar phenomenon of "shareholder primacy" which means that the short-term interests of the shareholders of a company enjoy supremacy as opposed to the long-term interests of the company, especially those of its employees and many times its clients and its environment.

There is way too much power in the hands of those who are not worthy of controlling the way we live our lives and the way our societies are organized. Observing history we find that every single civilization had crashed one after the other. The only exception may be, curiously, China which has gone from empire to a weird combination of communism and capitalism, which is now happily marching toward the step-by-step creation of a full-on digital dictatorship via a social credit system to have total control over its population while trampling on civil rights and environmental and health safety concerns.

All our evident ingenuity in creating art and wonderful technologies seems to be lacking in the field of economic and social organization. As if someone or something were deliberately blocking us from finding, creating, developing and successfully maintaining a well working, fail-safe, people-friendly economical system.

Mark Shepard, author of the brilliant book, *Restoration Agriculture, Real-World Permaculture for Farmers*[18] says that every single human society that has relied on annual crops for staple foods has collapsed. Why? Because they gradually stripped off all the forests and other, more complex biomes to convert the fertile land into new growing areas for annual crops: grains, potatoes and the like.

Growing annuals year after year in semi-barren land where a large percentage of the soil is not covered throughout the year, completely strips away nutrients from the soil, also because the land is fully exposed to erosion by wind and rains.

Once a society had cut down all its forests and once its agricultural soils had turned infertile, famine came and it lead to the demise of that civilization. Shepard proposes to develop agricultural systems that imitate perennial ecosystems with trees and bushes that provide renewing crops, interplanted with annual crops. Such systems would be more in line with the complexity of natural ecosystems and we could get not only food but also building materials, fuels, and other uses like medicinal herbs from our own farms or backyards.

What does this have to do with money and the recurring cycles of the economy? Well, there is a similarity between how our forests and other complex natural ecosystems have been, and are being, destroyed to be turned into annual crop growing mega areas and how societies are being eroded by the irresponsible use of unhealthy currencies that are lent out for interest.

As more and more fiat currency is being pumped into the economy to feed the system by creating more debt so that the already existing debt can be repaid so that banks could get their cut, the natural, otherwise self-sustaining human communities turn into barren sociological semi-deserts where the individual has to fight over resources against everyone else. Cities are concrete jungles where hardly any solidarity or genuine care can be found, unless you have the money to pay for them.

The only solution for the desertification of our society would be to create healthy money and healthy currencies that are not based on debt. But how could we achieve such a feat? A radical change can only happen if we abolish the store of value and tool of speculation functions of money and only use currencies for what they need to be used for a healthy and just economy to work: namely, as a medium of exchange and a unit of account.

If we did not allow money to be used as a store of value and a tool of speculation, society would look completely different. Imagine that there are no stock exchanges, no financial firms and wealthy individuals who bet on the future of currencies and basic agricultural and industrial products, or create obscure derivatives, no mega rich people shorting everything under the sun for their own gains, causing enormous harm to the economies at large and to each and every person who loses his purchasing power as a consequence.

In theory, we could get back to gold standard for fiat currencies, and make it illegal to increase the amount of bank notes in circulation of these currencies. This, coupled with the abolishing of interests on loans, other than maybe service fees to be paid to banks which could then serve as public utility companies owned by cities, rather than by states, instead of being for profit corporations, would put an end to the menace of the debt spiral. Of course, for such a complete overhaul we would need to strike the national debt of all countries as well, and possibly jail the top banksters who have been sucking the lifeblood of nations for so long.

In such an economic situation we could surely use money backed by gold or other metal, or even other non-perishable goods as a true store of value without having to hoard it in the hopes of getting interests for it. Our purchasing power would not diminish continuously. So, why is it not happening? Has this not occurred to anybody yet?

The sad fact is that we, the people, are not allowed to issue our own, customized moneys and currencies. That is illegal, remember? There have been numerous attempts to create alternative currencies in the past hundred years or so, and a couple of them showed great initial success. Let's see a number of those initiatives, what novelty they proposed and whether they were a viable way to support communities or they proved to be dead ends.

5

Can Negative Interest Be Positive?

The existence of interest on borrowed money not only siphons time and energy (i.e. money) off from the population, companies, and countries; according to Lietaer, it is also one of the most systematical causes of the destruction of our environment globally. Interest is the reason why the present net value of any income which can be realized in the far future is negligible.

In practice what this means is that financially it makes more sense to cut down a tree today and put the money you receive for selling it into the bank than leaving it alone for decades so that it can continue to grow, provide habitat for life, retain humidity in the soil, prevent desertification, filter the air and provide oxygen.

If interest did not exist, your money in the bank would not grow simply by virtue of the passing of time, so it would make no sense to destroy something today that in itself would be of value for a longer time, such as a tree.

Demurrage currency

Demurrage currency would be probably the best instrument to eliminate such ecologically and societally negative outcomes from our economy. Demurrage currency has a "negative interest" which is applied because the currency is viewed as a public utility, just like street lighting, for the use of which we have to pay a small amount of handling and maintenance fee.

As a result, the nominal value of this currency decreases each month, so it is not worth hoarding it. Imagine if we had such a currency (let's call it "dec" now), and that you received 100 dec on January 1. If the handling (or demurrage) fee is 1% per month, on February 1 you would only have 99 dec left. If you put your 100 dec into the bank, or under your mattress, when you wanted to take it out again on January 1 of the following year, you would have 88.64 dec available as the amount would be reduced by 1% each month.

Under such circumstances you are not incentivized to keep your money in the bank or to just hoard it, letting it lay about while it is silently losing its purchasing value.

If you observe humans, it is easy to see that, in general, we act according to our best interests, or rather according to what we think is, or what common sense tells us to be, in our best interest. (Isn't it curious that the same word "interest" signifies both "what benefits me" as in "what is in my interest" and also "money I receive passively for hoarding or lending out my money"? This is quite an interesting piece of mind control language use to ponder.)

Out of their best interest people would not hoard a demurrage currency, but instead they would spend it as quickly as possible. Those who would receive the money from them in exchange for their goods and services would also do the same; they would try to spend the money as quickly as possible before it loses more of its value.

This negative interest is what makes demurrage currency an economical hot potato. Everybody would try to pass it on to somebody else to avoid losing out on purchasing power. The increased velocity of transactions would result in faster economic activity, significantly more transactions, and as a result many new jobs would be established.

The decisions about the economy and the development of the urban environment and infrastructure would also be decentralized to a great extent, because those who would like to spend their demurrage currency would actively participate in spreading the money (by paying with it for goods and services), and as a consequence, they would create many jobs.

The lack of interest on money would also mean that a good, livable and sustainable future would be more valuable to people than present day income. People would concentrate on the long term consequences of their present day actions. They would buy products with a longer shelf life. They would construct their buildings if not "for eternity", but taking into consideration what would be beneficial for the coming generations too. For example, they would spend all surplus income on further insulation and other developments that make the building more cost efficient and environmentally sound.

The government would not have to offer a tax deduction or "educate" people to act in an environmentally responsible manner because they would already do so out of their own self-interest. The negative interest of the demurrage currency would reprogram the "invisible hand" of financial self-interest.

It is important to note that the negative interest of a demurrage currency is not the same as the zero or negative interest of our current fiat money. We have seen in the past few years that when you put your money in the bank, it is disappearing at a very slow rate, because national banks started to stipulate zero or even negative interest rates.

The bank is taking your money because it is sitting on your account while it can happily lend out a large part of it to others. This makes it a bad option to just leave your money in the bank, but it doesn't make you think long-term as demurrage currency could do and it sacrifices future benefits for present-day gains.

The theory of demurrage currency was developed by Silvio Gesell[19] at the beginning of the 20th century, but the most well-known experiments for its use took place at the beginning of the 1930's. It all started when Max Hebecker, the owner of a bankrupt mine in Germany tried to pay with coal instead of the official currency, the Reichsmark in Schwanenkirchen in 1929. He issued a temporary local paper money called "Wära" which could be exchanged for coal. Wära could be translated as "lasting currency".

The Wära remained valid only if its owner purchased stamps for a small amount of money and stuck one of them onto its back side each month. The negative interest administered in the form of these stamps was necessary to cover the storage costs of the coal which was used to back up the currency.

Given that everybody who accepted the Wära as a currency had self-interest in convincing the rest of the community to accept it, the movement became so successful that one year later there were over two thousand similar currencies called "stamp scrips" in circulation throughout Germany, all backed by various products. It comes as no surprise that the German national bank, referring to its monopoly on issuing money, prohibited the further use of stamp scrips in 1931.

A movement started in 1932 by the mayor of a small Austrian town called Wörgl came to a similar result when in the midst of the world economic crisis he managed to convince the city council to issue "stamp scrips" worth 14,000 Schillings which were backed by the same amount of Schillings deposited in the local bank in order to reduce local unemployment which at the time was at 35 percent.

As a result of the introduction of this local demurrage currency, unemployment in Wörgl disappeared in two years, while the inhabitants of the town constructed a water pipe system, renovated the streets and the majority of the houses. At the same time, people paid local taxes before deadlines and even planted new forests around the city.

Individual initiatives of people using these stamp scrips were aimed at harnessing long term advantages. All this due to the fact that the demurrage currency did not incentivize people for hoarding it.

Lamentably, the local money of Wörgl had a similar fate to that of the Wära; after more than two hundred Austrian municipalities adopted this model, the Austrian national bank prohibited the use of local currencies.

As a surprising and instructive data, it is worth mentioning that the circulation rate of the local currency of Wörgl was fourteen times greater than that of the official currency, which means that during the same time period the local currency created fourteen times as many jobs as the Austrian Schilling.[20] That is an enormous difference.

Present day community currencies

Today the majority of the more than one thousand nine hundred community currencies currently in use do not apply demurrage. They are mostly free of interest, but as the example of these community currencies proves, that in itself does not incentivize their holders to invest in the future or to spend those currencies as quickly as they can. As a consequence, the majority of community currencies only help people build their local communities, but they do not create more jobs and they definitely do not pump up the local economy notably.[21]

If indebted countries chose to introduce demurrage currencies (first maybe locally or regionally, and later across the nation), they would be able to pay back their debt relatively easily, as the economic growth would increase manifold without an increased negative impact on the environment or on sustainability. Such countries could even lower the tax burden of their population.

And now the bad news. It does not take a rocket scientist to see why there is no chance of this ever happening until we live in what is called a representative democracy (not to mention the global, not so hidden, centralizing efforts of the controllers, as clearly visible from the history of the European Union).

It would be worth allowing the use of demurrage currencies at least locally, which could peacefully coexist with the official currencies of the given country. Regional governments and municipalities could issue electronic cash tethered to the official currency of the country, so that the value of the local coin would be tethered to the national money 1:1, and accept it for tax payments. This would solve the issues of the growing unemployment, as well as the isolation of people, lack of community and the near extinction level environmental damage which are unsolvable with the tools currently in use.

Another, more idealistic stream in the alternative-local currency move-ment is that of time banks. A time bank is a kind of ledger where people who form an association can trade their services not based on their actual perceived value but on the amount of time they employed in providing those services. This, in theory, honors the fact that there is no way that we can buy more time, so time is our most valued wealth (although do not tell this to the proponents of the currently flourishing transhumanist movement who, fully immersed in their hubris, are trying to extend their physical lives into immortality by merging with machines). We talk about normal people here, ok? No transhumanist psycho freaks (pardon my French).

Unless our societies become way more ethics oriented and unless we adopt real integrity and truth as the main driving forces of our everyday existence, there is very little chance that time banks could ever create much positive change. For one, they already exclude the exchange of physical products.

Or what if you are a heart surgeon and just did a seven-hour life saving operation on somebody who belongs to your time bank? It just happens to be that you would receive seven units of the time bank token. Would you be able to receive back the same amount of value by paying a cleaning lady with your seven time bank tokens to clean your house for a total of seven hours? Some people would say yes, but surely many would be completely against this model of equality. Clean floors are laudable, but saving somebody's life seems to be incomparably more valuable.

Participatory economics, where money is not the culprit

Not everyone says though that money as we know it is flawed and needs to be reformed in order to create a just economy and a more livable society. We must mention here the peculiar theory of participatory economics created by Michael Albert[22], an alternative economist from the United States. Michael Albert does not think it necessary to change the current characteristics of money because, according to him, the system he suggests would bring forth such a complex structural change that only that in itself would be sufficient to create real societal and economic equality. Even despite the current characteristics of money that encourage hoarding behavior.

Before we start to party, there is one problem though with participatory economics (or *parecon*). To be able to introduce it, the working class (and maybe the more progressively thinking members of what Albert calls the coordinator class) should join forces to cooperate on a large enough scale that would be necessary to change the structure of society.

To be able to do that, first the philosophy of parecon should be widely spread and the population should be mobilized, which likely would be a herculean task. At first glance such requirements do not give much hope for parecon to be ever introduced successfully, but let's see what Michael Albert suggests as a possible solution.

The uniqueness of participatory economics lies in the fact that it is the only theoretical system (and we have to emphasize that it is theoretical) which is not doomed to fail by the existence of social classes. Albert thinks that the hitherto tried systems (capitalism, socialism, and communism included) have contained in themselves the main cause of their failure; the fact that they divided society into classes of different value and status.

Albert says that in capitalism apart from the capitalist class and the working class there is a third, intermediate class which he calls the coordinator class. These people usually do not have capital but play managing, directing roles in organizations and corporations, and their weight within society is much greater than that of the working class. Lawyers, medical doctors, engineers and the like belong to this group.

He thinks that the fault of communism was that even though in theory its aim was to abolish class differences, in practice the earlier coordinator-coordinated structure was maintained intact and when communism was introduced, the place of the capitalist class was simply taken over by the coordinator class. Coordinators had more power than the worker class and could make decisions over the head of the workers and on their behalf, which explains why communism is not about equality, but is a system of inequality. The reason for this is the existence of classes, which excludes the creation of any kind of true equality.

Albert seems to be on track, but he does not touch on the root cause. There are not only capitalists, coordinators and workers. He imagined *parecon* to be a system that combines community ownership, allocation done in a participatory process of planning, balanced complex jobs, wages paid based on the onerousness of a job and the level of "sacrifice" it takes to perform it (in this sense thinking similarly to time banks), participatory self-management, and a lack of class differences. He would like everybody to have the same chance to participate in the economy and to benefit from it.

This would only be possible according to him, if instead of the current job specialization we would create complex jobs and the leaders and managers of today would do administrative and physical tasks as well. In this way the low level workers who are doomed to brain death and boredom would also get a chance to do more exciting, more responsible, different tasks too, of course in harmony with the needs of the company and society.

Is Michael Albert seriously delusional? Can such an economic system work with the same old debt based money and solve the problems of our society? His clear goal is the abolition of the privileged status of the capitalist and coordinator classes and the creation of real equality of chance. He deems it immoral that some people earn 5-10-20 times more than others with the same time and energy expenditure, and thinks that the only just system would be if work would not be remunerated according to the social ladder or the knowledge necessary for its execution, but according to how much time it takes to do it and how onerous or dangerous it is.

Only these criteria would provide true equality of chance according to Albert, because the less talented or less educated people would have the same chance to make a good income than those who are more talented, more educated or more lucky. The creation of complex jobs would result in the opening up of the possibility of a more fun, more humane, more creative work life for those belonging to the working class.

Parecon tries to avoid authoritarian structures, its planning process includes continuous internal dialogue and constant reconciliation. Production tools should be owned collectively, and consequently each and every decision needs to be a collective process. Albert envisions work councils and consumer councils working in unison to balance supply and demand within the economy. He thinks that central planning bureaucracies would not be necessary, and people would have to be involved in the planning of every facet of the economy, which would lead us into a real democracy.

It all sounds interesting, but seriously, without changing the root cause, the debt-based money system, how could such a participatory economy be plausible? Before the development of the blockchain technology the concept of participatory economy could be easily ignored as a pipe dream of an overly idealistic person who is completely unaware of the realities of how our society works. However, once we dive into the possibilities of the blockchain technology, we will briefly get back to the question whether blockchain could make things possible that seemed unattainable due to corruption and centralization.

Maybe participatory economy is too much, and jumping from today's crocodile capitalism into something so spookily idealistic would be too abrupt a change. Maybe what we need is a gradual, step by step breaking of the mental, technical and legal chains of having to operate under a corrupt, structurally, internally flawed money system.

Parecon has a hardcore ultra-communistic feel to it, as all that planning, all that coordinating done through committees does not seem very natural and is too process based. Because people would have to be involved in these input-heavy processes continuously, there is actually ample room for corruption to occur at any point, which could wreck the entire system. It also resembles China's marxist authoritarianism. If for nothing else, it is worth contemplating that there are alternative models for the organization of society not wildly known and we could always come up with something new that could actually work, although that wouldn't be parecon.

In any case, if we could just change the basic characteristics of money, eliminating interest, and separating the store of value and tool of speculation functions from the medium of exchange and unit of account functions, that would mean the first step in the right direction.

Now, with the appearance of cryptocurrencies and the blockchain technology this process seems to have already started. We have seen that traditional alternative currencies which are currently in use are only a solution to local economic problems because the state authorities and national banks do not approve of them, so they are not allowed to be adopted in entire countries.

Also, more importantly, these alternative currencies cannot be used for paying taxes, which limits their practical value. They are useful, however, for keeping wealth in the local community and not letting all of it siphoned off by multinational corporations.

But for a more systemic overhaul we really need to change our official currencies and the way we see money. In the following we will examine whether Bitcoin, and cryptocurrencies in general, could be a solution to the problems plaguing our society. We will talk about what cryptocurrencies are, what benefits they can provide and the possible issues which may arise from their use. We will also discuss what blockchain technology is, and how it can potentially change life on Earth as we know it.

6

Enter Satoshi

The global financial crisis of 2007-2008 began with the crash of the housing market in the United States. The banks had been offering mortgages up to 100% of the purchase value to practically anybody who requested them, and when real estate prices suddenly fell more than 30%, everybody panicked. This bubble was caused by the introduction of some very toxic new financial products like credit default swaps which are securities backed by home loans as collaterals. Once real estate prices fell while interests rose on mortgages, many people became unable to pay their mortgages.

The crisis came to a point where banks did not want to lend money to each other and this created a critical situation. As a result, in the United States an act was passed with the aim to prevent banks from taking on too much risk. "Too big to fail" banks had to be bailed out with tax payer money because these banks had too much influence on the economy.

The crisis revealed how the privately owned, profit oriented banks were unable or unwilling to regulate themselves and that actually they were a constant danger to the economy. They simply have too much power because they could cause another global financial crisis at any time.

This crisis was exacerbated by the actions of financial speculators who instead of real estate now focused on oil and food, which triggered a huge increase of the global price of cereals and directly caused the death of millions of people in developing countries. We cannot talk about ethics or empathy when it comes to the controllers. And sadly, many speculators went for the short-term gains instead of acting as a responsible, compassionate person should. We have been so suppressed, so much of our money (and time and energy) has been stolen from us since birth and the indoctrination is so strong that the default setting of individuals, and of corporations more so, is to move toward self-interest at any cost to others.

It was in such turbulent circumstances that the concept of Bitcoin was introduced in the form of a whitepaper, distributed to a cryptography mailing list. This whitepaper was written by a mysterious developer who called himself Satoshi Nakamoto. For many years nobody knew who Satoshi Nakamoto was, as he chose to stay in anonymity. Although he had interacted with people online for some time, he completely withdrew from public communications in June 2011.

There have been various "candidates" who people theorized could be Satoshi. Some believe that Satoshi is not one person but rather a group of developers. Others say that it could be that the NSA or the CIA are behind the creation of Bitcoin. They base this hypothesis on the fact that the blockchain uses the SHA-256 protocol which was developed by the NSA and subsequently registered by the National Institute of Technology and Standards. There could be many reasons for the real Satoshi to want to stay hidden so we will not dwell on his identity, but rather will take a look at what he brought to the table of technological development.

Cryptography is used to provide security for electronic systems by encrypting information. One common use of it is the pin codes for credit cards. Satoshi sent the Bitcoin whitepaper to a mailing list to developers interested in cryptography because he wanted to create a system which would be unhackable and safe enough to eliminate the need for trust in a third entity when making transactions. Currently we must trust a centralized power (banks) that they will not do anything dubious.

Satoshi Nakamoto's 2007 whitepaper was titled *Bitcoin: A Peer-to-Peer Electronic Cash System.* He then went on and wrote the code and introduced Bitcoin, the first *decentralized digital currency* to the world in 2009. The abstract of the whitepaper explains the goals which made him develop Bitcoin.

"A purely peer-to-peer version of electronic cash would allow online payments to be sent directly from one party to another without going through a financial institution. Digital signatures provide part of the solution, but the main benefits are lost if a trusted third party is still required to prevent double-spending. We propose a solution to the double-spending problem using a peer-to-peer network. The network timestamps transactions by hashing them into an ongoing chain of hash-based proof-of-work, forming a record that cannot be changed without redoing the proof-of-work. The longest chain not only serves as proof of the sequence of events witnessed, but proof that it came from the largest pool of CPU power. As long as a majority of CPU power is controlled by nodes that are not cooperating to attack the network, they'll generate the longest chain and outpace attackers. The network itself requires minimal structure. Messages are broadcast on a best effort basis, and nodes can leave and rejoin the network at will, accepting the longest proof-of-work chain as proof of what happened while they were gone."[23]

According to the whitepaper, Bitcoin was created to provide *"a solution to the double-spending problem using a peer-to-peer distributed timestamp server to generate computational proof of the chronological order of transactions."* It sounds convoluted, but stay with me here, ok? It will become clear as we break down Satoshi's statements.

Bitcoin: a peer-to-peer electronic cash

The standard processing of making electronic payments today involves a "trusted third party" (banks or money transfer companies). The role of these trusted third parties is to prevent cheating both by the sender and the receiver. We need to involve them because there is no way for us to know whether the other party will "behave" or will want to use the transaction to steal our money.

Financial institutions are relatively reliable as the middlemen to ensure that neither party cheats. However, there are some weaknesses of this system which regularly cause problems to those who want to engage in electronic transactions.

One of the issues is that transactions can be reversed. If you provide a service which cannot be reversed like cutting somebody's hair, when you are paid via electronic transfer, your client could later decide to reverse the payment for whatever reason. If he convinces the mediating bank or credit card company to reverse the payment, the money he sent you will disappear from your account and you obviously cannot recover the time and energy wasted in cutting his hair. This creates a serious trust issue between merchants and clients.

Another drawback is that the transaction fees of these middlemen are high because of the possibility of the bank having to mediate between the two parties, which costs money. These high transaction fees are not optimal if you want to make a smaller transaction because the transaction fee will be too high compared to the small amount of money you want to send. This is especially true for international payments which can have surprisingly high transaction fees, as you are charged not only for the potential mediating costs but also for the processing of the wire transfer and for exchanging your money to another currency.

Moreover, the speed of electronic transactions, especially international bank transfers is unjustifiably sluggish. An international bank transfer can take several days, which is far from optimal in this age, after all it is all electronic.

Security is another key issue with having to use financial institutions for electronic transactions. Banks are not entirely secure, although we like to think that they provide enough security to put our trust in them. They are relatively secure, but security breaches can and do happen quite often.

For one, some unethical or badly treated, indignant employee could steal from the accounts of many clients from inside the system. Then there is the risk of hackers attacking the servers of the bank who could successfully take over the control of the entire network and access all the accounts of the bank. The risk is even greater because the system of banks is centralized; they tend to be run by servers located in one place, so once a hacker gets to that central core, the security of the entire system is breached.

Bitcoin was developed against the backdrop of such a centralized and less than 100% secure electronic transaction system. Bitcoin is a *decentralized* electronic cash operated on a peer-to-peer basis. This means that it does not use central servers of some financial institution, nor is there a central server of the Bitcoin network. There are no trusted third parties involved in the processing of transactions. There is no central governing organization or corporation that can have access to, and control, the entire network.

Instead of having central servers, the system is comprised of the computers of users which make up a decentralized network. The advantage of this structure for Bitcoin users is that governments or financial authorities cannot shut down the network by simply turning off its main servers because there aren't any.

The Bitcoin network is made up of many nodes that are very difficult to locate at the current level of technology, and even if authorities would be able to locate some nodes and shut them down simultaneously, the Bitcoin network would be slower, but still operational even with a relatively small portion of its normal infrastructure.

The reason why the Bitcoin network would be able to remain functional (though slower) if say 10% of its computing power were shut down is because it is a distributed ledger using blockchain technology which means that information is continuously being updated and recorded throughout the entire network, so each computer/node has the latest version of the distributed ledger. Even if somebody managed to turn off 90% of the computers, 10% of them would still contain a copy of the latest version of the distributed ledger, so the information would not be lost or blocked forever.

The most important feature of Bitcoin is that it is set up as a decentralized peer-to-peer network. This is achieved by keeping a distributed ledger on every computer/node that belongs to the network. A distributed ledger is just like any simple database, but instead of being stored in a central place, it is constantly copied from computer to computer so that in any moment the majority of the computers have the latest, correct version of the transaction history.

Each node updates its copy of the distributed ledger independently. So those computers that were turned off in the above example, once reconnected to the Bitcoin network, would be able to download the latest version of the entire history of the blockchain as if they had never been disconnected.

The blockchain technology is just one way of creating a distributed ledger. The blockchain organizes data into blocks which are validated by the entire system of nodes.

The Blockchain

A blockchain is a distributed ledger which uses cryptography based on digital signatures, and a peer-to-peer network based on the blockchain protocol. It is called blockchain because it arranges transactions into blocks and uses special cryptography to create a link between them.

The blockchain technology was created by mixing three already existing elements: private key cryptography (digital signatures), the internet (the infrastructure for creating a decentralized peer-to-peer network), and a protocol which is based on the self-interest of users to maintain the distributed database (incentivization).[24]

Unlike traditional ledgers, which are held and updated by one central authority (like a bank), distributed ledgers are decentralized. This means that each participant keeps an identical copy of the transaction history, and all copies are constantly updated via the blockchain protocol. When a user joins the network, he downloads the latest, up-to-date copy of the entire blockchain from the very first block to the present one onto his computer. A computer that keeps a copy of the blockchain is called a node. Because of the way blocks are verified, the blockchain gets updated on each and every node of the network after each new block.

The most important factor in transactional relationships is trust between the parties. However, we often need to transact with people and organizations we cannot trust (because either we do not know them personally and can't be sure that they are who they say they are, or because we do not know if they will try to cheat).

When you transact in cash and you only have a 20 dollar bill, once you have given it to somebody in exchange for something, you cannot spend the same 20 dollars again. You also normally receive the product you spend the 20 dollars on right away because everything happens face to face, so you have full control of the transaction.

Centralized electronic ledgers solve the problem of trust by having a central authority which is able to verify the identity of both participants of a transaction, as well as whether the sender has the funds he tries to spend. This excludes cheating between parties because all transactions go through a central authority which only allows a transaction to take place after verifying that both the sender and the receiver are who they say they are, and that the sender has the money he wants to send to the receiver.

When you send money using the centralized electronic network of the banking system, the bank as the central authority makes sure that you are unable to cheat and spend same money twice, by always verifying if you have the necessary amount on your account to make a payment. (In practice, double spending still occurs in centralized systems because people can reverse transactions in bad faith and spend the money again, but the banks have mechanisms to stop people from doing it or at least mitigate the damage.)

In an electronic system there is always the possibility that a nefarious person might try to spend the same money twice. For example, if he only has 20 dollars in his bank account and purchases a product online for 20 dollars, once the payment is confirmed the merchant will ship the product to him. Our nefarious guy, however, could reverse the transaction right after he receives the confirmation of the merchant that the product was shipped to him, and he could spend the same 20 dollars buying something else. The result of the cheater's double spending is that he ends up with 40 dollars' worth of products while he has only spent 20 dollars, and the first vendor never gets paid and loses 20 dollars on the sale.

Double spending is a major problem that decentralized electronic systems like cryptocurrencies where the participants of transactions cannot know whether the other is trying to cheat must solve to create and maintain trust in the system and have people keep wanting to use it. Without finding a solution to the double spending problem a peer-to-peer network would very quickly fail. Once people started to lose money because of bad actors, they would abandon the system due to lack of security.

The internet, specifically because it is difficult to know who anyone is, has made it very easy for scammers and fraudsters to cheat people out of their money. When Satoshi Nakamoto came up with his version of a peer-to-peer electronic cash, he needed to find a solution to create trust in an electronic environment where nobody can trust the other because of the difficulty to know whether a person really is who he claims to be, and whether he is trustworthy.

A distributed ledger is a decentralized database that does not require the parties to trust each other or a central authority. The blockchain is a trustless record of the digital interactions of its users where trust is created by the impeccability of the blockchain protocol.

Blockchains are called trustless systems because the record of the digital interactions of their users is resistant to alterations caused by attackers and because trust is established by private key cryptography and a consensus algorithm that makes sure that a transaction can only be accepted as valid if at least 51% of the verifying nodes accept it as valid.

The permanent, immutable nature of the blockchain is the result of the way information is structured into blocks where each block is cryptographically intertwined with the previous block in a way that if an attacker wanted to change the already recorded information on the blockchain, he would have to change all the following blocks as well, which is nearly impossible.

This immutable relationship between blocks of the Bitcoin blockchain is due to the 256-SHA hashing algorithm and the proof of work consensus algorithm used to verify transactions. Other blockchains use other cryptographic algorithms and consensus algorithms.

The *256-SHA Secure Hash Algorithm* is the cryptographic hash function used in Bitcoin to provide the necessary security and a sufficient level of privacy on the blockchain. The 256-SHA hash function generates a 256-bit

(64-digit) code from any input of any length. No matter if the input has only a few characters or several thousand, the protocol will always translate it into a unique 64-character *hash* which is a kind of digital fingerprint of the input.

If even one character of the input is changed, the resulting hash will be completely different, but for the same input the resulting hash will always be the same, which is useful to detect any alteration of data in a block. Moreover, it is impossible to figure out from a hash what the original input was, which provides a secure way to prove the identity of the sender of a transaction without having to unveil his private data.

The original data occulted by the hash could only be discovered from it by using a brute-force search which means that the attacker would need to try all possible character combinations until he finds the correct combination by chance. Modern cryptography is based on this one-way hash function.[25]

The security and privacy of the blockchain are achieved by cryptographic encryption of user information (such as the addresses of the sender and the recipient, the transaction ID, the amount sent, and time of the transaction). The cryptographic hash function transforms all this data into a 64-digit hash, i.e. a string of 64 characters of numbers between 0-9 and letters between a-f.

The private key cryptography used provides at least pseudo-anonimity (and full anonymity in case of certain privacy-focused blockchains like Monero or Zcash). In the case of Bitcoin we only have pseudo-anonimity. The personal information of Bitcoin users is disconnected from their account, and a public address is used instead which is a seemingly random set of 34 digits, and nobody within the Bitcoin network can find out to whom a given public address belongs, unless the owner lets them know.

However, in practice it is possible to find out to whom those public addresses belong (and blockchain analysis companies or government agencies actually find the owners of public addresses). So although within the Bitcoin network users can be considered anonymous, for outside observers they are relatively easily identifiable. That's why the Bitcoin whitepaper suggested that users create a new wallet for each transaction to avoid being identified.

Each user has a *private key* which is used to identify him and demonstrate ownership of the coins he wants to spend. The *public key* is derived from the private key, and the *public address* is derived from the public key, by using a one-way hash function. This means that it is very difficult to find out the public key from the public address and the private key from the public key.[26]

When a user joins the Bitcoin network, he will get a software program called a *wallet* which "facilitates sending and receiving bitcoins and gives ownership of the Bitcoin balance to the user".[27] The wallet does not store bitcoins as separate electronic tokens (because bitcoins do not exist as such), instead it stores the transaction history related to the owner's private key.

The idea is that users generate a new public address with its corresponding single-use private key and public key for each transaction. A wallet is basically a string of different public addresses, it is "similar to a key ring because it holds a copy of each private key and its corresponding address"[28].

A Bitcoin wallet address (or public address) consists of 35 (and sometimes 26) characters, while the public key is 64 characters long. The public key serves to prove that you are the owner of a public address which can receive money.

When you want to send bitcoins, the transaction is broadcast to the nodes closest to your wallet. Each of those nodes broadcast it to the nodes closest to them and this propagation goes on until the entire network is aware of your transaction. Once it is verified that you have the sufficient funds to make the transaction, it is placed into a temporary depository called the *memory pool* (or mempool).

The integrity of the blockchain is maintained by *miners* in exchange for an incentive called *mining reward* which they receive when they manage to create a new block that is added to the blockchain.

Miners check if the transaction is valid and if it is, they put it into their mempool which temporarily stores unconfirmed transactions. The miner then picks a transaction from the mempool either in chronological order, or choosing one which pays higher transaction fees (which also go to miners), and sooner or later each transaction will be picked up and placed into a new block by the miner.

The miner runs the private key and the transaction through the 256-SHA hashing function and places the resulting hash into the block. He then keeps picking up transactions and after hashing them together with their respective private keys, adds their hashes into the block until it reaches the maximum allowed size. A Bitcoin block can usually contain anywhere between 300 and 3000 transactions, depending on transaction size.

In the header of the block the miner must include the version number (which tracks software and protocol upgrades), the *nonce* (a random number which the miner has to find in order to be able to add his block to the blockchain), the hash of the previous block in the blockchain, and a current timestamp.

The hashes of the transactions in the block are arranged into a *Merkle-tree*: they are paired up and hashed together, then the resulting hashes are paired up with other resulting hashes and hashed together similarly to how we get from the tips of a tree to its roots. This pairing and hashing goes on until only two hashes remain. When the algorithm creates a new hash of these last two, the resulting single hash which is called the *Merkle-root* will be included in the block.[29]

Because each miner works on different transactions at the same time, a consensus must be achieved about which of those blocks will be added to the blockchain, and as a result which miner will get the transaction fees of all the transactions in his block, as well as the mining reward. In order to win this competition, a miner has to solve a very difficult mathematical puzzle which can only be achieved by trial-and-error, checking every possible combination until one of them turns out to be the correct one.

What miners are searching for is the nonce, a random number added to the other information within the block to make the proof of work algorithm create a hash matching the mining difficulty. The Bitcoin protocol for example adjusts difficulty so that every 10 minutes a new block can be mined. "The end goal is to get a hash that's smaller than this difficulty, usually indicated by the number of leading zeros in a hash. Once such a hash is calculated, the nonce is considered the solution, and used as a confirmation mechanism for other nodes (miners) in the network which then confirm that the block is indeed valid."[30]

Once the miner finds the nonce, he can finalize the new block by hashing together the version number, the previous block hash, the Merkle-root, the timestamp, the nonce, and the difficulty target (which determines how difficult it will be to find the nonce).[31]

After adding a new block to the blockchain, the system will wait for newer blocks to be added and then confirms the block, which means that it is now permanently recorded on the blockchain.

To compute the hash of a block the algorithm always includes the hash of the previous block. As a result, blocks are connected in a way that if an attacker wants to change a block, he will have to change the hash values of all the blocks that come after it in the blockchain. As this is extremely difficult to achieve, it makes the blockchain a trustless system.[32]

When a node validates a transaction it means that the node verifies that the transaction is legal (not malicious or involved in double-spending). But in order to agree on the order of events, the order in which validated transactions will be included in the blockchain, the nodes of the network must reach a consensus.[33]

When transactions are made, they are broadcast to the whole network, but each miner can pick up a different set of transactions to include them in a block, likely based on transaction fees. Every miner who includes your transaction into his block can add totally different transactions to it. So that miners who all build different blocks can come to agree on a single, common ledger history, they have to come to consensus about which miner's block will be added to the blockchain next.[34]

If a miner's block is not chosen to be the one included in the blockchain, he will have to create a new block and start mining again in the hopes to win the next time. The most common consensus algorithms used in blockchains are *proof of work* and *proof of stake.* In blockchains with proof of work algorithms (like Bitcoin) whichever miner finds the nonce first, gets to add his block to the blockchain.

Where the proof of stake protocol is used (like in Ethereum), only those users called validators who have paid money (their stakes) into a validator account have a chance to add a new block to the blockchain. The algorithm picks a coin randomly from the coins staked, and the person whose coin was picked can add his block to the blockchain.[35]

"Digital signatures provide part of the solution"

Bitcoin has to provide a way for transactions to be safe and verifiable without the need to have a trusted third party. One of the solutions for achieving the decentralization of Bitcoin is the use of *digital signatures*. A digital signature is a form of cryptography that can be used to keep any information you want to send to somebody from being read by third persons.

There are two basic cryptographic ways to secure a message electronically: *symmetric key cryptography* and non-symmetric or *public-key cryptography*. The simpler type was already used by Julius Caesar. To secure messages the way it was done in Caesar's time you would have to take the original message (the *plaintext*) and substitute each letter of it with another letter according to a pre-determined rule. The resulting text (the *ciphertext*) could only be deciphered if the person trying to read it knew the rules of the ciphering process. In the cryptography of Julius Caesar this pre-determined rule was to substitute each letter with the one 3 places to the left in the alphabet.

The recipient only had to apply the rules backwards and substitute each letter of the ciphertext with the letter 3 places to the right in the alphabet. The rule used to get to the original message from the ciphertext is called the *cryptographic key*.

This type of cryptography has two main issues: first, anyone who wanted to read Caesar's original message would only need to capture somebody who knew the ciphering rules and make them talk, and also, for a cryptographer it is very easy to decipher, so ultimately there is no need to beat anybody to pulp. Because you can take the ciphertext and by using the cryptographic key you can turn it back into the original text, this type of basic cryptography is called *symmetric key cryptography*.

Breaking a code similar to that of Julius Caesar is easy. However, there are symmetric key cryptographic cyphers that are much more advanced. The

Advanced Encryption Standard (AES) is ridiculously secure at our current level of technology. Even the NSA uses it to encrypt protected information. This AES encryption has versions that are comprised of 128, 192 or 256 bits.

In theory, information encrypted using the AES protocol could be deciphered by a "brute force attack" which is one of the most popular ways to decipher protected information. A brute force attack means that the computer keeps trying all existing combinations until it hits the right combination by chance, so if given enough time, it could decipher the whole text.

The largest key which such a brute force attack has ever been able to find only had 64 bits, and it took 1,757 days for a total of 331,252 computers to decipher the code. Now it may seem that there is not such a big jump in difficulty between 64 and 256 digit encryptions, but each digit added increases the difficulty exponentially. Having a key length of 256 bits means that there are 2^{256} possible combinations. This is a 78-digit number so large that the fastest supercomputers we currently know of would take millions of years to crack it.[36]

We don't know, however, how quantum computers will change the game of deciphering. IBM just announced its first quantum computer called IBM Q System One, which is the world's first "integrated universal approximate quantum computing system designed for scientific and commercial use"[37].

MIT has already launched a course on quantum computing, so it seems that quantum computers are going to be the next big thing in information technology. So much so that Google just claimed in a paper published on a NASA site that they have achieved "quantum supremacy" which means that they were able to develop a quantum computer that outperforms a traditional computer. The Google quantum computer solved a problem in twenty seconds which would have taken 10,000 years for the fastest supercomputer. However, it doesn't necessarily mean (yet) that Bitcoin encryption is in danger.[38]

While in the document which was later deleted from the NASA site Google said that its quantum computer currently has 53 qubits (quantum bits), theoretically, one would need 2,000 qubits to be able to break the encryption used for Bitcoin's digital encryption, and even more for breaking the SHA-256 protocol. They expect a double-exponential growth rate in computing power for their quantum computers. This means that quantum computing has already appeared, and Bitcoin and other blockchain based systems must develop quantum-proof ways to keep their encryption unbreakable in the following decades.[39]

At least, for the immediate future we do not have to worry about them. Bitcoin uses the very safe 256-bit encryption in its SHA-256 protocol which we will touch upon later. However, it goes further than that and also applies a more advanced version of cryptography called non-symmetric or *public key cryptography*.

Public key cryptography means that if you encrypt your message using the encryption code, the recipient will only be able to decipher the ciphertext if he has another specific key which proves his identity.

The *public key* is used to encrypt the information, and no matter how many times you encrypt data, you will always use this very same public key for encryption. To be able to read the ciphertext you have to have a specific *private key*.

If you do not know the private key, you cannot decipher the encrypted text. The difficulty is that it is impossible to find out what the private key is if you only know the public key. If you share your public key, people can use it to encrypt information to send it to you, but they will only be able to decipher the information if they also know your private key.

Satoshi solved the security issues of the decentralized Bitcoin network partly by incorporating *digital signatures* into the transactions. A digital signature is created when you add your private key to the data you want to sign. All this happens by using a specific algorithm. This algorithm converts the information you want to protect and your private key into the ciphertext. Everybody can verify if this ciphertext contains your signature (meaning, whether your signature is valid) by using your public key.

The use of digital signatures provides an acceptable level of security to Bitcoin operations. Because there is no central power to do the verification on behalf of the users and to provide the necessary authentication, data integrity and non-repudiation for a transaction to be safe, it is very important that the users of the Bitcoin network be able to prove that they are the rightful owner of a specific Bitcoin token, and also that they can safely transfer this specific token to anybody without having to fear that it gets into the wrong hands.

We talk about "specific Bitcoin tokens" because, as you will see later on, each bitcoin is individual and recognizable, so they are not as fungible as fiat money. Normal bank issued money is fungible because there is no way for the user to track where any banknotes or coins came from, so nobody can refuse accepting a banknote based on the transactions in which it had been used earlier. The everyday user cannot refuse to accept a banknote or coin if it was involved in illegal human trafficking or some other criminal activity because there is no way for him to track the route that specific banknote took from its printing up to the moment it was handed to him.

A bitcoin is not an actual token or coin that has a separate entity like a code sitting in your wallet, but just a balance in the ledger. If you want to find out how many bitcoins you have, you need to scan the blockchain, list all the inflows and outflows of your address and subtract the outflows from the inflows. This balance is a certain amount of bitcoins.

A digital signature can provide authentication of the sender of a transaction, as well as data-integrity (meaning that nobody will be able to mess with your transaction and steal the money you sent to somebody), and non-repudiation (which is making sure that nobody can deny your identity if you can provide your digital signature).

Each individual bitcoin is in fact different from the rest and is identifiable because a bitcoin is a chain of digital signatures. Each owner transfers the coin to the next by digitally signing a hash of the previous transaction and the public key of the next owner, and adding these to the end of the coin. A payee can verify the signatures to verify the chain of ownership.[40]

Hashing is a protocol that translates data of any size into a predetermined character-size ciphertext. So it does not matter if you have four or four thousand characters, you will always get a ciphertext with the same character length. In the case of Bitcoin such a ciphertext or *hash* always has 64 characters.

Hashing includes a complex mathematical equation that is not arbitrary, which means that if you hash the same message the resulting hash will always be the same, but if you make any change to any of the characters of the message the hash will be completely different. This is important in the verification of the transaction.

Digital signatures cannot be falsified (at least not easily), and they are recorded together with the transaction itself. The next transaction includes information from the previous transaction, and this is one of the reasons why your coins in storage are safe, even if the network were to undergo a 51% attack.

To prove that a specific bitcoin is yours, you have to present a valid digital signature. When you want to send your bitcoin to somebody else, you attach their bitcoin address (called public key) to the bitcoin to be sent.

The concern for a user when using a decentralized electronic cash system like Bitcoin is that their bitcoins could be stolen or could disappear. Making the digital signatures part of a transaction and not treating and verifying them separately means that a transaction will only be validated and the bitcoins involved in the transaction deposited onto the account of the recipient if a corresponding signature is included in the transaction and published on the blockchain. Because digital signatures are difficult to falsify, a thief would have to obtain the private key to steal the money.[41]

However, digital signatures in themselves are not enough to prevent double-spending.

"The main benefits are lost if a trusted third party is still required to prevent double-spending"

If I want to send say 10 bitcoins to you, I have to publish my transaction to the network and the closest nodes will scan the entire network to check if I have enough money to make the transaction, and that I haven't already sent those same 10 bitcoins to someone else.

So basically, the nodes have to check the ownership of the bitcoins that I want to include in my transaction and check if I intend to fraudulently spend the same bitcoins twice. In case of a central authority like a bank, preventing double-spending is easy, but when you deal with a decentralized network where you do not know any of the users, you cannot just "trust" that all of them will behave ethically.

You have to actually exclude the possibility of cheating. Bitcoin does this by a protocol called *proof of work which* is used to validate transactions and to add new blocks to the blockchain.

Once 51% of all the nodes of the network have confirmed that you really had the sufficient funds and you did not try to double-spend the money, your transaction can be included in a *block* by miners, and a block containing your transaction will eventually get attached to the previous block. The network stores the history of all valid transactions in a chain of unchangeable blocks, that is why this technology is called blockchain. Transactions can't be undone or tampered with, because it would involve having to redo not only the block in which they are included but all the blocks that came after it.[42]

To be able to understand the double-spending problem it is important to notice that Bitcoin does not keep your actual balance of your account, but instead you have to run the history of all your past transactions to follow incoming and outgoing money and to arrive to the actual balance this way. It is done like this because each bitcoin is a chain of digital signatures, each provided by its owner, and as obviously each individual bitcoin has a very different history having been passed from one owner to the next, they are not identical among themselves.

This means that the only way the Bitcoin network can determine whether you have the sufficient funds to make a transaction is to check if the individual bitcoins that you want to send have been sent earlier from your account to someone else. This seems obvious, but because of the individuality of each bitcoin and each satoshi (the smallest fraction of a bitcoin) and their distinct history on the blockchain it is not as easy as you may think.

Each bitcoin is non-fungible, meaning that the individual bitcoins are not really interchangeable the way dollars or euros are. When you go to the store and hand a 20 dollar bill to the cashier, she does not have any way to determine in what kinds of transactions your bill had been involved earlier. She can maybe detect if your 20 dollar bill is false, but if it is not, she must accept your bill, even if it was earlier used to pay for something illegal (of which she cannot be sure).

In contrast, bitcoins are created by different miners through the process of mining which we will discuss later, and from the moment a particular bitcoin is mined, "it has a human and social context. Every last satoshi has/is a permanent and transparent record. Each satoshi is its ledger history just as much as a unit of account, and none of them can be interchanged with another as they all have distinctive histories, permanently."[43]

The very fact that the Bitcoin blockchain is public and cannot be changed (or at least only with very substantial effort by way of a 51% attack for which somebody would have to be powerful enough to grab hold of at least 51% of the network) makes individual bitcoins and satoshis non-fungible.

Even though the public perception is that Bitcoin is anonymous and users are protected because nobody can trace back from mere public keys to whom those keys belong, it is, unfortunately, not true. It is possible to track the history of any individual bitcoin on the public ledger and there are many Bitcoin and blockchain analytics companies, and even government related agencies that already monitor blacklisted bitcoins.

External entities can also apply information to individual coins to "taint" them. Such tainted bitcoins are monitored and many exchanges simply close the accounts of anybody who happens to receive a deposit of such tainted bitcoins, and people's accounts are actually being shut down by the likes of Coinbase, Circle and Cash App, so you can only sell your bitcoin as if it were fungible outside of exchanges, directly to another person without middlemen, but that can be risky too.[44] Even the Europol, the police of the European Union is reportedly tracking people who use Bitcoin for payments, in case they are up to something illegal.

When you want to send bitcoins to somebody, you have to include as many earlier transactions in which you have received bitcoins as necessary until the total of these transactions reaches the full amount which you want to send, or more. So if you want to send say 10 bitcoins and you have a total of 15 bitcoins which you received in four transactions of 3, 3, 4 and 5 bitcoins, respectively, you will have to include only three of those transactions (3 btc+3 btc+4 btc) because the total of these three is 10 btc.

The reason you have to include these "inputs" is because the Bitcoin network does not keep a record of your actual balance, but instead you have to run through all the history of your past transactions to come to your current balance. By including these so called *inputs* (the transactions in which you received bitcoins), you prove that you have sufficient funds to send 10 bitcoins to the recipient and that you indeed own those specific bitcoins.

To prove that you are the rightful owner of the bitcoins of an earlier transaction (that you now include in the transaction as "input") you have to generate a *digital signature.* The digital signature is there to prove your identity and it is generated by appending your private key to the transaction and hashing it. The new hash is your digital signature. The earlier transaction includes your public key as it was sent to you, so the nodes now can check if the input you include in your new transaction actually has your public key.

They do not have to be able to see your private key to be able to confirm your identity because your signature together with the transaction and your public key can be used to verify your identity. As the signature depends on the transaction (because it is created by hashing the transaction and your private key), the signature will be different for each transaction you will ever make.

Before the transaction is validated by 51% of the entire network, it is placed into a kind of depository for unvalidated transactions. People like to compare this to putting your money into a public locker and placing a puzzle on it for everybody to solve. Once a person is able to solve the puzzle, they can unlock the locker and remove the deposited amount. The actual puzzle solving is called bitcoin mining.

Before your transaction can be executed, the nodes of the network must verify whether these inputs (earlier transactions in which bitcoins were deposited onto your account) had been used before as inputs in another already verified transaction of yours. If they had, that means that those specific bitcoins are no longer available for you to spend and that you are trying to cheat the system.

If nodes find that the inputs you included in your transaction have been used earlier, your transaction will be sent back to the pool of unverified or unordered transactions which are waiting for being picked up by miners to be put into blocks. So the process of checking if the inputs you use for the new transaction have ever been used is one component of how the Bitcoin protocol prevents double-spending.

Once the nodes confirm that you indeed have the necessary amount available, they will have to check your identity to make sure that your funds are not diverted fraudulently from your account by a fraudster, and that it is really you who wants to send money to the recipient.

Let's see an example of double-spending. In this scenario we are dealing with an attacker who wants to spend the same money twice. Say, Malicious Guy could send Innocent Lamb 10 bitcoins (or btc) as payment for a product that Innocent Lamb was to send him. Malicious Guy could wait until Innocent Lamb receives the payment and happily ships the product off to him. Once Innocent Lamb confirms that the product has already been shipped, Malicious Guy immediately starts a new transaction of 10 btc to Cover Pal (which is another bitcoin address of Malicious Guy or his buddy in crime), including the same 10 bitcoins that he has included in the transaction to Innocent Lamb. Malicious Guy is referencing the same inputs in the transaction with Cover Pal as the ones he included in the transaction with

Innocent Lamb.

Innocent Lamb could think that he is safe as the "Malicious Guy to Innocent Lamb" transaction was confirmed by the network. However, transactions get registered on the blockchain once a node puts those transactions into a block and solves the mathematical puzzle by trial and error (or brute force), looking for the random number called *nonce* that is part of the block which is used to create the final hash output of the block.

Once a nonce is found, the block is verified and it gets added to the blockchain. The node then sends the information to other nodes which update their own copy of the blockchain, adding this newly created block.

However, if Malicious Guy were able to amass the sufficiently large computing power (more than half of the hash power of the entire Bitcoin network), there is a probability that he will be able to solve the nonce first for the block in which he included on purpose the second, fraudulent transaction addressed to Cover Pal. At that moment the blockchain would have two slightly differing versions: the version where the last block contains the correct transaction addressed to Innocent Lamb, and the fraudulent version where the last block contains the transaction addressed to Cover Pal.

The protocol of Bitcoin is such that if a new block is created and a nonce found for it, the block must be added to the longest version of the blockchain. If Malicious Guy were able to find first the next nonce, he would add it to his fraudulent chain which now would contain one more block than the good version of the blockchain. This means that other nodes would automatically have to add any further blocks to this fraudulent chain because the protocol is to accept the longest chain as valid.

The distasteful result for Innocent Lamb would be that by this mechanism of auto-correction the fraudulent version would become the "good blockchain", which would automatically render the last block of the original blockchain invalid, and the transactions in it would be sent back into the pool of unvalidated or unordered transactions. Meaning that Innocent Lamb would lose his product because he has already shipped it off to Malicious Guy, and he would never receive the 10 btc either.

In fact, this Malicious Guy could create not only one, but many fraudulent transactions by "duplicating" (double-spending) the same bitcoins. This is the problem of double-spending. As you may remember, Satoshi wrote that the only way to confirm the absence of a transaction is to be aware of all transactions.

Double-spending on the peer-to-peer network would not only mean that users would be vulnerable to fraud and malicious attacks and could be living in fear of losing their precious bitcoins, but it would actually cause inflation because the amount of bitcoins in circulation would increase in the network. Of course, it would be the end of Bitcoin because users would immediately lose trust and would try to sell their bitcoins as fast as possible. The story would end in a downward spiral and with Bitcoin smashing into the ground.

One of the most important features implemented by Satoshi in the design of Bitcoin for it to be stable and resistant to centralized manipulation is the fact that there will only ever be 21 million bitcoins and that they are being mined into existence gradually at a constant pace. No matter how many miners are competing to create the next valid block and add it to the blockchain, the protocol ensures that new blocks can only be mined at a 10-minute pace.

Double-spending would not only take away trust in the currency, but it would eliminate the inbuilt scarcity of Bitcoin. That is why finding a viable solution to the double-spending problem is so important for creating a healthy, safe and reliable cryptocurrency.

As we saw, digital signatures alone are not enough to prevent people from committing fraud on a peer-to-peer network. The solution of Bitcoin to the double-spending problem is to make the transaction history public by using blockchain technology. Each user stores a copy of the entire blockchain containing all verified transactions, and checks this copy when wanting to verify a new transaction or before accepting a payment to verify that the specific bitcoins they are about to receive had not already been included as inputs in earlier transactions.[45]

"The network timestamps transactions by hashing them into an ongoing chain of hash-based proof-of-work"

When you open a Bitcoin wallet, your computer connects to several computers that also belong to the Bitcoin network and your computer receives the latest copy of the blockchain. The verification process of new transactions includes the nodes of the system downloading the updated copies of the transaction ledger, and the chronological order is proven by applying timestamps to the transactions.

However, there is an inherent issue with the nodes of such a peer-to-peer network: the selfish interest of each user would be to not include their own transactions in the global transaction history. Why? Because if your transaction is not included in a block on the blockchain, it will get rejected as an unverified transaction and while it is waiting to be picked up and put into a new block to go through the process again to eventually be included in a block which is then added to the blockchain, you have the chance to spend the same coins for something else. This is called the Byzantine Generals' Problem in computing.

Until the creation of Bitcoin the Byzantine Generals' Problem has not been solved. The question is how we can create consensus in a system where participants and communication channels cannot trust each other.

Imagine that there are two generals who decide to attack a city. They agree to attack from two sides, and to be able to communicate they have to send a messenger through the land of the enemy. If General A sends a message to General B saying when to attack, the messenger can be captured so that the message does not get delivered, or the enemy can substitute the message with a fake one.

General B does not know the original messenger, so he cannot be sure if the message he received comes from General A or from the enemy. He can send a reply to General A, but his message can be intercepted too.

If both generals decide to trust that the messages were delivered safely, they can both attack at the time mentioned in the letters, but if the message was false, that would mean sure defeat. The other option would be that neither of them would attack because they realize that there is no way for them to be sure whether the messages were intercepted.

The Byzantine Generals' Problem in peer-to-peer networks is how we can be sure of transactions being valid or not in a system where the communication channels are not clear and cannot be trusted. The question is how we can create trust in the system of the network in a way that eliminates the need for the users to have to trust other users whom they do not know.

While the double-spend problem arises from the difficulty to prove who the owner of a certain coin is, the Byzantine Generals' Problem stems from the fact that we cannot trust that those who check the record of ownership (the nodes who verify the transactions) act honestly and not in their selfish interest. At least more than 50% of those who verify the validity of a transaction have to agree on its validity. The question is how we can avoid double spending and the Byzantine Generals' Problem without a centralized server that would timestamp transactions.

Let's see how Satoshi managed to solve the issue of consensus even in a network of potentially dishonest nodes because, as Chris Pacia wrote, "this is where Nakamoto really showed off his brilliance"[46]. Satoshi's solution to the consensus problem was to shift the incentives so radically that otherwise selfish nodes now have it in their self-interest to act honestly.

The solution is in the mining process, the way nodes can verify transactions and how they can earn mining rewards. As miners are obviously motivated by the mining rewards, they will behave in a way that makes their mining activities more successful.

As there are no central authorities that could verify the transactions of users, when a user opens a bitcoin wallet his computer connects to several other users. When this user makes a transaction his computer broadcasts it to all its peers (the nodes his computer is connected to). Each node that receives the transaction has to perform various checks to find out whether the transaction is valid.

Once a node verified that a transaction is valid, it will broadcast it to all the nodes it is connected to. Those nodes will then start the verification process in the same way, and if they verify the transaction they will pass it on to their own peers. This process goes on until the transaction has reached all the nodes of the network.

However, not all nodes are miners. If you have a bitcoin wallet, you can make transactions and download a full copy of the entire blockchain from the beginning, but it takes too much space (140GB) so normal wallets generally do not keep a copy of the entire blockchain but only of those parts of it which are relevant to the user of the wallet. They use a simplified payment verification mode and will filter out anything that is not relevant to them. These are *partial or lightweight nodes.*

Then there are those users who choose to function as *full nodes* to maintain the integrity and strength of the Bitcoin network. These are computers with significant storage space. They keep a copy of the whole blockchain from day one. Lightweight nodes can use full nodes to broadcast their own transactions to the network, and full nodes will notify them when a transaction appears that is related to such a lightweight node. In this case the lightweight node downloads the relevant part of the blockchain.

A completely different type of nodes are called *miners.* Miners collect transactions and organize them into blocks, then by investing a very significant computing power they try to guess a random number called the nonce for a block. This only can be done by "trial and error", so the more computing power (or hash power) a miner has, the greater chances he has to find a nonce first. After finding a nonce, the miner has to add it to the entire "message" of the transaction and hash it to receive a new hash. This newly verified transaction will be added to a memory pool.

The miner has to repeat the process with all the transactions that go into the new block until he has verified enough to set up a new block. A block can contain from 100-300 transactions according to the original protocol. When the miner creates a valid block, he broadcasts it to the network and he is rewarded with newly created bitcoins. The reward is halved every four years, at the same time the mining difficulty increases. Currently, the mining reward for one new block is 12.5 btc until around May 21, 2020 when it will drop to 6.25 btc.

Of course, there are many other miners who have also received those transactions and who are working simultaneously on verifying them to create a new block for the mining reward. If the Byzantine Generals' Problem had not been addressed in the coding of Bitcoin, this would lead to a chaotic situation where competing miners would create "blocks with favorable transaction histories, relaying them, and creating multiple versions of the blockchain"[47].

Users could not trust the blockchain, as there would be no way to prove whether the version of the blockchain they use is the correct one, and it would be a fertile soil for all kinds of manipulation and cheating people out of their money. The good news is that the proof of work protocol successfully deals with this issue.

The difficulty of the mathematical puzzle is constantly adjusted to the total computing power of the Bitcoin network so that it always takes approximately 10 minutes for a miner to create a new block, which gives stability to Bitcoin because miners cannot suddenly flood the network with newly mined coins at a rate which would cause devaluation of the coin in the short term.

When the Bitcoin network was very small and there were much less transactions, it was also much easier to mine bitcoin, but as its price kept rising ever higher and more people started to buy and use bitcoin, more people took up mining and the difficulty increased. So much so, that currently you cannot mine bitcoin with a standard computer. You need to invest substantial money to buy all the specialized equipment, or you can team up with others by joining a bitcoin mining pool where you buy a part of the equipment in exchange for part of the mined coins.

"The longest chain not only serves as proof of the sequence of events witnessed, but proof that it came from the largest pool of CPU power"

What proof of work means is that miners have to expend quite some time and processing power to create a block, and the more processing (or CPU) power a miner has, the more probable it is that he will be able to create a block before others.

The proof of work protocol is designed in a way that makes it quicker to find blocks collectively, rather than individually. If there are competing transaction histories, i.e. if there has been a point where one miner managed to attach block A as the last one to the blockchain while another miner attached block B, the blockchain has branched out temporarily into two different versions. The event of creating such different versions is the creation of a *fork*, the same way as a fork in the road offers more than one options for travelers to choose from.

If there is a sufficiently large number of miners who accept the version of the blockchain containing block A, and also a large enough number of other miners who accept the version ending with block B, both groups of miners will continue to work on the version of the blockchain which they accepted as valid.[48]

The more hashing power a miner has to carry out his "trial and error" process in search of the nonce, the more his probability of creating a new block first increases. So if the global mining power of those miners who voted for the version of the blockchain containing block A is greater than those who voted for the version with block B, the miners of the block A version will be able to create new blocks earlier, which means that over time the version containing block A will be longer than the blockchain containing block B.

"The chain with the most processing power devoted to extending it will always be the longest chain. If chain A has 51% of the processing power and chain B has 49%, those mining chain A will collectively solve the math problems more quickly. As a result, the more time passes, the larger the gap between blockchains A and B will become."[49]

"As long as a majority of CPU power is controlled by nodes that are not cooperating to attack the network, they'll generate the longest chain and outpace attackers"

An individual miner has the incentive to always want to mine on the longer, majority blockchain because it is not very likely that the community of users will accept the minority chain, so there is no monetary incentive in trying to mine blocks that will be worth nothing instead of 12.5 btc. Voting for a shorter, alternative chain will not be worthwhile just because the transaction history of the alternative chain would be more favorable to him. If some ill-intentioned miner just made a payment which he does not want to be included into the next block to be mined, he could start mining another block which does not include his transaction. But unless he is able to amass more than 50% of the total hash power of the entire network, he will unlikely be able to mine the alternative block before somebody else in the network manages to mine the good one containing his transaction.

Even if he does not give up his attack and keeps working on mining his alternative block, when he finally adds it to the blockchain, it will be ignored by the majority of the nodes because the next block has already been added to the blockchain before he could add his fraudulent block. In this way the transactions in the attacker's block will be returned to the pool of unordered transactions.

The only chance of the malicious miner is to keep mining to add newer and newer blocks to the alternative chain in the hopes of being able to "outmine" the correct version of the blockchain. Once the alternative chain is longer than the good one, it will become the main chain. But the chain which is accepted by the majority of the processing power will always grow to be the longest chain, so unless the attacker manages to gather 51% of the full processing power of the network, he is doomed to fail.

The total processing power in September 2019 was close to 100 million tera hashes per second, which means the Bitcoin network outweighs in processing power the top 500 supercomputers in the world combined. Even though in theory there could come a time when another type of computing could bring a qualitative difference in the chance of hackability of the Bitcoin network, for the time being it seems to be nearly impossible.

The protocol was created in a way that incentivizes miners to behave ethically and to always accept the network consensus by accepting the largest chain as the correct version instead of trying to enforce their particular versions for their own self-interest. This incentive is what guarantees that the users will be able to agree on a single transaction history. As Chris Pacia says, Satoshi "designed Bitcoin in such a way that it essentially channels private self-interest into public good. Miners are led as if by the invisible hand of Satoshi himself to come to a consensus."[50]

7

Bitcoin to the Rescue?

A s we saw, the aim of Satoshi was to provide an alternative to centralized currencies in the form of a peer-to-peer decentralized network
that would be safe, unhackable and immune to manipulations
from central powers or authorities. Let's see whether Bitcoin lives up to
its reputation to be the number one candidate to become a currency that can
transform the world for the better.

We have to look at Bitcoin from various aspects. We discussed so far
that Bitcoin is a decentralized alternative to digital currencies, based on
its revolutionary blockchain technology which eliminates the need for trust
between users because the technology itself makes it (almost) impossible
to cheat (as cheating would only be possible if you could grab control of
the majority of the computing power of the entire network, which is for the
moment also very difficult to do).

This blockchain technology is reliable and available continuosly, without
downtimes as there are always nodes that are operational, even if some
computers are out of service at any given moment. Even if the majority of
the nodes were disconnected from the network, the blockchain would still
be safe on the ones that are up and running, and the system would still work,
although it would likely clog up very quickly and transactions would become
sluggish until the rest of the nodes would get back online.

In theory, the Bitcoin network should be safer than normal centralized payment systems because it cannot be hacked. There have been a couple of hacks that happened, always via the hacking of a centralized cryptocurrency exchange, but the Bitcoin network itself has not been hacked. The problem with centralized cryptocurrency exchanges is that if you use one to buy your bitcoins, you do not actually hold your private keys. It is the exchange that has all the private keys of its users. So if attackers are able to hack into the central server of a cryptoexchange, they will be able to grab the private keys and steal the money of many people all at once. This is why *decentralized exchanges* are so important because they would be extremely resistant to attacks. Such exchanges have already started to appear.

Due to the ingenious proof of work protocol the blockchain can only be compromised if the attacker manages to amass at least 51% of the total hash power of the network. So we have a public ledger which keeps track of the entire history of the network from the genesis block to the present day. This history is open and searchable to anybody: something that would be impossible with the current monetary system.

Since the middlemen are eliminated from transactions, transaction times can be much shorter as there is no need for a third entity to do checks and act as an arbitrator in case of disputes. The transactions are secure and irreversible (which can be a positive or a negative, depending on which side of the fence you are). If you provided a service for which you will not recover your time used and the buyer is not happy with your service, he cannot refuse to pay you. The system is hacking-proof and cheating-proof.

Double spending is impossible because the proof of work procotol does not incentivize dishonest behavior of miners who approve transactions. The distributed ledger is public, out there for everybody to see and check. It does not mean that they will be able to identify who did a certain transaction because only your public key will be visible, but the average user cannot associate it with your personal data.

As for velocity, it turns out that sending Bitcoin is quicker and cheaper than centralized international money transactions, although this is not always true (more on that later).

The big question is whether Bitcoin is really as safe and as decentralized as people would like to think, and whether the Bitcoin network can overcome the various issues of scalability it is currently dealing with.

Bitcoin can only be adopted on a larger scale as a *de facto* alternative currency that provides freedom and gives people back their power from central authorities and powers if these issues are solved.

Without solving these issues, if Bitcoin gets adopted on a massive scale thanks to the current involvement of the controllers who try to push for the use of Bitcoin as another asset (a store of value or digital gold) that can be used to make speculative money like they do on the stock exchange, with futures and Bitcoin ETFs, including the launch of Bakkt on September 23, 2019, which is a trading platform, or as they call it, "a global regulated ecosystem for digital assets" created by Microsoft, McDonalds, Starbucks, and ICE (the parent company of the New York Stock Exchange) to buy and store bitcoin, to trade bitcoin futures, and to use bitcoin to buy goods and services, it could happen that certain characteristics of Bitcoin will be used against people, which could give much more power to the controllers and the authorities over people's lives.

Remember, the blockchain keeps a history which cannot be changed and is there for everyone to see. Is this enough for the controllers and public authorities to behave ethically? Well, I suggest you decide only once we have discussed the below issues which Bitcoin still needs to solve.

If you want to transfer money to your mother from your bank account, you enter the transfer order in the system and the bank then verifies that you have enough money on your account to make the transfer. Next they contact your mother's bank to make sure that her account is valid and can receive the transfer. Once your mother's bank confirms that everything is OK with her account, your bank will subtract the transferred amount from your account and your mother's bank will add the same amount to her account.

Your bank also charges you a transaction fee in most cases. If you happen to live in another country, you will also be charged an exchange fee. The whole process may take up to several days, depending on the countries involved. But even in case of banks within the same country, it can take a day or two for your money to reach your mom's bank account.

Imagine what would happen if you wanted to send bitcoins to your mom instead. Bitcoin is not stored on any central server but instead on all the computers that belong to the Bitcoin network. You would submit the transfer order by indicating the wallet address (a unique, digital identificator which serves as an address, similar to that of an email address) and the amount you want to transfer.

The computers of the Bitcoin network would start to verify the transaction, checking if you have the right amount to transfer, and then the individual nodes would verify your transaction as valid or invalid. If more than 51% of the system validates it, it gets recorded in the ledger of the network and automatically copied onto all the computers of the system. Once your transaction is thus verified, your transfer takes place. In practice this may take up to ten minutes in an ideal situation. Still not instantaneous, due to some technical characteristics that we will discuss later, but much quicker than bank transfers. Also, there is only a very small transaction fee compared to those of the banking system.

The scalability issues of Bitcoin

By the second half of 2019 the majority of people in Western countries certainly have heard something about Bitcoin, probably they even know that it is a cryptocurrency, but many few are actually using it to pay for goods and services. There are some Bitcoin ATMs where you can exchange bitcoin and cash, however, if you want to pay with bitcoins when you are shopping, or in a restaurant or for any services, your choices are still quite limited.

There are good reasons why people have not started to use Bitcoin for everyday payments, but rather buy them to "hodl" (to hold the coins as an investment in the hopes that their value will eventually rise to where they can get a juicy profit from them), or for speculative trading. One of the reasons why the majority of people who buy bitcoins prefer to use them as investment only and do not use them for payments is the issue of transaction speed.

We talked earlier about how some bank transfers can take various days, especially international ones, and not only are they slow, but they also come with hefty transaction fees. Bitcoin officially should not have high transaction fees, but unfortunately, it is increasingly not the case. And the reason is tied to the transaction processing capacity of the Bitcoin network.

The sad truth is that in practice the Bitcoin network can process a maximum of only 7 transactions per second, while the network of Visa processes on average some 20,000 transactions, with the maximum being 50,000. Now that is quite some difference in speed. The sluggishness of the Bitcoin network is due to its growing size, because with its continued growth there have been more and more transactions to be processed.

The Bitcoin protocol automatically adjusts the difficulty of the mathematical puzzle to be solved by miners so that mining a new block will always take approximately 10 minutes. So even though there is more hash power applied throughout the network, only one block will be mined in every 10 minutes.

The hash power has increased due to the increased competition between miners for the mining rewards and because it is getting increasingly difficult to find a nonce, which means that the Bitcoin protocol inherently calls for the need for ever growing computing power on behalf of miners who want to be successful.

Not only is the mining speed inbuilt and kept at a steady 10 minutes per new block by the Bitcoin protocol over time, always adjusted to the growing difficulty of finding nonces, but also, the size of a block cannot exceed 1MB. In practice this means that a block can contain 100–300 transactions.

As a result, as the network became too big for it to be efficient with its original parameters of operation, more and more transactions were left in the pool of unordered transactions waiting for somebody to process them. Instead of minutes you could be waiting hours for your transaction to be verified. Miners could not add extra processing power to their operations fast enough to be able to keep up with the avalanche of transactions due to the exponential growth of the Bitcoin network.

Now that is definitely an issue if you want to pay with bitcoin in a shop, unless you are happy to linger around for an hour until the merchant receives confirmation that your payment was verified.

As the core developers of Bitcoin did not want to touch the block size (and we will see later why not), the miners started to offer priority in processing to transactions for which the sender was willing to pay a special fee.

The problem with mining companies offering to process your transactions before other transactions for an urgency fee is that it is totally against the ethos of Satoshi's Bitcoin. It is no longer the completely decentralized one-CPU-one-vote system Bitcoin was created to be, where each node had the same chance to vote for the validity of transactions and blocks.

Bitcoin transactions should be free, and keeping the 1MB block size could lead to a situation where users have to pay more and more, in a way bidding their transactions into priority position for processing, while the transactions of those people who did not pay an urgency fee to some miner could be parked in the pool until the end of time.

This means that Bitcoin no longer can seamlessly process the transactions running on its network, and the solution mining companies found to this issue has created a situation where mining companies start acting like banks in certain aspects. They take payments to process your transactions, and they can choose not to process your transactions if you did not pay them. The ever growing power of the mining companies has created a situation which is pointing towards centralization once again.

Electricity costs

With the growth of the Bitcoin network and the increasing mining difficulty, currently only large mining pools can compete for being the first to create a new block that will reward them with newly created bitcoins for their efforts of validating transactions on the network, and the cost of electricity involved in mining bitcoins is increasing. The global energy consumption of the Bitcoin network has already exceeded for example the annual electricity needs of Denmark.

Many people say that this is a problem and that Bitcoin will use up all the electricity that we can produce and cause pollution etc. But it would only be true if we could not use alternative, renewable energy to provide electricity for the Bitcoin network. Many mining companies are strategically based in countries where the cost of electricity is low, obviously to maximize profit. Many of them realized that the cheapest form of electricity they can get is from renewable sources, for example geothermal energy in Iceland. We as a society have to find renewable ways to produce all the energy we need. If there is political will (and if the controllers do not try to keep us away from purer, less polluting energy sources) this can be done without causing damage to the Earth.

It has been repeated incessantly by the media, especially earlier, when Bitcoin bashing was more so the order of the day, that should Bitcoin be adopted as a payment system, it would eat up the energetic resources of the planet because it is already consuming more electricity than certain countries. This was being pounded into the minds of people, so much so that people just believe it without checking its veracity.

The surprising truth is that if you compare the costs of running and maintaining the current fiat money system versus the Bitcoin network, they are not even in the same order of magnitude. While the yearly electricity consumption of the Bitcoin network is $3.5 billion, just the electricity cost of the entire banking system amounts to $63.8 billion. That is 18 times more just for the electricity costs for maintaining the banking system. To this we have to add the costs of gold mining ($105 billion), gold recycling ($40 billion) to back official monies, as well as the printing costs for bank notes ($28 billion). The total banking system cost comes out at $1,870 billion per year.[51]

Even if Bitcoin will be adopted en mass, the costs for gold and paper production and handling, as well as the manpower, bank building maintenance etc. costs would not be necessary. The difference is now over five hundred thirty to one between the banking system and Bitcoin. This is just one example of how skewed some of the "public opinions" propagated on purpose can get.

Of course, if a mass adoption would occur, there would likely have to be way more full nodes and more miners, which would significantly add to the electricity needs of running the system. However, we could forget about the $173 billion yearly extra cost related to gold and paper used in relation to the money system, as well as about bank CEO bonuses and customers having to pay for the operations of banks.

Compared to other mining systems of other cryptocurrencies, like proof of stake mining, proof of work indeed is labor intensive and on purpose requires miners to expend significant time and energy (using electricity to solve a mathematical puzzle) to validate transactions, and as a consequence, mine new coins.

The cost of electricity associated with proof of work has been one of the reasons why there have been continuous debates in the crypto community whether proof of work is sustainable going forward, or whether there is another way which could provide the same level of security to cryptocurrencies without having to expend that much energy. This exactly has been one of the key questions around which various changes and hard forks have been made.

Centralization: Bitcoin becoming its own antagonist

At the beginning it was very profitable to mine Bitcoin. You could find a block per day with a standard PC and back then in 2009 the reward for finding one block was 50 bitcoins. Since early 2013, however, as the difficulty in solving the puzzle grew and as the mining reward was halved, it was no longer worthwhile to mine Bitcoin at home. The ASIC miners appeared in that year and they quickly took over as the most efficient equipment specifically developed for Bitcoin mining.

People started to group together and built mining pools to aggregate the enormous CPU power necessary to have a chance at still being profitable. Currently, on present day dollar value Bitcoin mining is not very profitable and one has to have entire warehouses filled with thousands of ASIC miners with cheap electricity to be able to stay in business.[52]

The proof of work protocol is what makes Bitcoin trustable without its users having to trust each other. However, it is exactly the nature of proof of work, the fact that a miner has to expend significant amount of time and energy to be able to validate transactions and maintain the consensus of truth on the blockchain, that has an unfortunate consequence. Because the difficulty of mining and the amount of transactions to be processed have been continuously increasing, its proof of work protocol in a sense became a hindrance to Bitcoin.

But as Satoshi wrote in his whitepaper, "as long as a majority of CPU power is controlled by nodes that are not cooperating to attack the network, they'll generate the longest chain and outpace attackers". If miners want to increase their chances of staying profitable, they must create ever larger pools, continuously increasing their hash power. In practice this process lead to a situation where Bitcoin is no longer truly decentralized.

By June 2018 two mining companies (BTC.com and Antpool) owned by Bitmain, the Chinese company that manufactures the leading ASIC Bitcoin miners, together mined 42% of the bitcoins over a given period. At that time Bitmain also controled more than 20% of the hash power of the Bitcoin Cash network.[53] (Bitcoin Cash is a separate cryptocurrency which was hard forked off Bitcoin in 2017 as an attempt to solve Bitcoin's scalability problem by increasing its block size from 1MB to 8MB while rejecting the idea of Segregated Witness. Both Bitcoin and Bitcoin Cash use the SHA-256 protocol, so the ASIC miners can be used to mine both.)

"The ASIC or Application Specific Integrated Chips used in the Antminer line are designed to handle the SHA-256 hash code used by BTC. These advanced mining chips produce far more hashing power than GPU or CPU mining efforts. In many instances, ASIC chips are capable of calculating the Proof-of-Work 100,000 faster than their GPU counterparts."[54] This means that Bitmain came very close to the 51% hash power threshold that would make it possible to dominate and attack the Bitcoin network.

This development caused quite some havoc which only calmed down when by August 2018 Bitmain's hash power shrank back by 9% and "only" had 33% share of the Bitcoin network hash power. However, this may not be entirely due to competitors getting some leeway to build up their participation because, as it turns out, Bitmain was at that time working on expanding to the West and tried to establish a Bitcoin data center and mining facility in Texas.[55]

In October 2018 experts estimated that Bitmain controlled somewhere around 51% of the Bitcoin network. As David Hamilton put it, "Bitmain now controls the destiny of Bitcoin in terms of development. Any changes to Bitcoin's protocol must be approved by the mining community"[56], or else miners will not continue to work under the changed protocol.

Bitmain has managed to secure their position as the industry leader by providing the miners with more powerful ASIC mining options. This has also given Bitmain incredible power within the BTC network. Bitmain now controls the destiny of BTC in terms of development. Any changes to BTC's protocol must be approved by the mining community. This means that Bitmain had the ability to weigh heavily on future protocol updates and have Bitcoin developments move in a direction that better serves the interests of the company. With 51% of the hash power Bitmain was able to reject transactions if they wanted to,[57] which was really bad news for anyone wishing to maintain the Bitcoin network secure, impartial and safe to operate on for everybody, independently of whether they use Bitmain products or not.

Bitmain made some bad decisions, for example investing too much in Bitcoin Cash, which resulted in a loss of over $500 million in the third quarter of 2018, and in the first part of 2019 its leading position was being threatened by a new player, Canaan Creative IPO[58], which makes a 51% attack less probable either by Bitmain or by any contender to the mining race. However, it doesn't exclude the possibility of any big firm growing so large in the future that it could be a threat to the security of the Bitcoin network.

To date Bitcoin has never suffered a successful attack, but in 2018 there have already been two successful 51% attacks against Verge, which is a proof-of-work cryptocurrency (currently number 68 of the list of Coinmarket-cap.com based on market capitalization).[59]

As we saw, the centralization of mining means that there is a chance that enough of the miners could convince 51% of the nodes to accept a new block that contains fraudulent information. Not only it is a matter of security, but according to the interpretation of the majority of people into Bitcoin, it also goes against Satoshi's idea of decentralization. Once the mining companies get to a certain power, they could start requesting transaction fees for validating the transactions. And that would bring us back to square one; mining companies would turn into just another type of banks.

However, Craig Wright who seems to be one third of the team called Satoshi Nakamoto, as we will see later, says that Bitcoin was intended to be decentralized but not in the way most people believe. According to him, the decentralization should take place in the peer-to-peer nature of the network, and due to the nature of proof of work Bitcoin was destined to be mined mostly by mining pools.

In fact, for long there has been a debate on how the network would be maintained operational once the last bitcoins were mined into existence (which should happen somewhere around 2140, so you probably do not have to worry about it, unless you plan to merge with the machine, in which case I have an advice for you: don't do it). If miners could not receive new bitcoins for doing their work to maintain the consensus of the network, they would not be incentivized to keep providing this service. So at that point, if Bitcoin will still exist, miners would have to receive compensation in other forms, and that could be transaction fees.

Miner companies already started to offer to prioritize "urgent" transactions for a processing fee. As mining will be more and more labor intensive while rewards get halved every four years, even though the value of Bitcoin will likely increase so much that mining would still be profitable, sooner or later processing fees would have to be introduced. However, at this point in time, when we are still at the beginning of the history of Bitcoin and its reach is so small (only 0.45% of the global population have bitcoin wallets[60]), it is more crucial to maintain decentralization so that by the time Bitcoin is adopted en mass, it can be a more just electronic payment system and not a space age equivalent of the current, corrupt monetary system.

The centralization caused by mining pools is why the people behind *Bitcoin Gold* forked the main chain and created Bitcoin Gold to shift its proof of work from using the secure hash algorithm called SHA-256 to Equihash-BTG. This protocol change immediately rendered the ASIC equipment manufactured to mine Bitcoin (primarily by Bitmain) obsolete for mining Bitcoin Gold (at least that is how they interpreted Satoshi's intentions).

The goal was to give the chance to mine bitcoins back to the small fish, the single miner as it was possible in the beginning, by using common GPU equipment.[61] The Bitcoin Gold team wanted to restore the decentralized nature of Bitcoin as Satoshi imagined it.

The irony of the situation is that even though Bitcoin Gold was created to get back to the ideal of decentralization of Bitcoin, just like Litecoin Cash and Monacoin (both smaller cryptocurrencies), Bitcoin Gold has suffered a successful 51% attack in May 2018.[62] Unfortunately, a 51% attack is much easier to execute against a smaller cryptocurrency using the proof of work protocol because the attacker has to amass way less processing power to gain control of the main chain.

The centralization issue reaches even further than just to the dominance of Bitmain. As of October 2018, 80% of the hash power of the Bitcoin network belonged to only six mining companies, all based in China. Although by April 2019 the first six mining companies only controlled a little less than 72% of the hash rate[63], it is still true that around 80% of the total hash rate of the Bitcoin network is controlled by mining pools based in China.[64]

This is bad news because the Chinese government has shown over the past several years a hostile and completely erratic behavior toward cryptocurrencies and even banned cryptocurrency exchanges and ICOs. This, coupled with the general trend that shows a high likelihood of China being in the process of becoming the next economic superpower once it manages to dethrone the United States, is even more alarming. And not only for the US. China has started to buy up large areas in Africa, which is quite disturbing.

China is an authoritarian society that somehow managed to mold the worst aspects of both capitalism and communism into its own unique economic model, based on heavy-handed control of public opinion and life options for its people, regular violation of human rights, the silencing of people who oppose the regime, inhumane working conditions, and non-existent food and product safety rules, to mention just a few. All this is accompanied by a total disregard for the sustainability of natural resources and the planet. In contrast to Western societies, the Chinese work ethic is basically to live to work and not the other way round.

What is even more alarming is that China is currently conducting a beta test of an electronic social credit system, for the moment on a voluntary basis. It is quite blood-clotting, actually. Participants are being continuously monitored digitally via all manners of electronic devices in their homes and in public; using cctv cameras, mobile phones, social media applications, you name it. The social credit system adds or subtracts social credit points for each of their actions.

If they buy too much alcohol, or tobacco, or maybe natural health products that do not serve the pharmaceutical interests, they are penalized. If they say something that goes contrary to the government's guidelines and official opinions, be it either in the "privacy" of their bedroom, in public, or on social media, they are penalized.

Such penalized individuals are then restricted in their options, for example they are not allowed to buy train or airplane tickets, or to leave the country. What if in the future they will not be allowed to get an employment, or buy food, or rent a home, or leave the place they are confined in?

And the really Orwellian part about it is that the system is designed in a way that if you do something that the system does not want you to do, they penalize your entire family. In this way people will quickly learn, because they are negatively "incentivized" by the social credit system, to police the members of their own family.

Now imagine if this were introduced on a mass scale because rest assured, they are planning to roll it out, this is not just an interesting social exper-iment. Next, imagine what will happen when China becomes the absolute super power. Would you say the controllers would benefit from that? I think they would be ecstatic. This would mean the end of free thought, free speech, and definitely would put the last nail in the coffin of love based human relationships.

Now, in light of all this, maybe you think twice before you invest in mining companies that contribute to the centralization of Bitcoin, or at least in the ones operating in China. Even if you buy Bitcoin, perhaps you want to look into other cryptocurrencies also (called altcoins), and select the ones that are in line with your personal values.

Malleability issues

There are various types of malleability, but the one worth mentioning in relation to Bitcoin is *transaction malleability* because it has been the subject of debates, and attempts to solve the issues with it even caused a hard fork. As we mentioned earlier, the data of a transaction together with the digital signature of the sender is hashed during the processing protocol. We also saw that transactions that have not yet been verified are deposited in the memory pool.

Now imagine that a miner or a hacker changes the transaction identifier (the transaction hash) according to certain rules: for example, instead of a positive value he puts a negative value. In such case the digital signature would still be accepted as valid, just like in the case of physical signatures: we do not have to reproduce the perfect copy of our signature every time we sign a document for it to be accepted as a valid signature.[65]

But the fact that the transaction identifier can be changed means that it is possible that miners would include the modified transaction instead of the original one. Some people even say that the attack of MtGox in 2013, when bitcoins were stolen from the exchange in a value of approximately $575 million could possibly have been done this way. If this was the case, the attacker withdrew money from the exchange intercepting the transaction and changing its transaction identifier. The transaction was still valid, which means that the attacker could receive the bitcoins, but the transaction identifier was not included in the block so the balance of the attacker did not decrease.[66]

While certain groups tried to blow up malleability as a very important problem of Bitcoin, it is actually "'baked into' the design of Bitcoin"[67], as the individual behind the pseudonym Jonald Fyookball suggests. The malleability of transactions can only cause problems when a transaction is included as an input (or transaction parent) as reference in a new transaction.

Imagine that somebody sent you bitcoins and the transaction already appears in your wallet, but has yet to be confirmed. If you do not wait for it to be confirmed and include this transaction into a new transaction you want to make, you have to use the transaction hash of the first transaction adding it to the data of your transaction plus your private key, and hash all that information together to get a new hash.

Everything will be all right if nothing malicious happens, but what if a miner or a hacker decides to change the transaction identifier of the first (parent) transaction? As Bitcoin uses the SHA-256 hashing algorithm, changing even one digit will result in a totally different hash. Which means that now the new transaction will not be valid because the input you used to generate its hash came from a transaction identifier that does not exist.[68]

Before the transaction identifier is changed, it exists in the mempool of nodes and miners. After a miner has changed it and he puts this new, slightly changed identifier into a block, the original transaction will disappear from the mempool because those outputs will now be spent. Which means that the new transaction you are trying to send is guaranteed to fail.[69]

It seems that the need to fix malleability was an issue that was blown out of proportion by those groups that wanted to benefit from it. Actually, this transaction malleability of Bitcoin makes the coding, and consequently the implementation, of the *Lightning Network* easier. As the Lightning Network is a privately owned enterprise that is built as a second layer or *layer two application* over the main chain of Bitcoin, it seems that those who wanted to introduce the Lightning Network and get it adopted by the entire Bitcoin community tried to lobby for it by saying that the issue of transaction malleability was absolutely crucial to fix.

Although malleability is not a crucial issue in the case of Bitcoin, it is important to mention because of the efforts made on behalf of the creators of Bitcoin Core which is a popular Bitcoin client used by almost 95% of the Bitcoin network. The https://bitcoin.org website states that Bitcoin Core is "a full Bitcoin client and builds the backbone of the network. It offers high levels of security, privacy, and stability. However, it has fewer features and it takes a lot of space and memory."[70] Well, that right there is a good motivation to try to implement a layer two application such as the Lightning Network in the hopes of making the network much faster without using up additional space and memory on the main chain.[71]

There are two possible approaches to fix the transaction malleability issue of Bitcoin. One of them is to add consensus rules that give precisely detailed rules on how signatures should be generated so that miners could not make minor changes to them. Proponents of this approach suggested this improvement, but it was withdrawn, likely because changing such consensus rules would actually result in a new hard fork.[72]

The other approach was to modify the structure of blocks and transactions in such a way that signatures are no longer a part of the transaction hash. This is the approach that was adopted by the *SegWit soft fork*, which was implemented on Bitcoin as of August 1, 2017.[73]

So, Bitcoin is now running with Segregated Witness (SegWit) incorporated, which means that transactions and digital signatures are no longer hashed together, even though the signature is still put into the same block. However, the problem here is that if we look at the definition of Bitcoin by Satoshi in the whitepaper, i.e. Bitcoin being an electronic coin as *a chain of digital signatures*, we come to the conclusion that since the implementation of SegWit Bitcoin is no longer Bitcoin because the signature gets separated from the transaction.

SegWit actually decreased the security of Bitcoin, because clients who have not upgraded to SegWit can choose to include or not include signatures, and signatures can be discarded by anybody.[74] Moreover, SegWit only fixes malleability for SegWit transactions, which by October 2018 reached only 53% of all transactions.[75] In the following year up until September 2019 the transactions performed with SegWit oscillated around 40%, going as low as 25% and as high as around 48%. Although it seems that the volume of transactions done using SegWit reached as high as 86% (in February 2019) and 95% (in August 2019), generally it has been oscillating between 40% and 60% until June 2019 and between 40% and 80% from July to September 2019.[76]

As not everybody was happy with the SegWit soft fork, the malleability issue has actually caused a *hard fork* on 1 August 2017 when those in the

Bitcoin community who did not agree with separating the transactions and the digital signatures opted for increasing the block size instead to 8 MB from 1 MB and *Bitcoin Cash* was born.[77] We will see a bit further whether this was an optimal solution.

Slow adoptability

Mass adoption of any technical innovation can only occur if it is easy to adopt the new technology. The difficulty to understand how the new technology or device works, or if people cannot easily try it out to see for themselves if it really works can be obstacles to mass adoption. At the moment we seem to be lingering in the gap between the early adopter phase and the early majority phase, at least in the developed nations.

The fact that the Bitcoin network can only process a maximum number of 7 transactions as opposed to the regular 20,000 transactions per second of the Visa network is certainly hindering its mass adoption. Another very important factor is that the price of cryptocurrencies in general, and especially of Bitcoin, is very volatile due to massive market manipulation by whales.

Whales are those traders, including institutions, who own thousands of bitcoins and can make the price of Bitcoin fall or rise by dumping on the market a couple of thousand bitcoins or by buying enormous amounts at once. It is still an unregulated, Wild West situation in cryptoland. However, regulation is not entirely positive. Why not? We must remember who the regulators are and what their goals are.

Since the introduction of *Bitcoin futures* the price of Bitcoin has been much more heavily manipulated, so much so that technical analysis which could bring relatively solid results in traditional financial markets has become almost worthless on the crypto market.

The planned Bitcoin Exchange Traded Funds (or ETFs) would generally increase trust in Bitcoin, but likely instead of supporting it as an electronic payment option, it would turn Bitcoin even more into some kind of digital gold. And it could make financial institutions and corporations hoard it as people would do with gold.

There are also a couple of corporate initiatives like Bakkt, which is a collaboration effort between Intercontinental Exchange (ICE) and entities like Microsoft and Starbucks, which aim at operating a separate ecosystem related to Bitcoin. Bakkt is interesting because its parent company is Intercontinental Exchange which also funded the New York Stock Exchange. ICE claims in its website that it "builds, operates and advances global financial and commodity markets"[78]. The plan of Bakkt was to settle its futures contracts in physical bitcoins, so they also wanted to custody those bitcoins in a physical warehouse. Although the people at Bakkt estimated that the Commodity Futures Trading Commission would grant them the necessary approval by November 2018, in the second half of April the CFTC still had not granted Bakkt the necessary approval.

Bakkt eventually decided to self-certify their Bitcoin futures with the CFTC, so that they can keep their promise to launch their user acceptance test net on July 22, 2019[79], which they did.[80]

Meanwhile ErisX, an exchange backed by Fidelity Investments, TD Ameritrade and Digital Currency Group has obtained authorization to launch a physically delivered Bitcoin futures product.[81]

Bakkt finally received approval from the New York Department of Financial Services and it announced that it would launch its Bitcoin futures and warehouse product to institutional clients on September 23, 2019.[82]

Virtually everybody in the crypto space thought that when Bakkt and ErisX would finally go live, many institutions would step in and buy bitcoin in great quantity from them. However, the catch is that Bakkt and ErisX would withhold the actual "physical" bitcoins and users could only trade virtual bitcoins. They could take out loans in bitcoin, they could pay in bitcoins, but those bitcoins would be exchanged into fiat when paying for example in Starbucks. What clients would really own would be simply IOUs of bitcoins, while the actual private key of real bitcoins would be kept in custody by the clearinghouses of Bakkt and ErisX. The same situation as when people buy promises of gold instead of obtaining real, physical gold immediately upon the purchase.

However, the trading volume of Bakkt's "ETF-like" Bitcoin futures product has been surprisingly low in the first weeks of its launch. Institutions don't seem to be that interested. The common expectation was that the more institutional money enters the crypto market and the more those institutions invest in Bitcoin, the closer mainstream adoption could be. However, whatever bitcoin accumulation may be happening must likely take place in over-the-counter trades. Binance Research, the research team of the biggest crypto exchange confirmed that they think the launch of Bakkt's Bitcoin futures could have been one factor which caused a 2,000-dollar dip in the price of Bitcoin on the crypto market: "Bakkt was touted by many 'crypto-observers' as an additional primary channel to bring large institutional flows into cryptocurrency and digital asset markets. It may certainly still do so in the future, as illustrated by the CME futures sluggish start and subsequent pick-up in volumes. Short-term wise though, Bakkt's disappointing start seems to have been a contributing factor to the recent price decline."[83]

All these derivative Bitcoin related products could just as well push Bitcoin into being more of a gold-like store of value instead of an actual digital cash. And this is exactly what we have seen happening. As institutions and old world actors are building up their businesses for selling Bitcoin related financial products, the price of Bitcoin will increasingly become a target of financial market speculators. Consequently, Bitcoin is being pushed towards only being seen as a store of value instead of as a practical decentralized electronic cash.

Safety, anonymity and privacy are also very important aspects to consider when it comes to using a blockchain based cash system and there are certainly some things that we must discuss as it relates to Bitcoin, but we will do it in a later chapter about privacy coins. For now just keep in mind that not everything is as it seems at first sight regarding privacy, anonymity and safety in Bitcoin land.

8

Forks in the Bitcoin Road

A s a natural process for an open source software which does not have an all-powerful central authority to decide how and in which direction to develop the program, there has always been different groups with different ideas about what would be the best for the development of Bitcoin. As developers were trying to tackle certain issues as those came up, some proposed changes went against what the majority of Bitcoin miners preferred to see for the future of the network. Miners obviously play the most important role in the functioning of the network, so whatever they opt for becomes consensus about which is the best way to go.

If miners cannot agree on a new development or some change to the protocol when the new protocol is implemented on the blockchain (always beginning from a predetermined block), those who do not want to accept the change can choose to continue to build on the old blockchain without upgrading the software and act as if nothing has happened. After the predetermined block, which the developers announced to be the last block operating with the old rules, the updated blockchain will work according to the new rules.

There are two kinds of software changes: if the old software will not recognize the new blocks created according to the new rules, the change of rule in the software is called a *hard fork*. A hard fork *loosens the rules* of the protocol that has been enforced by full nodes, for example if you want to change the original block size of Bitcoin from 1MB to 2MB, after the hard fork a block which exceeded 1MB but did not reach 2MB in size and was earlier considered invalid would now be considered valid.[84]

When a hard fork is executed, all nodes that agree to accept the new rules must upgrade their software, or else they will not be able to operate on the blockchain anymore, so this change is similar to a fork in the road where users either keep walking ahead without making any changes in direction, or they start walking in a new direction, adopting the new protocol.

However, if the old software can still recognize new blocks that were created according to the new rules, the implementation of that change is called a *soft fork*.[85] A soft fork *restricts the rules* of the original software.[86] A good example would be if instead of the original 1MB block size there would be a change to 500K blocks. As a result, the nodes that do not upgrade their software would see the new transactions created under the new rules as valid (because 500K is less than 1MB, which is in line with the original block size rule), but if these nodes mine new blocks, those new blocks will be rejected by the upgraded nodes (because those blocks will have a 1MB block size which is not acceptable by the new rules).

This means that for a soft fork to not cause any issues, the majority of the hash power must be behind it, supporting its implementation. If a soft fork does not get the support of the majority of the hash power, it can become the shorter chain and be abandoned by the network, so basically the new changes will quickly be taken out of operation.

The other possibility is that, if there is enough activity or "political" power behind it, one chain can split off, although soft forks are less likely to cause the splitting up of the network than hard forks.[87]

It can happen that during a hard fork not everybody is convinced of the usefulness of the new rules which are to be implemented, normally on an ideological basis, and this can lead to a split of the network.

Those who think that the proposed change goes against the ethos of that specific cryptocurrency, if they can group together and create what they think is a better alternative solution, or if they think that the best solution is to keep the blockchain as it is, can create a completely new cryptocurrency.

In such cases the new cryptocurrency that does not adopt the changes of the hard fork simply continues to work from the original blockchain and follow its rules.

One good example of such a split is the birth of Ethereum Classic (which, essentially, is the original Ethereum with the original, untampered blockchain, created by those in the Ethereum community who did not want a central authority, the Ethereum Foundation to make changes to the blockchain after a major 51% attack, so that they can pay back some 50 million dollars' worth of stolen Ethers (the cryptocurrency of Ethereum) from The DAO which was an organization created on the platform of Ethereum.

The Ethereum Foundation which has been the guiding force behind changes to Ethereum wanted investors in The DAO to get their stolen money back, so they decided to alter the blockchain "manually"; something which goes against the concept of a decentralized blockchain. So the group of miners who were less than enthusiastic about such an act of central control decided to create their own cryptocurrency by simply sticking to the original, unaltered blockchain. In this specific case there was no software change involved, but rather a central, "51% overriding action" to remove the fraudulent blocks from the blockchain.

When a chain split happens, there are two or more versions of the blockchain that share the same history up to the block where their rules diverge. A chain split can be caused both by a soft fork and a hard fork, but it can also be avoided in case of soft forks and hard forks. However, hard forks are more likely to result in a chain split because the hard fork renders those full nodes that do not upgrade to the new software incompatible.[88]

As described in some of the scenarios above, in a chain split there are two or more competing versions of the blockchain that share the same history up to the point where their rule sets diverge.[89]

It can also happen that the majority of nodes that upgraded to use the new software may return to the old rules in order to avoid a chain split. This happened for example in March 2013 when an already implemented change unintentionally caused a hard fork of the Bitcoin blockchain, meaning that a block was produced that was acceptable by the nodes that upgraded their software, but was unacceptable by nodes that did not. In August 2013 they had to deploy a hard fork to fix the bug that initially caused the chain split. Once the bug was fixed, the development team in charge made a public request asking miners to voluntarily get back to the earlier software version to maintain the integrity of the Bitcoin network, which they did. [90]

After this introduction, now let's take a quick look at the most important hard forks of Bitcoin.

Litecoin

Litecoin was created by Charlie Lee who has been a software engineer for Google two more years after launching Litecoin. From Google he went on to work as an engineering manager and later director of engineering of Coinbase, one of the most important centralized exchanges (with traditional bank owners) until mid-2017. The Litecoin network went live on October 7, 2011.

Lee's intention was to create a more versatile, more agile cryptocurrency based on the Bitcoin Core, code which would appeal to more people and could have more success in real life use adoption. For this reason he improved the graphical user interface compared to Bitcoin to make it more user friendly and simpler to use, but of course that is of lesser importance compared to the other changes made to the original Bitcoin version.

Litecoin's answer to the scalability problem of Bitcoin is the decreased block generation time from 10 to 2.5 minutes, which means that it can process four times as many transactions as Bitcoin, although this speed is really not much to write home about either.

What's more important is that the SHA-256 hashing protocol used in Bitcoin has been replaced by a new hashing protocol called Scrypt. Scrypt "favors high-speed random access memory instead of processing power"[91], which means that Litecoin miners must have access to quite a lot of memory, so mining pools are at a disadvantage when it comes to mining Litecoin.

Scrypt requires from miners the heavy use of computing resources, particularly memory, not just the processing unit. Unlike when mining

Bitcoin, you cannot just stack processing units the way Bitcoin mining pools do, but you would also have to have a proportional amount of memory, which makes mining expensive for a large-scale operation.

As Charlie Lee said, "it makes it difficult to run many instances of Scrypt in parallel in a graphics card" which makes manufacturing ASIC miners developed for dealing with Scrypt much more expensive than for SHA-256.[92]

Scrypt can be efficiently run on standard central processing units (CPUs) and on graphics processing units (GPUs), so the price of entry for mining Litecoin is significantly lower than for mining Bitcoin. This makes Litecoin less prone to centralization by large mining pools and more secure because 51% attacks are more difficult to execute successfully.[93]

Mining Litecoin still requires quite a lot of computing power because of the mathematical nature of proof of work systems, including Scrypt, so in the end the computing power any particular miner has will be a large determining factor in his mining results.[94] Even so, there is ASICs hardware which can be used to mine Litecoin.[95]

Although Scrypt is not more secure as a hashing protocol, it is faster, easier, and it requires less energy than SHA-256.[96]

Litecoin has continually been upgraded and developed since its inception, mainly due to the various security vulnerabilities it had in the first place. It even pioneered the implementation of the Lightning Network, a second layer solution that allows almost instantaneous and very cheap transactions off the blockchain. Also, Charlie Lee was the first person to perform a Litecoin-Bitcoin atomic swap in September 2017, which means that he exchanged his litecoins for bitcoins on a peer-to-peer basis without having to use an exchange.[97]

Litecoin has been regarded by many as digital silver, always compared to Bitcoin, which is often regarded as digital gold. Consequently, it has not suffered such dramatic price spikes and dips as Bitcoin, although in 2018, together with all altcoins, it suffered a huge loss of value in dollars due to various kinds of manipulations of the market from which it has not recovered yet. Its relative stability could make Litecoin a more desirable cryptocurrency for merchants because its price fluctuations are smaller than those of Bitcoin.[98]

The SegWit soft fork and the creation of Bitcoin Cash

By 2015 the Bitcoin network has grown too much to be able to work optimally under the original protocol. The bottleneck effect that slowed down the network was the maximum allowed block size being only 1MB which means a miserly maximum 7 transactions per second. Due to the increased traffic, many transactions had to wait several hours to be verified and mining companies started to charge urgency fees in exchange for giving priority in the processing of transactions.

In practice, transaction fees skyrocketed from a few cents to 5-10 dollars per transaction for priority handling. The transactions of people who did not pay an urgency fee could be lingering around in the mempool for many hours, even up to three days.[99]

It was clear that something had to be done if Bitcoin was ever to become a more widely adopted and effectively usable cryptocurrency, and not just some asset that could potentially give good returns to investors.

For such a wider adoption the scalability problem had to be addressed. However, there were two very different opinions about how this issue should be handled. One group wanted to implement a hard fork by increasing the block size with the aim to be able to cram more transactions into one block, which would automatically lead to more transactions being verified in the same amount of time.

This solution would entail that any full nodes that did not adopt the new rules implemented by the hard fork would not be able to validate the new, increased sized blocks because they would still keep operating with the rule that says the block size cannot exceed 1MB. This would inevitably lead to a chain split if the developers were unable to convince the majority of the owners of hash power of the network to go along with the hard fork and upgrade to the new, modified software.

However, there was another group of developers who opposed this approach and who wanted to avoid increasing the block size and a hard fork.

They proposed in December 2015 to decrease the amount of information that a block can contain instead of increasing the block size. The idea was to separate the transaction data (like amount, sender and receiver) from the digital signature that authorizes the transaction.

In a normal Bitcoin block the transaction data is linked to the digital signature because they are together hashed into a "ciphertext" (or hash). The idea behind this proposal was that if the digital signature is not added to the transaction, then more transactions could fit into a block, which would then make the network quicker without the need to increase the maximum block size.

They called this technology *Segregated Witness* (or SegWit) because it segregates the actual transaction data from the "witness" or digital signature. After a long time of debating the developers finally announced a soft fork to implement Segregated Witness on the Bitcoin blockchain. As it was going to be a soft fork, not all full nodes were required to adopt this software change. The SegWit soft fork took place on August 1, 2017. In the beginning it did not have a very extensive support, but eventually by October 2018 already 54% of the hash power has adopted it.[100] However, it decreased to around 40% in the following months, largely due to the fact that in the bear market there were not enough incentives for large crypto exchanges like Binance, Bitmex or Bittrex to adopt it.[101] Still, in September 2019 more than half of the miners did not use SegWit.

The group that was opposed to SegWit decided to split off and hard fork the blockchain by implementing an increased block size. On August 1, 2017, the same day that Segwit went live they created *Bitcoin Cash (BCH)*, a new cryptocurrency. The maximum block size of Bitcoin Cash was 8MB, which in theory meant an eight-fold increase in the validation time of transactions. It must not have provided the needed effect though because less than a year later, on May 18, 2018 Bitcoin Cash was hard forked, this time to further increase its block size to 32MB.[102]

The problem with SegWit is that it changes one of the fundamental characteristics that actually define(d) Bitcoin. Satoshi's definition says that "an electronic coin" (and obviously, he meant Bitcoin) is a chain of digital signatures. The bad news is that SegWit actually breaks the chain of digital signatures which were originally meant to be used as a way to check the integrity of the blockchain and the ownership of each transaction.

Digital signatures in Bitcoin are used to prove the ownership of a coin. "The fact that signatures cannot be forged is one reason that your coins in storage are safe, even if the network were to undergo a 51% attack."[103]

Satoshi's Bitcoin requires the signature to be part of the transaction, and the transaction data and the signature to be hashed into the input of the next transaction. This provides an important data integrity check because a coin cannot be removed from one account and put into another one without the correct signature of the current owner of that coin. This signature must be included in the transaction and published on the blockchain.[104]

Signatures cannot be forged (at least it is very unlikely), the only way somebody can steal a coin is by getting hold of the private key of its owner. When somebody uses a stolen private key to divert funds, you can later check on the blockchain to verify that indeed it was a theft because the signature is false.[105] Well, the situation is that for the moment around half of the nodes have implemented SegWit, which means this crucial integrity check is not there anymore for those coins and transactions related to SegWit nodes.

It is important to note that SegWit "allows for layer-2 solutions to be built on top of the immutable blockchain, one of these second layer advances is the Lightning Network"[106]. So while the implementation of SegWit fixed transaction malleability which posed only a very minor threat, in turn it removed one of the basic elements of what Bitcoin initially was meant to be. The big question then is whether the Segwit soft fork was only a clever move on behalf of those who wanted to make the integration of the Lightning Network possible on Bitcoin, or whether it was just an imperfect solution to the problem of scalability.

Many believe that Bitcoin was hijacked by the banksters through Blockstream which is a for profit corporation founded in 2014 by Dr. Adam Back, Gregory Maxwell, and Matt Corallo, all well known Bitcoin developers. Bitcoin Core is a software which is considered as Bitcoin's reference implementation. Bitcoin Core is itself a node of the Bitcoin network and also provides a bitcoin wallet.[107]

Bitcoin Core is an open source project, thus anybody can contribute to it, but it appears that the developers of Blockstream have tried to steer the Bitcoin project into a direction that would keep the Bitcoin blockchain "dumbed down" so that Blockstream can sell its Bitcoin related products to companies.

At least this is what Adam Back communicated. "Blockstream plans to sell side chains to enterprises, charging a fixed monthly fee, taking transaction fees and even selling hardware — a fact that has caused the big blockers to protest that Blockstream and the engineers it employs who are also Bitcoin core developers want to keep the block size small so Blockstream can profit. Back says this isn't true because, beyond a certain point, side chains won't really solve scaling."[108] However, this argument is not valid because Blockstream will benefit until the network reaches that certain point mentioned by Back.

Back also alluded to the increasing of the block size as if it were a more important feature of Bitcoin than having the transaction data and the digital signature hashed together. "Back says the community shouldn't remove Bitcoin's signature features in order to scale the network." As he said, "If we're going to get centralized into a big datacenter somewhere, as in the PayPal case, it's basically guaranteed the company running it will get national security layers and black lists and all the things banks do, and regulations will apply to them."[109]

What managing to stir its development into the direction of using sidechains/second layer solutions means for Bitcoin is that the transaction fees go to the developers of those sidechains and not to the miners (because the amount of transactions recorded on the Bitcoin main chain is reduced). So if Bitcoin is more capable of managing everything without the need of sidechains in terms of speed, low transaction fees, fungibility, security, and immutability, the less need there will be for sidechains.

"Blockstream doesn't make money on what Bitcoin can do, Blockstream makes money on what Bitcoin can't do."[110] Bitcoin has to be scalable, reliable (in respect of transaction times and low fees), and capable of handling smart contracts to avoid the use of sidechains/second layer solutions and the hijacking of its network by private interests. Actually, "BTC is the only coin in existence with intentionally limited on-chain capacity".[111]

Since 2015 the following changes have taken place in the development of Bitcoin, which all seem to support the theory that Blockstream has tried to hijack Bitcoin to profit off its users.

The maximum block size remained 1MB. This 1MB limit was added to the Bitcoin code by Satoshi in 2010 as a temporary measure against spammers and with the understanding that it would later be removed. As the block size limit naturally kept transaction speed low, it became the subject of continuous discussions among developers whether they should increase the block size. As a consequence of keeping the maximum block size at 1MB, transaction fees became not only very high due to the increased traffic of the Bitcoin network, but fees also fluctuate widely.[112]

The operation codes for zero-confirmation instant transactions and smart contracts were removed from the Bitcoin code, so instant transactions and smart contracts which were earlier possible on the blockchain would have to be executed on sidechains. The developments that took place since the involvement of Blockstream with Bitcoin Core were upgrades that, curiously, made Bitcoin compatible with the second layer solutions which Blockstream just happened to be developing in the meantime. Such sidechain protocols of Blockstream are Liquid which went live in October 2018 and the Lighting Network.[113]

Liquid's platform provides a sidechain that enables 1-to-1 exchange of Bitcoin between chains and its aim is to make Bitcoin transactions faster and more secure for exchanges and institutions. The only issue with it is that instead of the proof of work protocol it uses a "federation of trusted functionaries", which means that it doesn't even pretend to look decentralized.[114]

The Lightning Network is a low fee sidechain for micropayments faster than Visa, that was developed by Blockstream and two other companies. Each company created its own iteration that are fully compatible with each other. Blockstream's *cLightning* iteration went live in February 2018. The decentralization here happens in the form of transaction fees being taken by Blockstream instead of going to Bitcoin miners.[115]

A third, related project of Blockstream was the launching of satellites to provide Bitcoin transaction capabilities to people in regions with low internet accessibility. Of course, that would also come with a price tag as it is a private service provider.

As we saw, Bitcoin Cash was born as an opposition to the implementation of SegWit. The Bitcoin Cash folks wanted to solve the scalability issue by increasing the block size from 1MB to 8MB and then a year later to 32MB. The problem with this approach is that block size heavily tips the scales in favor of miners with the most resources because the bigger the block size, the more data must be processed to validate all the transactions in a block. Also, the cost of entry becomes more prohibitive for people with less resources. These points have been frequently reported by Bitcoin Core fans as the major issues with Bitcoin Cash.

Jimmy Song, one of the contributors to Bitcoin's development and the author of a book titled *Programming Bitcoin: Learn How To Program Bitcoin From Scratch* said that Bitcoin Cash is actually fiat money because it was created by a simple act of will without further effort (by hard forking Bitcoin and increasing its block size), created from an authoritative determination. According to Song, while Bitcoin intends to be a tool of liberation from government by decentralizing power, which is shown in its "classically liberal, anarcho-capitalist and Austrian" [116] characteristics, it is a sound money and has cypherpunk roots. In contrast, Bitcoin Cash is "interventionist, paternalistic and Keynesian befitting its corporate roots and is a fiat money"[117].

The Austrian and Keynesian economic theories differ in their notion of how markets are controlled. The Austrian school believes that markets are self-regulating systems where the actors of the market following their self-interest behave in a way that will maximize their profits, without any intervention from any authority with centralized power. This inherent self-interest causes the markets to be self-regulating. In contrast, Keynesian economics preaches that markets need a central governing hand to dictate the direction in which the economy should go, and to regulate the market by direct action (i. e. manipulation by a central bank).

Well, it is again a very good example of the two-sided thinking so prevalent in our culture. Either the market is controlled by a centralized power that does what it wants without taking into consideration the values and wishes of everyone else, or the market regulates itself without central governance but then the individual actors have to fight with all the rest for their share.

All individual Bitcoin coins are created in the process of mining, so once Bitcoin Cash was forked off Bitcoin, the Bitcoin Cash network indeed created the same amount of coins that had been mined on Bitcoin up to the fork, so in that sense Bitcoin Cash could be called "fiat money". However, for the developers and miners who chose to keep working on the Bitcoin Cash version instead of the Bitcoin one, the Bitcoin Cash blockchain was only the organic continuation of Bitcoin. Also, all the Bitcoin Cash coins created as duplicates of the Bitcoin blockchain up to the point of the hard fork refer to the same transactions, to the very same money that Bitcoin users moved around. So Bitcoin Cash is not a "fiat money".

What we see now is that even though Bitcoin was created to be decentralized, until hoarding it makes no economic sense, and especially until speculating over its price is no longer possible, with or without Bitcoin we will still be bound by the dog-eat-dog type Darwinian, survival-of-the-fittest style fight for money. This could be avoided with the use of demurrage currencies as it was demonstrated successfully in this part, however, definitely not with the zero or negative interest rates of the central banks coupled with their shameless printing of more money called "quantitative easing" until hyperinflation strikes and kills the currency. Which is exactly what the Central Bank of Europe just announced to do again in September 2019. The Federal Reserve has also started pumping billions of dollars daily into Wall Street around the same time. But we digress. Back to Bitcoin Cash now.

It is interesting to see how a major proponent and contributor to Bitcoin protocol improvements, Jimmy Song describes Bitcoin. He sees a fundamental difference between Bitcoin and the rest of the cryptocurrencies:

according to him, Bitcoin provides sovereignty over your money because each individual is free to decide which software they want to run, which features they utilize and which use cases they prioritize.[118]

This is what Bitcoin being decentralized really means. People have property rights over their own bitcoins and each person chooses from the possible solutions to any problems based on stable and immutable rules.[119] That is why Bitcoin cannot be censored and why it does not have a single point of failure.

Bitcoin actually is the only cryptocurrency that provides users sovereignty over their own money. All altcoins, i.e. all cryptocurrencies except Bitcoin have "a single point of failure or control which can be co-opted by another entity and thus users really aren't sovereign over those tokens."[120]

We must take into account, however, that the decentralized nature of Bitcoin does not mean that today or whenever you are reading this the Bitcoin network will be decentralized and there is no danger of a 51% attack caused by the exceedingly big chunk of Bitmain and similar large mining companies. What Song means is simply that at the time of making any change to the Bitcoin software, each user can decide autonomously, no central governing team pushes decisions down the throat of the Bitcoin community. If mining centralization ever reached over 50%, the majority mining company could steer the development of Bitcoin in a way that would be beneficial to them.

In practice this means that this theoretical free choice (we are back to Austrian school economics where decisions are made based on personal self-interest, without the need of a central governing body) has already resulted in the serious deviation from the original intention of creating a safe, non-corruptible, peer-to-peer electronic cash system that can provide safe and (relatively speaking) free transactions, without constant fear of being hacked or attacked.

Now the situation instead is that, as we saw it, Bitmain has already crossed once the 51% threshold as regards to total hash power of the network. While those nodes that do not agree in the future with any of the potential changes made to the software or a new way of operation of the Bitcoin network which Bitmain or its future competitors and those who own and operate

ASIC miners stand behind, they will have no choice but to adapt or leave the system because they will be unable to compete with the majority mining company when it comes to processing speed. And processing speed will directly decide who will build the largest chain: the guy with the most hash power.

So, in the sense of Austrian school economics Bitcoin may still be a decentralized cryptocurrency, but knowing that the controllers are there, as they always have been, makes thinking in Austrian terms a bit outdated. When looking at day-to-day operations it is clear that the SegWit soft fork turned Bitcoin into a shadow of its former self. It is not as safe because of the separation of the signatures from the transaction data, and although it did increase speed, obviously neither of the proposed options were meant to turn the Bitcoin first layer (the blockchain itself) into a true rival of the likes of Visa with thousands of transactions processed by the second.

Rather, the goal was to try to implement layer two solutions above the blockchain and deal with the issue of speed in this way. Essentially, both SegWit and Bitcoin Cash were just different approaches to trying to solve the issue of scaling of the Bitcoin network. So we now get back for a moment to the statement that Bitcoin Cash is fiat money. The pseudonymous writer Jonald Fyookball believes that Bitcoin Cash was born out of a community split over the question of how to best scale the Bitcoin network, so it is definitely not a fiat money as Jimmy Song claims, but it is actually Bitcoin as it functioned up until 2015, without an artificially limited transaction capacity and high fees as an electronic cash.[121] Well, the block size is still limited, but at least the limit was raised.

As an interesting side note, Roger Ver, the figurehead of Bitcoin Cash and later of Bitcoin ABC offered $1.25 million to a developer company to build the Lightning Network on Bitcoin Cash but they declined it due to "political and ideological" questions. So while they first increased the block size to retain the sovereignty of the original Bitcoin blockchain by not having to rely on layer two solutions to provide scalability, later he wanted to implement the Lightning Network on Bitcoin Cash. Just one of those weird cases where we do not have all the pieces of the puzzle, but it might have had to do with the war between legacy Bitcoin Cash (Bitcoin ABC) and Bitcoin Satoshi Vision.

When I keep referring back to Satoshi's definition of Bitcoin, I do not do it in the Satoshi-is-god-and-we-must-not-stray-from-his-vision sense. What I want to draw the attention to is whether the changes done to the protocol make Bitcoin safer, more secure, more private, more scalable and more decentralized, or whether they are diverting from the original ideals.

Bitcoin was not necessarily perfect the way it was created (or at least we do not have the knowledge to judge its potentials), but it is worth looking for ways it can be improved along the lines of the ideals of a decentralized, truly workable digital currency to have a better overview of whether certain protocol changes help or not to turn Bitcoin into that ideal cryptocurrency.

So while we must remember that Bitmain already had control over more than half of the hash power of Bitcoin as of October 2018 and theoretically it could get back over 50% in the future, it is also important to know that Bitmain itself was one of the entities behind the creation of Bitcoin Cash, even though it owned only 5% of the total supply. Also, there is nothing strange in a mining company supporting Bitcoin Cash if it means that the protocol remains the same when it comes to who gets the transaction fees, instead of standing behind the SegWit implementation which opened up a new way for the introduction of second layer solutions that syphon transaction fees away from miners.

The contrarian view is that Bitcoin Cash has its centralized developer group that follows its own roadmap and forced upgrades on everyone through authoritarian hard forks that everyone must follow, or they will not be able to keep operating on the Bitcoin Cash blockchain. They push issues to the front which they deem important, and not just handling the issues as they are raised by the community of Bitcoin Cash users, like for example the use of smart contracts or the method of payment.[122] Actually the March 2018 hard fork that raised the block size to 32MB was linked to their aim to concentrate on smart contracts as the new block size makes transactions swifter and leaves enough space within blocks to include smart contracts.

According to Song, Bitmain was acting like a central bank of Bitcoin Cash; it tried to maintain a peg to Bitcoin which they use as their reserve currency, but they could not keep this peg because all altcoins fell in value much more than Bitcoin did in 2018, so Bitmain had to keep selling its Bitcoin reserves to keep the peg to even 0.1 btc. As they run out of Bitcoin reserves, eventually they would have to artificially inflate the value of Bitcoin Cash, the same way regular central banks do to fiat currency, basically putting a tax (inflation) on money.

The only appeal Bitcoin Cash has as a cryptocurrency, according to Song, is quicker transactions, but then they were not quicker than Visa, and the promise they kept marketing is that they will act better than fiat central bankers. Having a "benevolent ruler" after getting rid of the "evil central bankers" is not a real solution when you can have your sovereignty over your own money, and there are many altcoins that do what Bitcoin Cash does and they are superior as methods of payment.[123] We must agree with him regarding the notion of "benevolent rulers", if nothing else.

Bitcoin Cash managed to stay among the top cryptocurrencies in terms of market capitalization largely due to their extensive marketing efforts. Roger Ver, the figurehead of Bitcoin Cash is the CEO of Bitcoin.com which is a website providing information on all things related to Bitcoin. Bitcoin Cash has maintained its position quite steadily as number 4, only preceded by Bitcoin, Ether and Ripple. Even after it was hard forked and split into two new currencies, the "victorious" version (Bitcoin ABC) stayed as number 4 on the top list.

There had been an internal fight going on for the control of Bitcoin Cash between Bitmain and an Australian businessman called Craig Wright. The latter has posed recently as Satoshi Nakamoto, supposedly signing a transaction in front of a couple of insiders with the private key of Satoshi. The funny thing is that Vitalik Buterin, the guy who wrote Ethereum and previously was involved with Bitcoin and allegedly has an IQ of 257, publicly laughed at the allegations made in May 2016 that Craig Wright would be Satoshi. Gavin Andresen, one of the early developers of Bitcoin described at a conference how Craig Wright signed in his presence a message chosen by Andresen, using the private key from block 1, the very first mined Bitcoin block on a computer and with a software that Andresen was convinced had not been tampered with. He said that this convinced him that Craig Wright is the inventor of Bitcoin.

Buterin commented on the statement of Andresen saying: "just a syllable of controversy for fun, I'll explain why I think he's probably not Satoshi. First of all, very...very simple signaling theory: if you had the opportunity to take two different paths of proving who...of proving that he's him, one path would have been to make that exact kind of proof, make a...make a signature from the first a....from the first Bitcoin block, put the signature out in public, make a very simple ten-line blog post that anyone...you know including people...including, you know cryptographers...you know like Dan Bernard and Dan Kaminsky and so forth that can verify that it's him, and just post that out there and let the cryptography community do it. Instead, he's taken this path where he's wrote this big long blog post with 200 lines it's so confusing that even Dan Kaminsky said it's too confusing, and tried to get...only show that signature to a few select people and we're supposed to trust them. So, in general, signaling theory says; if you choose...if you have a good way of proving something and a noisy way of proving something and you choose the noisy way, then that means, you know...chances are, you...that means you could be...it's because you couldn't do it in the good way in the first place."[124]

The Faketoshi, as he is called by many, wrote a long and complicated letter to prove that he is Satoshi Nakamoto, but various cryptographers said it was nonsensical and lacking concrete proof of him being Satoshi. Craig Wright later became a public proponent of Bitcoin Cash. Many people believe the opinion Shaurya Malwa points out in an article, that if Wright really were Satoshi Nakamoto, he could not possibly abandon his creation, Bitcoin and go with a new cryptocurrency, Bitcoin Cash instead. "With all this in mind, there's little doubt as to why a visionary like Vitalik Buterin would waste the chance to call such uncredible figures a 'fraud'."[125], thinks Malwa.

However, one has to take into account the fact that Bitcoin in 2015 was not the original Bitcoin whitepaper, and Bitcoin Cash was more in alignment with the original Bitcoin, so Wright didn't abandon "his brainchild", but created a fork to keep the original blockchain free of harmful alterations. The same happened with the forking of Bitcoin Cash. For Wright, Bitcoin Satoshi Vision is the real, authentic Bitcoin, so in this sense what he abandonded is the overtaken, corrupted forms of Bitcoin.

Also, those supporting Wright believe that if he is indeed Satoshi Nakamoto, he may have had very good reasons not to provide a proof publicly that would without doubt prove to everybody that he is the inventor of Bitcoin. However, the story does not end there. On February 14, 2018 the estate of Dave Kleiman, a paralyzed coder who died in 2013, filed a law suit against Craig Wright, demanding 1,100,111 bitcoins (currently worth over $12.9 billion) and intellectual property related to the Bitcoin software.

The suit filed on behalf of Ira Kleiman, Dave's brother and the representative of his estate alleged that Wright and Kleiman mined bitcoins together in the early days of the cryptocurrency and that since Kleiman's death Wright has "perpetrated a scheme" to "seize Dave's bitcoins." Ira Kleiman was not sure about how many bitcoins Wright has appropriated, but his lawyers based the lawsuit on Wright's statements and extrapolated that he owes Ira Kleiman one million bitcoins, which is the full amount that Wright and Kleiman allegedly mined.[126]

The lawsuit alleged that Dave told his brother in 2009 that he was creating digital money with a wealthy foreigner, also alleging that Kleiman, Wright and two other people conducted a Bitcoin transaction on January 12, 2009, nine days after the first Bitcoin block was created by Satoshi. According to Kleiman's claims, Dave Kleiman and Wright ran a company called W&K Info Defense Research LLC that aimed to develop Bitcoin-based technologies from 2011 until Kleiman's death in 2013. The lawsuit called Wright a "business partner" of this venture but names Dave Kleiman as the "sole member" of W&K, giving him ownership of all bitcoins mined within the framework of the company.[127]

The lawsuit alleged that after Dave Kleiman's death Craig Wright emailed Dave's father claiming that he, Dave and a third person were the team that invented Bitcoin. The lawsuit alleged that the Kleimans only learned about Dave's supposed involvement with the creation of Bitcoin from Wright's letter. The lawsuit also said that Wright sent over several documents showing that Dave Kleiman had transferred the ownership of W&K's assets to Wright but claimed that the documents were "backdated and fraudulent, and that Kleiman's signature was forged with a computer font."[128]

At the same time, Craig Wright sued Vitalik Buterin and Roger Ver, among others, for supposed defamation after he claimed that he is Satoshi Nakamoto. In the case contra Ver, which Wright initiated after Ver called him a fraud, the UK court ruled against Wright stating that they have not found enough evidence of the defamatory nature of anything that Roger Ver posted regarding Wright.

The latest development of Bitcoin Cash was called *Wormhole*, developed by Bitmain as a second layer smart contract protocol. It would allow transactions of asset tokens and crowd sales on the Bitcoin Cash blockchain.[129]

The Wormhole protocol was meant to "allow anyone to create tokens on top of the Bitcoin Cash blockchain", projects allowing to raise funds and backers to contribute to the projects. These tokens would have the same functionality as the ERC-20 tokens of Ethereum and any dealings of such projects would happen in smart contracts.[130]

Wormhole is a fork of the Omni Layer protocol which is "an open-source, decentralized asset platform built on top of the Bitcoin block chain. This means that Omni transactions are Bitcoin transactions except the Omni platform provides more features."[131]

With this development Bitcoin Cash ceased to be "cash only". The Bitcoin Cash software now allows for more complex smart contracts, lower fees and a message service similar to Twitter.[132]

Wormhole is a platform similar to Ethereum on which smart contracts and new tokens can be built. It has its own token called Wormhole Cash, but there are more than 180 different tokens that have been created on Wormhole so far and Roger Ver already talked about potentially launching an ICO for the gaming part of his business on bitcoin.com.[133]

This was a really interesting development as it would have replicated what Ethereum is, being its own platform on which anyone can build new projects, new tokens, launch ICOs and set up smart contracts. It remains to be seen whether legacy Bitcoin Cash, now Bitcoin ABC, with its proof of work procotol could overtake Ethereum which is operating under mixed proof of work and proof of stake but definitely transitioning toward full proof of stake work, and become number two in market capitalization, but it is not very likely.

BitcoinToken, the first programmable token and smart contract engine built on top of Bitcoin Cash was introduced as a concept in August 2018. The platform is very user friendly because you can write smart contracts in assembly code or use predefined libraries and launch tokens by writing a few Javascript lines.[134]

Interestingly, Satoshi wrote an email to Mike Hearn who had worked as a Bitcoin developer for a couple of years before abandoning the project. In the email Satoshi basically confirmed that the 1MB block size limit was just a quick safety hack which would be removed later on. Also, he said that he always wanted Bitcoin to be able to compete with Visa style transaction speed and that it was technically possible to make Bitcoin way faster than the Visa network.[135]

Satoshi also mentioned in that email that computer speed would stay ahead of the number of transactions. Also, he thought that eventually most nodes would be run by specialists with multiple GPU cards (i.e. mining companies), so it was always clear to him that Bitcoin would be decentralized in the sense that each individual who participates in the system is able to choose what to adopt and what not, what equipment to use etc., but that the economic incentives inherent in the system would eventually lead to the appearance of one or a few big players similar to central banks (as is indeed the case now with Bitmain).[136]

Bitcoin ABC versus Bitcoin Satoshi Vision

Since its inception, the agreed protocol for Bitcoin Cash was to do a hardfork every six months in order to implement any upgrades and changes that have been under development, provided that there is consensus to the fork. The first hard fork in May 2018 happened without any turmoil and Bitcoin Cash continued as one cryptocurrency.

However, the latest proposals to be implemented during the planned

November 2018 fork were not accepted universally by the community, which caused the splitting of Bitcoin Cash into Bitcoin ABC[137] and Bitcoin Satoshi Vision.[138]

The changes that resulted in the creation of Bitcoin ABC (ABC meaning Adjustable Blocksize Cap) were proposed by Amaury Sechet, the lead developer of the most used Bitcoin Cash client called Bitcoin Cash ABC. The proposal wanted to keep the 32MB current block size and introduce certain code that would allow the blockchain to access external data.

Sechet's suggestions were aimed at making Bitcoin Cash "the most scalable, usable and extensible blockchain. It further opens the doors for non-cash transactions on the Bitcoin Cash blockchain."[139] This proposal was backed up by Bitmain too.

However, Craig Wright and his company, nChain opposed this proposal. They did not like the idea of using the Bitcoin Cash blockchain for non-cash transactions. They also did not want canonical transactions. According to them, these developments would be too early, not yet required, and also they had not been tested yet anyway. Instead, they proposed increasing the block size to 128MB, backed by one of the biggest Bitcoin Cash miners, CoinGeek who would have liked to see Bitcoin Cash to be restored to the original Bitcoin design.[140]

As the Bitcoin Cash community was divided, on November 15, 2018 the hard fork was executed and the Bitcoin Cash blockchain was split into two new blockchains: Bitcoin ABC (according to Sechet, Bitmain and Roger Ver interests) and Bitcoin Satoshi Vision (following Craig Wright of nChain, and CoinGeek). The two groups announced to fight until one of the blockchains is weakened and dies. Considering that both groups had similar economic and social support behind them, it promised to be a slow, very expensive war between the two interest groups, and one can ask whether the changes already implemented, together with the future ones that both teams planned for their respective coins, would in the end serve the public or only the interest groups themselves.

The roadmap of Bitcoin ABC (or BCHABC) shows moving their blockchain to "mankind scale" which they defined as 10 billion people being able to make 5 transactions per day on the Bitcoin Cash ABC blockchain.[141] Now that is one hell of an ambitious plan.

Bitcoin Satoshi Vision (or BSV) aimed to increase the block size to 128MB. It also wanted to re-enable some code proposed in the original whitepaper that was later disabled due to security concerns. Furthermore, Bitcoin SV planned to remove the cap on the number of instructions that can be executed in one go.

Charlie Lee of Litecoin used the opportunity of the hard fork to strike back at Roger Ver, the controversial proponent of Bitcoin ABC with a rather personal punch in his funny tweet: "Bitcoin Satoshi Vision is the real Bitcoin Cash. Karma's a BCH."[142] The reality, however, is that within one month from the hard fork, BCHABC was already way more popular than BSV. ABC had 50% more hash power than Craig Wright's SV.[143]

In practice, Bitcoin ABC is viewed as the new implementation of Bitcoin Cash, so when somebody mentions Bitcoin Cash nowadays they mean Bitcoin ABC.

At least officially mostly due to the behavior of Craig Wright, Binance, the largest cryptocurrency exchange decided to delist Bitcoin Satoshi Vision in April 2019. Their decision was quickly followed by Kraken, another large exchange. Such delistings could have meant a step on the road leading to the potential death of Bitcoin Satoshi Vision but then the Kleiman court case changed the narrative again when the judge ruled against Wright and ordered him to pay 50% of what they (Wright and Kleiman) mined together, which at the time of the ruling amounted to approximately $6 billion.

Although the court did not examine, or rule on, whether Craig Wright is Satoshi, it gave him a weird backing as they must have obviously believed that he and Kleiman did mine those 1.1 million bitcoins.

At the time of writing, in early October 2019 the total market capitalization of BSV is $1.47 billion and it ranks number 9 on the list of Coinmarketcap.com as opposed to Bitcoin ABC, which now appears in most exchanges as BCH, which ranks number 5 with a market capitalization of $3.7 billion.

Bitcoin Cash ABC has experienced an immediate surge in price due to the delisting of Bitcoin SV. Also, currently the majority of exchanges use the

BCH ticker for Bitcoin ABC (some even call it Bitcoin Cash ABC to refer to its origins) while Bitcoin SV is also mentioned as Bitcoin Cash Satoshi Vision with the ticker BCHSV.

Craig Wright published a book in August 2019 titled *Satoshi's Vision: The Art of Bitcoin* which puts things into a different perspective and which I highly recommend you read. He mentions in the book that the BSV team has already managed to scale the blockchain to a thousand transactions per second and they hope to be able to double the value that Visa does by the end of 2019.[144]

SegWit2x (B2X)

A group of developers were not happy with the SegWit soft fork, nor with the 8MB new block size of Bitcoin Cash. They proposed to solve the scalability issue by introducing segregated witness to Bitcoin while at the same time also increasing the block size to 2MB. They called this version SegWit2x.

As no consensus was made within the Bitcoin community about the implementation of both changes, its proponents decided to create their own blockchain and proposed to do a hard fork on November 16, 2017, but due to the lack of necessary support from miners it was canceled.

The implementation finally took place on December 28, 2017 when Bitcoin was forked and a new cryptocurrency called Bitcoin SegWit2x (B2X) was created, however, instead of the original proposal of increasing the block size to 2MB, the new developer team that stepped in increased the block size to 4MB, even though the reference to 2MB remained in the name of the fork and the coin itself.

On February 19, 2018 SegWit2x adopted *hybrid consensus*. This means to not only use proof of work for transaction verification but also proof of stake, which is the other most widespread consensus protocol to validate blocks on the blockchain.

Due to the nature of proof of work, networks using it as the only consensus protocol are vulnerable to 51% attacks because this protocol incentivizes amassing as much processing power as possible to be able to do more processing, which is the work in proof of work. For example in the case of Bitcoin, Bitmain has already once reached the level where it could have decided to not validate new transactions based on its own interest, and it could also have executed double-spend attacks.

In contrast, the proof of stake protocol allows miners to still be rewarded with minimal hardware and software resources. Miners have to deposit any amount they want to (which is their stake), and whoever has the largest stake has the chance to validate the transaction and receive the mining reward.

In SegWit2x miners who have been holding tokens for a longer time, as well as the largest amount are more likely to receive rewards. The new block creator is chosen in a deterministic way.[145]

According to the SegWit2x development team, the hybrid proof of work and proof of stake consensus maximizes user engagement and benefits everybody in the network. Every nine consecutive blocks are mined with proof of work and the tenth block is mined with proof of stake. If a user has B2X coins in his wallet he is able to mine the tenth block.

Once a user deposits his stake, he will be able to participate in mining activities after 8 hours and 100 blocks. Once a user received a mining reward, his funds get frozen for 100 hours. The biggest benefit of this hybrid protocol is that it makes 51% attacks impossible, or at least extremely difficult to execute.

However, SegWit2x, despite being one of the first cryptocurrencies to implement hybrid mining, did not gain many supporters or investors, mainly due to the fact that everything relating to the implementation happened behind closed doors, including the writing of the original agreement about the SegWit2x technology.

On the website of SegWit2x they state that their goal is to keep Bitcoin decentralized. However, while the SegWit2x can be seen a positive improvement because it increases transaction speed and takes away the unfair advantage of miners who use Google ASICBOOST, the increased block size leads to more centralization of power.[146] Plus the original integrity of the Bitcoin blockchain ensured by digital signatures is not there anymore.

In the summer of 2019 B2X appeared as number 2126 in terms of market capitalization on Coinmarketcap.com, with its value being a fraction of a

US dollar and the market capiitalzation was set to zero. By October 2019 Coinmarketcap.com is unable to provide figures for either its capitalization or its rank. At the same time, there seems to be two separate websites with two development teams of SegWit2x.

This is not what a bright future looks like. Even though the hybrid proof of work and proof of stake mining makes SegWit2x available to everybody and not just mining companies with enormous computing power, understandably, because it takes away their advantage, mining companies do not like B2X. Also, the fact that it is traded on the futures market does not help because it makes B2X very vulnerable to stock exchange manipulations, especially as its market capitalization is so low.[147] As it looks today, we can forget about this crypto for good.

Bitcoin Gold

Bitcoin Gold was created as a hard fork of Bitcoin only two months after the SegWit soft fork and the birth of Bitcoin Cash. The team behind this new cryptocurreny chose to tackle the growing centralization of Bitcoin by adopting a new encryption protocol instead of the SHA-256 secure hash algorithm used in Bitcoin.

They did not have a problem with the SHA-256 protocol itself, but with the fact that ASIC mining equipment specifically manufactured for large scale bitcoin mining has slowly started to overtake the mining ecosystem. The aim of this group of developers was to "make Bitcoin decentralized again", as they state on their website.[148]

Due to the huge costs of ASIC mining equipment and the fact that their main manufacturer, Bitmain also owns the two largest mining pools in the world and was already quite close to being able to execute a 51% attack, the Bitcoin Gold team changed to the Equihash-BTG encryption protocol.

You do not need special ASIC miners to be able to mine Bitcoin Gold; any generic CPU will do, so the price of entry has lowered considerably. Also, as ASIC miners are unable to mine Bitcoin Gold, this change automatically leveled the field for all users, at least for the moment creating a more decentralized cryptocurrency in terms of mining power.

On the official website of Bitcoin Gold the slogan is "make Bitcoin decentralized again", but ironically, Bitcoin Gold suffered a successful 51% attack in May 2018.[149]

51% attacks do not pose a threat to past transactions and can only alter present transactions, so the hackers cannot redistribute massive quantities of the attacked cryptocurrency to themselves. Even so, they can double spend and block transactions that are waiting to be verified.[150] And they certainly can torpedo smaller cryptocurrencies by causing their users to lose faith in, and eventually abandon, them.

In case of a smaller cryptocurrency 51% attacks are easier to execute because the amount of hash power needed to take over the system is significantly less, so size is an important factor when it comes to protection from 51% attacks. For example Bitcoin has a hash power which is an order of magnitude greater than other coins mined with the same SHA-256 algorithm. Bitcoin ABC, Bitcoin SV, and Digibyte are also using SHA-256, so they are more exposed to a 51% attack than Bitcoin because the attacker would have to expend less hash power to be successful. The same is true for the Equihash algorithm. It is used by B2X, Bitcoin Gold, ZenCash and Komodo that are much smaller than Zcash which also runs on Equihash, so Zcash is relatively safe from a 51% attack to the detriment of the other coins.[151]

For the above reason ordinary users are not at risk because attackers will go for the more juicy trophy which are exchanges, or if an ordinary user trades directly with an attacker without knowing that it is an attacker, then he is at risk too.[152]

Up until now, all the debates that ended in a hard fork have been battles of conflicting ideologies: those who opted for more perceived ease of use on the surface, but often out of corporate interest at the core, versus those who are adamant on maintaining (or in most cases trying to return to the ideal of) Bitcoin as a decentralized electronic currency, although not everybody means the same even by decentralization.

9

The Ethereum Ecosystem

D
evelopers, technical geeks, visionaries soon realized the significance of the appearance of the blockchain technology. The creator
of *Ethereum* himself, Vitalik Buterin said about Bitcoin that its
evolutionary nature lies in the fact that it wanted to revolutionalize at the
same time not only technology but the economy as well. Also, he added that
we cannot expect such a first development to do everything all at once. It
has been a big enough task to introduce these concepts within the context of
one electronic cash.

It only took a few years from the introduction of Bitcoin until the first
blockchain based platform, Ethereum was developed in 2014. Together
with Gavin Wood and Jeffrey Wilcke, Vitalik Buterin started to create a next-
generation blockchain with the goal to implement a general, fully trustless
smart contract platform.[153]

Ethereum is the first blockchain which has an official team dedicated to
its maintenance and continued development since its inception up until
the present, something which seems beneficial when you have a brand new
concept that takes many steps to develop and implement.

Numerous big corporations which are always on the look out for technologies and inventions that could potentially be disruptive to their business as
usual have already started to study blockchain and how they could use it for
their benefit. Governments and various institutions also took interest in

blockchain technology.

Obviously, the institutions of the old (current) system do not want only Bitcoin, as its decentralized network would disrupt the power balance if it manages to maintain its decentralization and gain popularity. However, they quickly realized that the blockchain isn't going anywhere in the near future and that they could either reap its potential benefits if they could create their own proprietary, private blockchains, or perish during the change of technology.

Interestingly (or depending on one's way of thinking, kind of suspiciously) the Peter Thiel Foundation paid $100,000 to the young genius, Vitalik Buterin to develop Ethereum at the age of 19. Buterin had been writing about Bitcoin for some time, earning 4 dollars per article (definitely not your average money hungry person) and he wanted to create something that was more general and not as specialized as Bitcoin. He was contemplating writing a programming language that would run on the Bitcoin blockchain and would make it possible for developers to write their own applications.

However, that would have meant that the Bitcoin base code would have had to be rewritten. So instead he created Ethereum which the Ethereum Foundation calls a "decentralized computer" with its own programming language, Solidity.

Although Buterin had the idea to make the blockchain usable for the creation of individual applications, the fact that the Peter Thiel Foundation backed this project makes one wonder what could have been the real motivation for initiating or at least supporting its development.

To put things into context, Peter Thiel founded PayPal together with Elon Musk. Thiel was also the first private investor in Facebook and has a 10% stake worth $2.5 billion in his secretive data company, Palantir.[154] Palantir collects and analyzes data of various databases and uses them for various purposes, including law enforcement, cyber security, intelligence, dealing with insider threat, and many other fields.

"Law enforcement accounts for just a small part of Palantir's business, which mostly consists of military clients, intelligence outfits like the CIA or Homeland Security, and large financial institutions. In police departments,

Palantir's tools are now being used to flag traffic scofflaws, parole violators, and other everyday infractions. But the police departments that deploy Palantir are also dependent upon it for some of their most sensitive work. Palantir's software can ingest and sift through millions of digital records across multiple jurisdictions, spotting links and sharing data to make or break cases"[155], writes Mark Harris.

How Palantir seems to operate is that they offer access to all the data they have gathered from other databases to an entity, be it police, a national institution of any sort, or a private company, in exchange for them having to install the Palantir software, which means that they give Palantir full access to all the information of the entity. "New users are welcomed with discounted hardware and federal grants, sharing their own data in return for access to others'. When enough jurisdictions join Palantir's interconnected web of police departments, government agencies, and databases, the resulting data trove resembles a pay-to-access social network—a Facebook of crime that's both invisible and largely unaccountable to the citizens whose behavior it tracks."[156]

So, it does not really make sense to think that a person who is so invested in maintaining the current order in which he has been more than thriving, would support and initiate the creation of Ethereum, a blockchain based platform that can be used as a basis for thousands of new applications, all decentralized, so that humanity can take back its power from the controllers.[157] This is very important to keep in mind as we learn about Ethereum.

Ethereum is that next level of development to which Buterin alluded when talking about Bitcoin being just the forerunner. Ethereum is a platform built on the blockchain which has its own programing language, Solidity. (Just something interesting to ponder: the name Ethereum comes from the word "ether" which is the fifth element, the "primordial water" from which all matter is said to come forth into existence. It is a very clever play with the words to call its own programing language used to bring ideas into existence "Solidity". From the ether you can materialize new applications, projects, cryptocurrencies, and smart contracts by applying some solidity to them.)

The two novelties that Ethereum introduced are smart contracts and decentralized applications. These together make the Ethereum platform very valuable for the blockchain ecosystem. But before we get into what smart contracts and decentralized applications are, let's just make one thing clear. Ethereum also has its own cryptocurrency/token called *Ether* which is traded on the cryptoexchanges as ETH, but in practice people in the trading world generally call it Ethereum instead of Ether.

Ether is used as a reward for the miners who validate the transactions of the Ethereum platform, and also as currency to pay the smart contracts that are made on the platform. Those decentralized applications that do not have their own private tokens also use Ether for payments.

Just as a note, Bitcoin too allows for smart contracts, although it is more difficult to program decentralized applications and smart contracts on it, but exactly this is what makes such applications and smart contracts more secure than the ones developed on the Ethereum platform.

Smart contracts

Smart contracts were first introduced by Ethereum, although recently many other cryptocurrencies have been working to make their blockchain apt for creating smart contracts on it. A smart contract is called smart because it is self-executing in a sense that there is no need for the intervention of lawyers to create the contract, nobody can dispute over how the contract must be or could be understood when there is a discrepancy between the parties in their understanding.

Smart contracts execute automatically, following a set of rules which are predetermined by the parties of the contract. For example, if you want to send ethers to somebody at a given future date, you can create a contract and record all the necessary information in it including amount, date and hour to send, the private code of the Ether wallet of the person to receive it etc., and it will execute the transfer according to the predetermined data of the individual smart contract.

Smart contracts can be seen as robotized wallets. Bitcoin wallets can only be controlled by a user. In contrast, Ethereum wallets can be controlled by smart contracts that are just computer codes recording rules agreed upon by the parties to the contract. These smart contracts will execute independently of human interpretation of the agreement according to the rules encoded in the contract.[158]

It is always the parties to a smart contract who decide how complicated or simple their contract will be, and the terms of the contract are enforced by the cryptographic code of the blockchain. If both parties follow what they agreed upon in the contract, it will automatically execute (i.e. it will pay to whoever is stipulated to receive the money in the contract). In case something does not go according to the rules agreed upon in the agreement (for example, if the receiver of the money does not comply with what is written in the smart contract), the contract automatically gets canceled. This auto-cancellation means that all data and all funds interchanged are returned to their original owners.

Smart contracts are in fact digital escrow services ruled and executed by rules, but they are cheaper than third party escrow services and more flexible because a third party escrow service could try to influence the parties to conform to its own terms regarding the contract and make them comply with conditions they otherwise would not want to.[159]

Smart contracts, just like the blockchain itself, eliminate the need for trust in other parties by placing the trust in the logical and correct functioning of the software. Ultimately, their appearance boils down to the unfortunate fact that we as a society do not and cannot trust our fellow humans because of the indoctrination and systematic exploitation on every level and in every facet of life we have been exposed to since the day we were born.

At first glance, using smart contracts to ensure "proper behavior" of the parties to any agreement may seem like an awesome idea, a great advancement which could ensure that our society finally becomes just and egalitarian. However, if you think back to the basic assumptions, doesn't it smell a bit like a typical problem-reaction-solution example?

Why? Well, the issue is not really that we cannot trust one another and that we must place our trust into soulless machines to regulate us and our relationships because we as a race are too immoral to do it naturally by ourselves.

The real issue, as I see it, is that, again, we are offered an *either-or* solution, as if we were told: "guys, we've done all we could, we had tried so hard to act in a civilized way among ourselves, but we failed, we humans just cannot be trusted, we cannot trust our fellow humans either, so we must put all our trust into the machines that will be just and provide guidance for us". This may sound exaggerated, but it is exactly what is behind the pushing of trustless systems.

There could certainly be a third solution. One that is not very likely to ever hit the main stream media. That solution would be making sure that we stop obeying the controllers, making sure that even if we choose to go with the machines because we find it more efficient, safer or more trustworthy to create smart contracts that will execute as they are etched into digital bytes. We would have to make sure that we do not let those who had always controlled all the processes, all the great movements of human evolution from behind the curtain hijack this technology and regulate and distort its use according to their interests.

Think of it as if you were trying to eliminate bamboo from your garden. In case you do not know, bamboos are very difficult to eradicate once they are settled in. Would it be enough to just cut the shoots off where they grow out of the soil? No, because their roots are still there, intact, hidden below the surface, ready to produce more shoots and offsprings.

Well, the same is true for the controllers. We could make sure to never let the controllers shape our minds and our behaviors, our economy and our society, but until we do, the blockchain revolution may just be a more sophisticated step in a chess game where the end goal is the total domination and exploitation of the human race.

Just keep this in mind as we go on exploring what smart contracts and trustless systems could mean for our future.

Decentralized Autonomous Organizations

A Decentralized Autonomous Organization (DAO) is a digital entity created to function autonomously based on predetermined sets of rules in a decentralized way. The goal to create such organizations is to eliminate the need for people in power who could distort or not take into account the rules of the organization during their day-to-day operations. A DAO eliminates corruption from the organization.

DAOs also eliminate the need for documents and make decision making transparent because they cannot be corrupted (always when not hacked, of course). Basically, a DAO is an organization with decentralized power created to carry out certain tasks.

However, first somebody must write smart contracts that will form the basis of the organization. The DAO will simply execute the rules contained in the smart contracts on an "if-then" basis, meaning that if something is fulfilled then something else will happen, and if that something is not fulfilled, then the result will be different but always predetermined.

Once the smart contracts are created, an Initial Coin Offering (or ICO) takes place which is a form of crowd-funding, where the goal is for people to provide funding to set up the DAO and put it into operation. ICOs, however, are not like equity shares in a company because token holders are not entitled to receive a part of the profit of the organization. These tokens only give people voting rights to determine the direction of the organization without granting them ownership. Decentralized autonomous organizations are usually not owned by anybody, they are just "software sitting on the Ethereum network"[160].

When a DAO starts to operate, people can make proposals on how to spend the money raised with the initial coin offering, and those who purchased tokens during the ICO can vote to approve or not the proposals. Smart contracts make it possible to get rid of much (or all of) the institutions and substitute them, at least partially, with decentralized autonomous organizations.

DAOs function by running various smart contracts to execute goals automatically that normally would be done by institutions. DAOs could be easily used in the areas of voting, healthcare, insurance, music and ebook sales, or education. The smart contracts applied could be used to manage all sorts of public records, to monitor patients, collect funds, or track the progress of projects in general.

Would decentralized autonomous organizations be better to manage certain facets of our society like registers, maintenance of infrastructure, roads, notary services, land registry etc? Favoritism would obviously be a thing of the past if certain powers were unable to make covert changes to the blockchain according to their interests, and it would also mean not having to spend hundreds of millions on the salaries of public administration workers who in many cases just make life more complicated for citizens (bye-bye, present day administration). Politicians could not put certain people into key positions in exchange for favors, and what's more; politicians could not be given big cheese top management level jobs as a "well deserved reward" for all the favors they had done to those companies during their time in power.

DAOs would be operating transparently because there would be no ways to break the rules (well, at least one would have to be able to hack the system to be able to rewrite the smart contract and that would be quite tedious to do, not like it is today when all kinds of corrupt activities go on behind closed doors).

DAOs would be obviously way cheaper and quicker than their present day counterparts, and the transactions would be frictionless. Eventually, they could replace all sorts of institutions, making society apparently more transparent and instead of having institutions control humans in their day-to-day lives, we would have efficient, impartial managers of necessary functions and processes of society based on equality and fairness.

Although the question still remains whether each and every institution could be simply replaced by smart contracts and decentralized autonomous organizations, and whether it is desirable to take the human element out of decisions pertaining to human lives completely because if we go with DAOs, it will be hard to factor in the human aspect into smart contracts.

What if somebody needs special consideration? What if a very rare constellation of circumstances takes place that cannot be rightly handled by smart contracts? Maybe we should leave human supervisors or a separate service to supervise and deal with such special cases if we can find a way to avoid corruption and not use such a service as an easy way out for the powerful bad guys from the grip of the rules applied uncorruptedly by DAOs.

We would have to work out a good working model, maybe combined with human supervision or a way for individuals to still be able to discuss their cases with, and explain their situations to, another human being.

Or maybe the solution would be to stop supporting the notion of government altogether (because there is ample evidence that governments do not make our lives easier and better), and take responsibility of our own lives, taking our own decisions in the framework of small communities where everybody's voice can, and should, be heard. What if the solution is taking our power back from external organizations and govern ourselves together with those living in our vicinity the way an enlightened community of psychologically adult individuals would do?

DAOs would basically be autonomous, intelligent technological entities that improve themselves (and their decisions) by learning and they have full autonomy. For the moment, officially such a DAO does not exist, however in 2018 the government of Malta has already proposed to grant legal personhood for blockchains, DAOs and smart contracts.[161]

As a side note, the Knights of Malta have always played an important role in monetary governance worldwide, although that might just be a mere coincidence. Maybe the granting of legal personhood to blockchains was what made Binance, the cryptocurrency exchange giant based in Hong Kong decide to move to Malta where Binance was planning to open the world's first blockchain based, decentralized community-owned bank with tokenized ownership, besides less regulatory control. In contrast to ICOs, this bank would issue legally binding equity tokens.[162]

Before we go any further, it is important to note that Ethereum was written in a Turing complete language (called Solidity) which makes it fundamentally different from Bitcoin which uses a Turing incomplete language (called Script). "Any system or programming language able to compute anything computable given enough resources is said to be Turing-complete."[163] There is a debate whether Bitcoin is Turing complete or not. Just as a reference, Craig Wright stated in 2018 that Bitcoin is Turing complete.[164]

Although there is a debate whether Turing completeness is a positive attribute as it makes a system more vulnerable to attacks, and whether it is necessary to create smart contracts and the likes, one thing is sure at least on the surface: Bitcoin was created to fulfill a more reduced, specific function, namely just to be a cryptocurrency, while Ethereum was written on purpose to be used as a basis for other blockchain based applications and functions.

There have been efforts lately both from the developer communities of Bitcoin and Bitcoin Cash to widen the usability of their respective systems. Bitcoin Cash announced that it is now possible for any developer to create smart contracts on *Wormhole Cash*, using the Omni Layer protocol we mentioned earlier. At the same time Bitcoin has come forward with new developments like *Rootstock* which is a Turing complete sidechain that allows for writing smart contracts that operate on the Bitcoin blockchain.[165]

Another new project is *Particl* which is a new coin built on the latest Bitcoin codebase. Particl focuses on decentralized applications and privacy while being compatible with Bitcoin and 100% open-source at the same time. Particl is the world's first decentralized marketplace, designed to accept the majority of cryptocurrencies and uses the privacy protocol of Monero, which shows that the limitations and rigidity of the Script language compared to Solidity does not necessary mean that the decentralized applications built on the Bitcoin codebase are somehow necessarily inferior to those built on Ethereum.[166]

Decentralized applications (dApps)

Using the coding language of Ethereum anybody can create their own decentralized applications, similarly to how anybody can create mobile phone applications for the iOS and Android operating systems.

Decentralized applications (or dApps) cannot learn or improve their decisions and they always have to follow the preprogrammed rules to execute the same types of transactions. In contrast, Decentralized Autonomous Organizations will also have self-improving autonomous software. (Basically, a decentralized application is just a set of rules and its own mechanism to enforce those rules, while DAOs are like a form of artificial intelligence that lives on a decentralized network.)

The Ethereum platform and the facility of the Solidity language to create decentralized applications, smart contracts, and DAOs could reshape our economy, our institutions, and society as a whole. But there are some caveats. Faster, more incorruptible, cheaper, yes.

But everything remains recorded on the blockchain, forever. And that is not necessarily a good thing if there could be anybody, people or legal entities, who could use all that information against you. The belief that transparency would eliminate corruption and would result in a just and egalitarian society has some flaws that few are willing to examine.

It seems that we are only at the very beginning of the blockchain revolution, but people well versed in technology and programming could quickly realize that the blockchain is a revolutionary new technology and many developers immediately started to work and experiment with it. Blockchain is already being implemented (or they are looking into implementing it) by certain governments and institutions (which reveals a lot about the importance of the blockchain because authorities tend to be slow when it comes to the implementation of technological changes).

But in this specific case they know that they are running out of time, so either they react and manage to incorporate blockchain into their legal and economic systemic operations, or shortly they would be out of control and booted by the people once decentralization gains more ground. Would you let that happen if you were one of them?

There are numerous important corporations that are developing their own private blockchains or are studying how they could implement blockchain as a part of their operations. The most well-known example is Bakkt, a trading platform created by corporations like Intercontinental Exchange, Microsoft, and Starbucks, which has launched its test net on July 21, 2019 without having obtained approval from the authorities, in the hopes that the approval was going to happen sooner or later.

They finally decided to go for the self-certification route and announced to qualify on September 23, 2019 and launched their physical Bitcoin future products. The Bakkt platform enables customers to purchase Bitcoin directly with fiat money and to spend it on goods and services offered on the platform. They store the bitcoins in their own warehouse and clients receive the actual "physical" bitcoins, once their contracts expire.[167]

Not an ideal development in terms of decentralization, and a clear example of how people who are currently on the top have been working to stay atop, come hell or high water. If those people are banking on the blockchain technology, it means that we, the ordinary people of the world will also have to deal with it because it is here to stay, at least for a while.

We have to adapt to this new development in technology which will bring huge societal and economic changes. We must stay ahead of the waves of change to benefit from them and avoid going under when the huge waves come.

The DAO hack and the birth of Ethereum Classic

A bit confusingly, there was one particular decentralized autonomous organization which was simply called *The DAO*. It was set up by the founders of Slock.it which is a car and home sharing enterprise similar to AirBnB that lets people share their vehicles and homes without being there personally to hand over or pick up the keys. A special code is used to unlock and lock the cars and the homes listed on Slock.it.

The founders of Slock.it wanted to fund this car and home sharing project by launching an initial coin offering and it was unexpectedly successful. In fact, it became the most successful crowdfunding project in history raising some $150 million (until it was "dethroned" by the Filecoin ICO in 2017 with $257 million).

The DAO did not develop its own tokens, instead it offered Ether tokens for purchase during the Initial Coin Offering. As it turned out, the Ether tokens that were exchanged for buying into the project represented around 20% of all the Ether tokens in circulation.

Despite some earlier warnings from several people about vulnerabilities in the smart contract, The DAO did not revise it and went ahead with allowing the transactions to be executed. It turned out to be the worst move ever because in June 2016 somebody managed to steal 50 million dollars' worth of Ether using the vulnerability in the coding of the smart contract.

This could have seriously damaged the reputation of Ethereum, even though the Ethereum platform base code was working perfectly and the issue was the integrity and security of the smart contract that only depended on its creators, those belonging to The DAO. Vitalik Buterin on behalf of The Ethereum Foundation proposed to intervene by executing a soft fork that would block any transactions from the account of The DAO and its child account which was created by the attack. This was a way to blacklist the attacker to prevent him from ever getting access to, or spending, the money that was stolen from The DAO account.[168]

They wanted to make it possible for token holders of The DAO to get their money back by this measure. Surprisingly, the unscrupulous attacker wrote an open letter in which he stated that The Ethereum Foundation cannot act like an authority about what happens in relation to a smart contract because smart contracts are supposed to be self executing and are bound only by the rules that were included in their coding. So, if The DAO smart contract allowed the attacker to transfer the stolen money to his own account, it was only possible because the smart contract allowed it. Consequently, the attacker argued that he didn't do anything illegal. He also promised to distribute 1 million eth and 100 btc among the miners that do not accept the soft fork and stay "faithful" to the original blockchain.[169]

Another, later proposal from The Ethereum Foundation was to do a hard fork, although many people did not agree with it because the whole decentralized blockchain concept and the concept of smart contracts being self-regulating and self-executing are completely opposite to such a central intervention, even if it is done with the aim of getting back stolen money of investors from an attacker obviously acting in bad faith.

Many people thought that such an intervention to "correct an error" or to act like an authority to arbitrate in a dispute caused by a smart contract would set a precedent for further requests for intervention on behalf of The Ethereum Foundation. The Foundation could then fork the blockchain whenever they saw it fit, which is obviously not how a decentralized network should operate. Should that happen, users would quickly lose trust in Ethereum as a platform.

As Chris Stewart put it, "the road to hell is paved with hard forks"[170]. It seems that once you hard forked your blockchain, it becomes easier to justify changing things "the easy way", also it is easier to do both technically and socially, but that means that the blockchain is no longer decentralized, so it is understandable that the Ethereum community was divided over this proposal.[171]

Despite all these considerations, they did hard fork Ethereum, as some think, partly because several members of The Ethereum Foundation had invested in The DAO. The new version of the Ethereum blockchain incorporated the blacklist order of The DAO and its child acccount.

Those who did not want to accept the idea that The Ethereum Foundation could intervene to act as an arbitrator regarding smart contracts, and who preferred to maintain the integrity of the original blockchain without a central authority being able to change it "when needed", maintained the old blockchain which they called *Ethereum Classic*.

Ethereum Classic (ETC) became an individual cryptocurrency. It is described on its own website with decentralization, immutability, and unstoppability being its main characteristics. *"Ethereum Classic is a decentralized platform that runs smart contracts: applications that run exactly as programmed without any possibility of downtime, censorship, fraud or third party interference. Ethereum Classic is a continuation of the original Ethereum blockchain - the classic version preserving untampered history; free from external interference and subjective tampering of transactions."*[172] From this description it is clear what they did not like about the hard fork.

At the time of writing this book Ethereum Classic is the 20th most popular cryptocurrency with a market capitalization of $524 million, which accounts for approximately 2.8% of the capitalization of Ethereum.

Initial Coin Offerings (ICOs)

Initial Coin Offerings (ICOs) were introduced by Ethereum first. As mentioned earlier, an initial coin offering is a blockchain based crowdfunding method used to raise funds for a proposed new project to be developed on the Ethereum platform.

ICOs became very popular because it lowered the bar for people to invest in startups. There had been several crowdfunding platforms operating earlier, but the startups using them had to conform to the rules of those platforms and also, they cost money because the platforms would take their cut from the raised money. In contrast, on the Ethereum platform anyone could initiate an ICO and anybody could buy the tokens offered and become an investor in as many new projects as they want.

The project starts by writing a smart contract and creating new tokens which are offered in exchange for ether. People can invest in the project by buying these project specific tokens (that is why it is called a coin offering). They either offer the discounted tokens, or the future delivery of discounted tokens, if the application is still in development.[173]

The project gets access to ethers (but they are held back by the smart contract) to fund its development. If the development goals are reached, the smart contract distributes these new tokens to the supporters, while it sends the ethers which were held back to the developer. If the project does not accomplish its goals, the ethers are sent back to the supporters. So, the smart contract is an escrow service that keeps the money of the supporters until the project reaches an agreed developmental stage.

ICOs became popular because it is very easy to crowdfund projects this way, and also because creating new tokens on Ethereum is not difficult, and according to 2017 and 2018 data, 84% of the ICOs were issued on the Ethereum platform.[174] In 2017 over $6,2 billion were raised in ICOs, and in 2018 that number increased to $7.85 billion.[175] However, there is the issue that if you are a U.S. citizen you cannot participate in ICOs, you would have to be an accredited investor because ICOs are considered to be "securities offerings".[176]

The SEC of course had to stop it and in April 2019 they issued a "crypto token guidance" that describes what types of tokens and networks fall under securities laws.[177]

The only thing a company searching for funding has to do is write a smart contract on top of an existing, trusted platform. What makes Ethereum a trusted, stable platform is its large mining community and the fact that it has the second largest market capitalization, right behind Bitcoin.

Ethereum has clear guidelines for creating new tokens called the ER-20 protocol. All tokens created under this protocol are exchangeable to other ER-20 tokens, which makes them a safer investment because investors can get out by exchanging them to other tokens if they see that the project is bound to fail.

Lately, there has been much talk about the fact that a large part of the ICOs did not deliver, alleging that many were used just for speculative reasons. There has been an effort in various countries to regulate ICOs because they may be very volatile and speculative with a high chance that some ICOs are just cash cows used by unscrupulous people to get easy money from uneducated investors without actually working on the proposed projects.[178]

Of course, the representatives of the traditional way of project financing, venture capitalists, etc. too are trying to discredit ICOs as a legitimate vehicle to fund projects and companies. As if there were any reason why individuals could not invest their money in startups just because they do not have as much money as the Wall Street guys. In that vein, lottery should also be prohibited to people with a net worth less than say 50 million dollars. You know, to protect people from losing their hard earned money.

Blockchain startups are also trying to be cautious in drafting their smart contracts with the aim to avoid the appearance of their ICOs being securities and thus being subject to the regulations of the Securities and Exchange Commission of the US. Undoubtedly, there indeed has been some cash cow ICOs that were seemingly set up to use the money raised for pump-and-dump style trading. Such tokens tend to lose their value quickly because there is no real project with real developments behind them, so people find out fast that they do not have real value.

But we must not forget that the sinking of many ICOs (according to estimates it could mean 80% of the ICOs) and their related coins may not have happened only due to the crypto space being a "Wild West" without proper regulation and a hoard of unscrupulous actors trying to get rich quick by ripping off unsuspecting individuals.

In any sector of the economy successful enterprises represent less than 10% of all the new businesses started. So it seems to be within the normal range of the economy as we know it. But the crypto space has one important characteristics that could be one of the main culprits for such bad statistics: in the "real world" startups do not immediately go public and their shares are not traded on the stock exchange right from the beginning.

In contrast, many crypto investors buy into ICOs to make a quick profit trading the tokens and don't care about the actual projects, so pumping and dumping tokens is a danger that the leaders of projects doing an ICO cannot avoid. A further uncertainty is that these startups need to pay in fiat currency (generally speaking), so a bear market like the one we have been in since December 2017 diminishes their power to stay afloat while following their original plans for the project.

It's true that due to their volatility, novelty, and unregulated nature cryptocurrencies and the crypto space in general are higher risk investments, so one must tread with caution.

Proof of stake consensus

Ethereum has a quite serious scalability (and thus usability) problem because the more miners there are in the network, the complexity of mining under a proof of work protocol increases without an increase of the bandwidth of the network. So it will still take the same amount of time to produce one block, even when there will be a thousand times more miners (independently of whether they are pooled together or work individually), and all this complexity of production would increase the cost of electricity. This would result in higher transaction fees.

Similarly to what happened on the Bitcoin network, as miners prefer to work on transactions with a higher value because their commission is higher, transactions with low commissions and those of lower transactional value are at risk of suffering serious delays or never being processed.

The pressure on Ethereum, however, is even greater than on Bitcoin, because Ethereum as a platform services many applications, so it can get saturated easier.

We saw earlier that the way Bitcoin guarantees security on its peer-to-peer network is by running the proof of work consensus algorithm to validate transactions. Ethereum initially was also developed to use proof of work. It makes the bad behavior of users nearly impossible (which only could happen if someone would be able to amass at least 51% of computing power of the entire network to override the good blockchain by sheer force), but this consensus protocol certainly has scalability issues.

To validate a block, miners have to do "trial and error" work to find nonces, hence the name "proof of work" because the likelihood to stumble upon nonces just by chance is very, very small.

The disadvantage of proof of work consensus is that it takes, well, a lot of work, meaning a lot of electricity, and the bigger a network is, the more transactions need to be processed which raises electricity costs. Also, the block size limit eventually creates delays in processing transactions which could take hours, or in severe cases even days. The result is the increasing transaction fees, as miners offer priority treatment for the processing of transactions in exchange for urgency fees.

We saw earlier that as the system matures and lesser and lesser new coins will be mined, Bitcoin will eventually need to turn to another type of incentive for miners instead of mining rewards in the form of newly created bitcoins, and that likely it will be the introduction of transaction processing fees, but currently, the use of such transaction fees has created a skewed system where many transactions without priority fees could linger in the limbo of the mempool until luck strikes, or until forever.

The other issue is the tendency of miners to form ever larger mining pools because besides reducing their technical and operational costs, the bigger a mining pool is, the better chances it has to solve the puzzle first and be rewarded with new coins.

Actually, this tendency is triggered by the Bitcoin software itself because all economic actors (except for the occasional crazy person) will act in their own self interest and joining larger and ever more powerful mining groups is just the logical thing for a miner to do.

This tendency has already created a kind of centralization both on the Bitcoin and the Ethereum networks. Currently, four big mining pools control more than 50% of the whole Bitcoin hashing power, and only three major mining pools control over 50% of the hashing power of Ethereum. In April 2018 Bitmain launched ASIC miners manufactured for mining Ether[179], which made Ethereum mining totally unprofitable for anybody who used simple CPUs, and currently the only way to stay profitable as an Ethereum miner is to join a large mining pool, most likely based in China where these ASIC miners are manufactured and where the cost of electricity is low.[180]

These developments do not go in the direction of safety and decentralization, so something had to be done.

Vitalik Buterin had mentioned in his earlier blog posts that it was inevitable that sooner or later ASIC miners would be developed specifically for mining Ether, and that no matter how hard Ethereum developers would try to keep the Ethereum code optimized for general-purpose computers, innovations would prevail that could outperform such generic devices.[181]

The developer team of Ethereum have been working to promote and implement changes in Ethereum in order to protect the blockchain against ASIC miners "meant to consolidate rewards in the hands of companies or individuals capable of operating at scale"[182].

After the appearance of the ASIC miners for Ethereum, certain developers even proposed to make changes to the software that would make ASIC miners unusable to mine Ethereum. Monero and Siacoin have already proposed such changes to their software to block Bitmain from grabbing control of their blockchains. Buterin publicly reacted to the news saying that it is not worth wasting time and energy thinking about the ASIC miner issue, but rather they should double down on their efforts to develop and implement Casper[183] (which is a new protocol that has been in development and under gradual implementation with the aim to move Ethereum away from the proof of work protocol to use *proof of stake*). Basically, Buterin meant that they were already in the process of making the change that would soon render Bitmain ASIC miners unusable to mine Ether, so there is no need to worry about their sudden appearance.

The developers of Ethereum have been working on the gradual implementation of the proof of stake protocol instead of proof of work in order to solve the problem of scalability and at the same time maintain decentralization by rendering ASIC miners obsolete to be used on Ethereum. The proof of stake protocol was first introduced in 2011 by a cryptocurrency called Peercoin which currently sits as number 356 in the ranking of Coinmarketcap.com.

The goal of the proof of stake algorithm is to validate transactions and avoid double spending on the network. Instead of miners who have to solve a mathematical puzzle and expend a significant amount of energy, the proof of stake protocol has *bonded validators*. Validators vote on the next block (if they accept it or not) and the weight of a validator's vote depends on the size of his stake. The process of choosing a validator is semi-random.[184]

Those who want to be validators have to deposit any amount of Ether in a special "virtual safe". This process is called bonding. The deposited amount is their stake in the "validator game" and is there to ensure that validators will have something to lose if they "behave badly". The reason it is not worth for a validator to act in bad faith is because not only will he lose the full amount of what he deposited as his stake, but he will also be banned from being a validator for life.[185]

It is completely up to each validator how much money they want to deposit, but the higher their stake, the higher their chances to be randomly selected to be the validator for the next block. Validators get a reward for their validation work. So while it is up to each validator how big their stakes are, the proof of stake algorithm periodically selects a validator randomly.

The validator who is selected will create one block and will get a validator reward which is the transaction fee because no new coins are mined during the validation process.[186]

At first it seems that the proof of stake protocol favors the wealthy as they can afford to deposit higher amounts, but validators are selected randomly, which means that it will not always be just the richest users selected to validate transactions and receive the transaction fees.

The Casper protocol

The Casper protocol is a hybrid proof of work/proof of stake algorithm that was developed to transition the Ethereum network from proof of work to proof of stake. It is called Casper as an allusion to the animated movie character, Casper, the friendly ghost because this protocol is an adaptation of certain principles of the Greedy Heaviest-Observed Sub-Tree (or GHOST) protocol used for transitioning from proof of work to proof of stake consensus.[187]

The Ethereum Improvement Proposal (EIP) 1011 about the hybrid Casper Friendly Finality Gadget indicates that the implementation of Casper is something that has always been accounted for since the beginning: *"Transitioning the Ethereum network from PoW to PoS has been on the roadmap and in the Yellow Paper [a formal definition of the Ethereum protocol] since the launch of the protocol. Although effective in coming to a decentralized consensus, PoW consumes an incredible amount of energy, has no economic finality, and has no effective strategy in resisting cartels. Excessive energy consumption, issues with equal access to mining hardware, mining pool centralization, and an emerging market of ASICs each provide a distinct motivation to make the transition as soon as possible."*[188]

Casper actually consists of two simultaneously developed projects, both aiming at transitioning Ethereum to proof of stake. *Casper the Friendly Finality Gadget (FFG)* lead by Vitalik Buterin can be seen as a first step which uses a hybrid proof of work/proof of stake model. Proof of work is still used to create new blocks, but Casper the Friendly Finality Gadget is layered on top using a smart contract. It was already introduced on May 8, 2018 for peer review with the goal to create a smooth and seamless transition to proof of stake.[189]

This Hybrid Casper uses the above mentioned GHOST protocol to modify the longest chain rule so that all, including unvalidated, blocks are taken into account when measuring difficulty, which increases the security of the network.[190] Casper FFG reduces the complexity of the entire blockchain.

The second element of the project is called *Casper the Friendly Ghost: Correct by Construction (CBC)* and is lead by Vlad Zamfir. It uses a safety oracle to fine-tune a partially built proof of stake protocol until the system has been completed. Casper CBC is also called *full Casper.*[191]

Casper was later redesigned into a new protocol called *Shasper* which refers to the merging of Casper and Sharding, the latter being another important effort to solve the scalability issues of Ethereum. *Sharding* is a process used to divide data across multiple servers instead of one in order to avoid the appearance of a bottleneck of traffic. Tables of data are split horizontally into smaller units called shards.[192]

On Ethereum the whole blockchain will be split across many nodes so that each one of them contains different fragments of the full blockchain. This liberates the majority of the network when it comes to having to save a copy of a particular transaction, as each transaction will only have to be broadcast and updated on the servers that contain the relevant part of the ledger. Sharding means that certain shards (of the entire information as a whole) are assigned to only specific nodes, which makes the verification process leaner and places less burden on the entire network.[193] Shards will be connected to each other and to the main chain in a way that each node can rely on the information of the rest without having to store the copy of the entire blockchain.

Originally, each node of the Ethereum network was meant to process every transaction of the network. This makes the blockchain very secure because approved blocks are validated many times by various nodes, but this proof of work protocol makes the blockchain slow. Each new transaction or smart contract code creates a new state of the blockchain, which with sharding does not have to be copied on each and every node, but instead the state of the network is split up into shards, each containing their own independent state and transaction history.

In Ethereum *state* refers to the whole set of information present on the system at any moment, including data on the current account balances, smart contract code, and nonces. This splitting makes Ethereum much faster. The main chain will be divided into separate chains that will still be connected to each other and the main chain. This makes parallel processing of transactions possible, increasing network speed. Nodes will only have to deal with transactions that belong to their own shard chain.[194]

Vitalik Buterin talked about the next iteration of Ethereum already in 2014 saying that "we will either solve the scalability and consensus problems or die trying" and by the second half of 2018 he confirmed that "there is no significant unsolved theoretical problem left for Ethereum 2.0." The software development phase of Ethereum 2.0 has started with the Beacon chain being its first component.[195] Based on the diagram of Hsia-Wei Wang on the original architecture of Ethereum 2.0, we can have a better understanding of the direction in which Ethereum is growing.[196]

The first layer is the *proof of work main chain* which was the original Ethereum Mainnet until the Constantinople hard fork finally took place on February 28, 2019 including the St. Petersburg upgrade which was implemented to correct a security error found in Constantinople. The Constantinople hard fork introduced proof of stake and converted Ethereum 2.0 into a proof of stake blockchain which will be further implemented when Casper will be fully operational, which is planned to happen still in 2019. In the resulting Ethereum 2.0 this main chain has the same function as it does now (only the proof of work protocol is replaced with proof of stake to do the same function).

This hard fork resulted in a couple of other changes including bitwise shifting which makes the processing of information use only 10% of gas it needed to use before. Gas is the measuring unit of computational power used for executing tasks on the Ethereum blockchain.[197] They also optimized large scale code execution on the blockchain, and made the pricing method better for contract storage, which will lower gas costs. Another change was the implementation of off-chain transactions and *state channels* similar to those of the Lightning Network, all aimed at improving the performance of the Ethereum network. And of course, the block mining reward was reduced from 3 eth to 2 eth.[198]

So while the way transactions are validated and blocks are created has changed on the mainnet (the original Ethereum blockchain), the real novelty comes from the three new layers which Ethereum developers are planning to add to the network because they extend the functionalities of Ethereum.[199]

On top of the Ethereum mainnet the second layer is the *Beacon chain*, which is being developed and tested at present. Users will have to deposit their coins as stakes on this beacon chain if they want to become *validators* and vote on occurrences on shards.

In October 2018 they announced the deployment of the Ethereum 2.0 Prysm demo release as a new chain known as a beacon chain, where validators can stake their coins and vote on occurrences on shards known as cross-links. The beacon chain is synchronized with the current proof of work chain's latest block hashes. Additionally, a contract will be deployed on the proof of work chain where users can deposit 32 eth for the beacon chain to become validators of Ethereum 2.0.[200] Ethereum 2.0 is announced to go live in January 2020 when the beacon chain could be activated too.[201]

After the beacon chain is implemented, the next step will be the implementation of a third layer composed of the *Shard chains*. The function of these shard chains which are units created by splitting the main chain into independent parts or shards is to make the network faster and energetically more efficient. The plan is that shard chains will aggregate transactions and come to consensus on how to order them, however, they will not execute the transactions.[202]

The *Virtual Machine* or VM layer is the last component which will be responsible for the execution of transactions and contracts.[203] The Ethereum Virtual Machine (EVM) is a software which is already currently operated by each node on the Ethereum network. The EVM prevents denial of service attacks and it also interprets and executes the programming language of Ethereum.

The EVM is a runtime environment for operating smart contracts. A runtime environment is the execution environment that an operating system provides to the software which can send instructions to the processor and access other system resources that would be inaccessible using the programing language of the software itself.[204]

The Ethereum Virtual Machine is a completely isolated environment for smart contracts. Every smart contract runs inside the EVM without having access to the network, its file system or other processes that may be running on the computer that hosts the EVM.[205]

Currently, Ethereum has the proof of work main chain which is in the process of transitioning into proof of stake, and the proof of stake beacon chain, and the connection between these two layers is provided by a smart contract for the staking deposit. The plan is that, eventually, the proof of work main chain will become a sidechain or contract on the proof of stake chain once the migration to proof of stake is completed.

On September 21, 2017 Byzantium, the first half of the Metropolis hard fork took place which added some code that now permits the execution of zk-SNARKS on Ethereum. Vitalik then posted that Byzantium verified its first zk-SNARK proof. *Zero knowledge SNARKS* (or zk-SNARKS) are used in zero-knowledge cryptography to verify a ledger entry without having to reveal the identity of any parties. The zk-SNARK protocol which was promoted by the altcoin Zcash, has been identified as the only truly anonymous transaction, although the developers of Monero would likely disagree.[206] During the October 2017 Byzantium hardfork the mining reward has already been reduced from to 3 eth from 5 eth.[207]

The second part of the Metropolis hard fork called Constantinople took place on 28 February 2019. The Constantinople hard fork was part of Ethereum's development plan to increase efficiency and help move the network from proof of work to proof of stake consensus. This included a further reduction of the mining reward from the current 3 eth to only 2 eth.[208]

The aim of this gradual mining reward reduction was to stop the high (7.4% per year) inflation of the price of Ether because it was expected that the lower rewards would serve as a disincentive to mine new coins, and the hope was that this would in the long run increase the price of Ether.[209] Since the appearance of the ASIC miners in 2018 Ethereum mining has become hardly profitable to the average user and there has been a concern that this lowering of the mining rewards would meet opposition from mining companies and that many miners would simply switch to mining other cryptocurrencies and stop supporting the Ethereum network.

However, when on October 14, 2018 the Constantinople upgrade was activated on the main testnet of Ethereum, there were some issues. First, the blockchain seemed to be stuck for a long time at the last block before the one where the hard fork should have been executed, and finally, when the new block appeared and the hard fork happened there were no transactions recorded on the network. The issue could have been that miners and developers did not agree on the necessity of the proposed changes of the Constantinople hard fork.[210]

Obviously, miners, especially the mining companies that invested in the new ASIC miners, were not happy to see the mining reward further decrease from 5 eth to 2 eth in the span of a little more than a year.[211] The plan was for proof of stake validators to receive 0.82 eth per block as a reward, which is significantly lower, and the validator reward was planned to eventually further decrease its final amount to 0.22 eth per block by the time the move to proof of stake is complete.[212] However, in light of the general discontentment, Vitalik Buterin suggested in April 2019 that the validator reward should be raised to 3.3% of the overall amount of 30 million eth staked by validators, which would be still way less than the proof of work mining reward.[213]

Apart from the apparent aversion of Ethereum miners to Casper, as it will eventually take their mining rewards away, other challenges and risks also exist regarding moving to proof of stake consensus. The first iteration of Casper only features maximum 250 validators, which means that a physical disaster, a regulatory change, or an area specific hacking attack occurring in an area that contains all the validators could disrupt the functioning of the entire network.[214]

Proof of stake could solve the mining centralization problem, but it is not certain that it will solve the problem of centralization once and for all. The fact that to qualify as a validator a user would have to deposit a minimum of

1,500 eth, currently worth approximately $260,000, automatically disqualifies anybody who cannot afford locking up that much money. This seems to put mining companies and whales at advantage again because mining companies could collectively place large amounts of Ether as stakes, just like "whales", the big time cryptocurrency investors.

Even though Vitalik said that likely the minimum staking requirement will be lowered to 32 eth, until we get there, Ethereum will still be far away from being and staying truly decentralized.[215] Although it makes sense to stake your own money if you want to be a validator so that there is actually the potential of losing your money if you behave unethically within the network, it does not take away the fact that proof of stake gives an obvious advantage to people with more money.

Repeated 51% attacks make no sense financially under the proof of stake consensus protocol because the attacker is risking losing all his stake. It also eliminates (at least for now) the possibility of mining pools using their technical advantage to overpower and centralize the network, although mining pools certainly could make large stake deposits with their members collectively bearing the costs. Switching to proof of stake reduces electricity costs. The amount of newly issued (mined) coins will be less because staking in Ether has no real costs, unlike proof of work mining. Once you want to stop acting as a validator, after a certain time you will be able to get back all the money you deposited as your stake.[216]

However, the proof of stake consensus certainly will raise an issue when the developers of Ethereum will want to do another hard fork once the network has moved completely to proof of stake. The issue is that while on a proof of work blockchain miners are incentivized to choose the branch which they think is the correct one (because they have mining costs which they obviously do not want to lose by choosing the wrong chain which will later be abandoned, meaning that miners who opted for that chain will lose out on mining rewards), the situation is different on a proof of stake blockchain.

Validators of the proof of stake Ethereum 2.0 could choose to deposit stakes for both forks of the chain because they have nothing to lose and doing it will ensure that they will benefit independently of which chain will turn out to be the winner.

If all validators stake both branches, there could be somebody who manages to amass and deposit say 1% of the total stake deposited in one branch. He only would have to put his transaction in one of the branches, then fork the blockchain and put his 1% of the stake in the branch which is winning. In such case this one person with only 1% of the total stake could double-spend.[217]

A possible solution to avoid such double-spending is called Slasher. It would penalize validators if they simultaneously create blocks on multiple chains.[218] Casper also has a system of penalties for validators who do not behave as they should. Depending on the severity of the fault, the penalty can be as high as 100% of the validator's stake. Validators can be fined if they are frequently absent from the network. If problems arise on the shard to which the wallet of a particular validator is connected, the amount of the fine will be 2% of his stake. If the shards of a group of validators are simultaneously out of order, the penalties will be in the double digits.[219]

Vitalik, however, also mentioned that this penalty scheme has its own flaws because if a hacker attacks the network, collective penalties can wipe out the deposits of the validators.[220] Another serious issue is the possibility of a long range attack on the proof of stake blockchain. Proof of stake clients can't stop users "who were around since the beginning of the chain if they want to revert all of the blockchain history and start a new, seemingly valid chain. In effect, every version of a blockchain that exists or has *ever* existed could be revived and run as its own chain, if the underlying protocol allows for it."[221]

As the attacker would not have to outperform in the time-intensive operation of proof of work mining, he could go thousands of blocks back, so unless this is prevented somehow, there could be a very high number of forks going back to earlier versions of the blockchain. In contrast, if an attacker wants to attack a proof of work blockchain, he would go back only a few blocks because of the massive hashing power needed to outperform the rest of the miners in creating his version of the blockchain faster. One of the proposed solutions is to timestamp blocks so that long range forks that revise blocks older than a finalized block are ignored.[222]

After the delays in late 2018 the Constantinople hard fork was scheduled to be implemented on January 17, 2019 to complete the Metropolis upgrade, but two days earlier a blockchain analysis company found some weaknesses in the new code that would potentially allow attackers to steal funds from Ethereum holders. After this news the core development team called off the execution of the hard fork, likely also taking into account that Ethereum Classic just suffered a 51% attack a few days earlier.[223]

The Constantinople upgrade finally took place on February 28, 2019 together with the St. Petersburg upgrade which was meant to correct the security error.

Possible scaling solutions for Ethereum

Ethereum can currently only process 15 transactions per second, which is very low compared to the 1000 which it is supposed to be able to do (not to mention the mainstream alternatives). The transaction delays can be due to various factors inherent in the design of Ethereum such as block interval time, mining delays, gas price, and empty block penalty.[224] According to Buterin, the speed of the Ethereum network must be increased to 100,000 transactions per second to remain in the game in the long run.[225]

Plasma is another project that is being developed to scale Ethereum. The project started as a cooperation of Vitalik Buterin and Justin Poon, the creator of the Lightning Network. Plasma is a second layer of smart contracts designed to be implemented on top of the main blockchain. Having a second layer for smart contracts means that the related transactions do not have to be broadcast to, and validated by, the entire network. The goal for Plasma would be to replace centralized mining operations with a truly peer-to-peer network where the community collectively runs smart contracts in a decentralized, yet scalable fashion.[226]

Plasma would drastically decrease the amount of data that individual clients need to process because nodes would not have to download the entire Plasma history, but users could generate "plasma coins" by sending a deposit to the contract. Plasma could protect Ether and ERC-20 tokens, should a hack occur on an exchange. Plasma would allow private chains to be anchored into a public chain. Coins on the Plasma chain are equal to coins on the public chain, so if the Plasma chain is hacked, you can use your Plasma coins to recover equal amount of your coins on the public chain. The plus is that transactions do not take up space on the public chain.[227] This means that people could deposit their Ether or ERC-20 tokens into the Plasma system which is auxiliary to the main Ethereum chain. Plasma would be, unsurprisingly, similar to the solution of the Lightning Network in that it would use "a series of smart contracts to create hierarchical trees of sidechains. The sidechains can be governed using their own set of rules and only relay information back to the parent chain of Ethereum."[228]

"That means that you have a system that can be used for issuing tokens at enterprise scale, whether it's governments or private individuals, while paying very low public chain transaction fees. And at the same time you get a lot of the public chain benefits."[229]

From the late September 2018 post of Vitalik in which he proposed zk-SNARKs as a new method of scaling without having to use layers as with Plasma, it is clear that there has been some extensive research work going on in the background within The Ethereum Foundation.[230] He estimated that with the use of zk-SNARKs Ethereum could scale up to 500 transactions per second which is good compared to the average 193 transactions per seconds processed by PayPal (but still significantly lagging behind the Visa network).[231]

Although we have to take into account that increasing transaction speed is not the most important thing. The security of transactions is more important.[232]

Zk-SNARKs were introduced by Zcash, an altcoin that places its emphasis on the privacy aspect as a cryptocurrency. Zk-SNARKs is an abbreviation of *zero-knowledge succinct non-interactive argument of knowledge* and means that it is possible to prove that somebody has a certain information (like a private key) without having to reveal the information itself and without the need for interaction between the prover and the verifier of such information.

A zero-knowledge proof allows the prover to prove to the verifier that a statement is true, while not revealing any further information about the subject of the verification.[233]

Because Ethereum has to support the traffic of all the various projects built on its platform, there has been increased pressure on developers to find a scaling solution. With the growing number of users who want to do P2P transactions and decentralized apps on the blockchain, plus the growing number of ERC-20 tokens created on the Ethereum platform, the Ethereum blockchain becomes less practical as a solution to outcompete traditional payment processing companies.[234]

One of the partial solutions that Ethereum tried was the integration of the *Raiden Network*[235] as a second layer solution. Raiden is a so called *statement channel* similar to the Lightning Network, where you can send transactions off the main blockchain instantaneously via previously established payment channels. Just like the Lightning Network, Raiden requires users to set up a payment channel and deposit money into it by broadcasting this as a transaction to the main blockchain network.

While Plasma has been developed by the Ethereum core developers, Raiden was created by a private company called brainbot labs Establishment[236] to conduct rapid transactions off the blockchain without the involvement of third parties to help solve the scalability issues of Ethereum. Similarly to the Lightning Network, users have to open a payment channel by creating a smart contract, and both parties of the payment channel have to deposit some money that will fund the channel. Transactions are initiated off-chain, but once users want to get access to their coins outside of the Raiden Network, they will close the payment channel and only the final balance of the channel will be recorded on the blockchain.[237] Raiden can be used by any ERC-20 token too.

The one transaction that gets registered on the blockchain could actually hold thousands of transactions conducted on the payment channel as part of various transaction routes of the Raiden Network. Because only one transaction is recorded, transaction costs can be divided among hundreds of users. Instant payments could take only minutes for the funds to become available.[238]

Ethereum privacy developments

Ethereum has adopted zk-SNARKs as part of the Byzantium upgrade in October 2017 due to the rising interest in privacy. Interestingly, though certainly not coincidentally, Vitalik Buterin is part of the Zcash team as an advisor (just as Gavin Andresen, ex-lead developer of Bitcoin).

The dApp developed for implementing zk-SNARKs on Ethereum is called *Miximus*. Miximus enables Ethereum to provide privacy protected transactions just like Zcash, but "any computation that can be done on Ethereum could now be done in such a way that nobody will know what the computation is actually computing. At most they can just verify that the transaction is a valid one."[239]

The developers of Ethereum also adopted privacy features similar to those of Monero. Ethereum has been working to implement these Monero-style privacy features under its own tumbler called *Mobius*. Mobius will provide privacy by using a smart contract with ring signatures and stealth addresses to obfuscate private information of transactions.[240] We will discuss these features later in the chapter about privacy coins.

A blockchain startup called Clearmatics has been entrusted with the implementation of Mobius but it has not been completed yet, though according to consensus the solution is quite simple and easy to implement on Ethereum.

With these developments Ethereum is getting closer to potentially being able to allow users to use anonymized data in smart contracts, as well as decentralized applications which include privacy features (also called *Zapps*) and anonymous token transfers.[241]

However, it is also interesting to consider what Vitalik Buterin replied to a user called WhalePanda on Twitter on May 8, 2018 when WhalePanda wrote: "if you really care about privacy, you would pick a decentralized coin". The reply of Buterin to this was: "Why? If I was using cryptocurrency for a high-privacy-demanding usecase, I'd go for what seems more likely to protect confidentiality and not give a crap about luxuries like decentralization."[242] Maybe it has something to do with his involvement with Zcash, or maybe we cannot see something he can see, but at first thought his statement is not reassuring at all for those who want more privacy and decentralization. It is clear that decentralization does come with some difficult technical issues and maybe that is what he alluded to, but who knows?

It seems that Ethereum has been following a roadmap working through any roadblocks that may appear, but they have to cope not only with the technical difficulties of development, but also with the different interests of the various interest groups that are invested in Ethereum. Whether Ethereum manages to keep interest in its platform itself despite the openly declared efforts to abolish mining rewards and substitute them with way smaller validator rewards, and despite its intention to prevent centralization of the network is yet to be seen.

Obviously, the negative impact of the reduction of the mining reward and the small amount of the validator rewards must have not been received with much enthusiasm by the mining community because Vitalik Buterin recently made a comment that the validator rewards will eventually be increased. We will have to wait to see how things will change for Ethereum once the migration to proof of stake will finally be completed.

It is clear that the goal is not amping up the transaction velocity of the main chain but instead to develop further layers with specialized functions to create a more complex and much more efficient and fast network that could finally solve the issue of scalability while maintaining decentralization and security. If they manage to do it without alienating a large part of the users of the Ethereum network, the platform will have a greater chance to survive, and possibly even thrive in the near future. Or at least higher probabilities to stay in the game for the long haul.

Banco Santander, one of the most important Spanish banks just announced in September 2019 that they issued a $20 million bond on Ethereum, which is the first ever end-to-end blockchain based bond.[243] This shows that Ethereum does have good chances to survive.

10

Your Privacy Is Important to Us

The privacy, anonymity, and fungibility of Bitcoin

Since the birth of the internet there have been continuous debates between those who saw the digitalization of our personal data as a way of welcome transparency that would bring more equality and order to the world, and those who are of the opinion that this transparency is a two-edged sword which can easily be used to gain more control over people than we have ever seen before.

One of the arguments of the mainstream media against Bitcoin has been that Bitcoin wallets are anonymous, so it is ideal for criminals and that it is being used for money laundering and illegal trafficking with weapons, drugs, or sex slaves, etc.

Well, if this were the case, what about the times before Bitcoin? Had there never been any fiat currency used for illegal and criminal activities? Were those pesky criminals 20 years back paying in cauri shells or perhaps marshmallows? Did the establishment try to ban dollars, euros or any other fiat currency because criminals were using them to conduct illegal activities? Obviously not, but then the logical response is for them to say "that's why it is important that authorities control the activity of Bitcoin users, or else criminals will have free rein".

It is really a question of ideology whether one sees the "anonymity" of transactions which Bitcoin is touted for as beneficial or not. It all boils down to the popular belief, or rather propaganda instilled into us that humans are inherently bad. That if there were no outside control imposed on us, we would rape and pillage, cheat, kill and lie until our last breath. This is radically opposed to the natural morals and goodness inherent in people (well, in the large majority anyway).

These opposite world views are also present in the debate whether the digitalization of our personal data is something we should worry about or if it lays the foundation of a more transparent, more equal society. Well, you may want to refer back to the earlier discussion on some basic assumptions. If so much energy is expended to inculcate in people since their early childhood that they should not really trust others, that we are all evil, greedy, hateful, jealous bastards, capable of the worst acts, who only behave well because we fear retaliation of the law, that might tell you something about how difficult it is to convince people of the inherent goodness of humans and the existence of natural morality.

Of course, we are able to do evil and become evil, however, generally something really wrong has to happen to us to push us into that direction. That something could be abuse, trauma, the inherent injustice in the system that is forced on us, etc.

Privacy "isn't necessarily about protecting against corporations that would sell your data, governments who want to use or control your financial activity, making 'nefarious' purchases on the darkweb [obligatory scary voice], or evading taxes. The Bitcoin network is a global and open network built from entirely open source software. This is about simply rebuilding the most basic privacy barriers between yourself and literally anyone on the internet."244

It is a basic human need to keep our private sphere and in a human-friendly world we would not need to be "transparent by being monitored" but rather by adhering to an inherent, natural code of honor of doing the right thing because that is what makes us feel good about ourselves. That is why we would not want "the default state of Bitcoin to be that anyone with a node and the motivation could see our purchases, balances, and entire history of our transactions."[245]

Even though we are being bombarded with this notion of Bitcoin being anonymous, if Bitcoin were to become more common and used en mass in transactions and not just as a store of value or as a tool of speculation (currently it is not that common to use it for payments), it would be really easy to find a connection between your other digital data and your public address. The authorities or criminals would only have to find out what your public address is and then they could trace how much your net worth is, what you did with your money and when, and they could use this information to rob you or kidnap you. Or in case of the legally authorized ones, tax you.

China has already been doing some really scary "testing", for the moment with volunteers, of a social credit score system. These volunteers each have a score card and are being monitored continuously via electronic surveillance, both at home and in public. The system gives them points according to their actions. If, for example, you happen to buy too much alcohol or tobacco, or something else that is deemed unhealthy or frowned upon by the algorithm like medicinal herbs, your social score will be lowered because you will likely cause more expenses to society when you will get sick and will have to be treated.

If you post opinions, or videos and blogs on social media that go against the establishment, you may be labeled as a "dissident", "anarchists", or maybe a "potential terrorist" by the algorithm, even if you simply just think differently than how the government wants you to think. Of course, all these unwanted behaviors would result in immediate lowering of your social score number.

Eventually, those whose social score is not high enough will be punished by applying various restrictions on what they can do and where they can go. In the test phase, for example, people are banned from traveling on airplanes or trains, or from going abroad.

What is even more Orwellian though is that you will lose points not only when you personally do something that the system does not want you to do, but also when somebody from your family does something "undesirable".

People within families are incentivized to censor and control other members of the family to avoid being punished themselves. This is a very clever but appalling use of peer pressure and group psychology where the algorithm trains the population to self-police itself to stay within the pre-established boundaries of what is allowed and what is sanctionable. A generation that grows up within such a system would become fully controllable flesh robots without hardly any individual thoughts or initiatives.

Not that privacy coins would be enough to avoid such an Orwellian future, but they are definitely one aspect to consider if you want to prevent our society from turning into such a nightmarish, inhumane world. And if you think it's just China, think again. China is currently being set up as the most likely next leading power of the bright globalist future and the cyber-collectivist social model the controllers would like to extend to all countries eventually.

Why is the combination of social credit systems with blockchain based cryptocurrencies without appropriate privacy features (or the basic right to opt out of those systems) a terrible thing? If your transactions are not protected by such privacy features because all your transaction history is publicly available on the blockchain forever, immutably (unless you have the computing power to hack the entire system, but normal people don't), once such a social crediting system is implemented, you could be sanctioned for your everyday choices and life habits. And without proper privacy of cryptocurrencies there would be no place to hide in the electronic world from the tentacles of a social credit system, the government, your competitors or some cyber criminals too eager to spy on your private economy, opinions, and habits.

You could be punished for having bought something that the system does not want you to have. Maybe the system would punish what it deems unhealthy foods, so it would be ultimately "guarding your health and doing you a favor"...(sorry, I had to laugh here). But what prevents the system from deciding whether you are able to buy say healing herbs, like chamomile or oat straw or anything that is not dangerous but that could take away the profit from some powerful corporations? Nothing. Google Codex Alimentarius.

Or what if donating money to an alternative media site or video channel that goes against the main stream were seen as undesirable and punished by taking away your social credits? We must seriously avoid such a dystopian world.

"Privacy is a basic human right. It is indicative of how out of balance our society is today, that governments, corporations, and authoritative institutions can completely take our privacy, and it is of no consequence. But then any attempt to get it back is treated as not only nefarious and suspect, but sometimes even criminal. There is no better future waiting for a society that values authority and control over freedom and equality."[246]

Not only idealistic, anarchistic rebels and criminals want privacy coins. It is clear from their popularity in terms of market capitalization that there is a great need for, and interest in, such privacy coins among people.

The popular argument is that if you do not have anything to hide then you should not have any issues with being monitored. Really? Would you like to be stalked continuously, even if you are a law abiding citizen? I wouldn't. *"It's not that I have something to hide. I have nothing I want you to see."*[247] Again, this goes all back to the notion so heavily drummed into the heads of people that unless we are not constantly supervised, controlled and observed, all hell will break loose. But if you are lucky enough to visit a tribe that lives relatively undisturbed and close to nature, you will see that it is not true.

Blanket style surveillance means that the government now sees everybody as guilty until there is proof of one's innocence, and not the other way round as it should be. This is already happening at airports where passengers are submitted to harmful radiation and humiliating body scans to prove that they are innocent. An inhumane and completely unnecessary practice indeed.

People and small communities can successfully self-regulate themselves. Interestingly, the upper limit of community size which is still manageable by humans is wired into our brains. It appears that the maximum number (called Dunbar's number) is around 150 people. So if we live in communities that do not go over approximately 150 people, the genetic predisposition of humans is to live peacefully and harmoniously within their small communities, tribes or villages.

The issue is not people being evil or sinful; it is the fact that we live within a framework forced onto us that is more similar to the organization of colony building insects like ants or termites. Millions of individuals crammed into one tightly managed infrastructure, called a city, the majority controlled from above. This is another important factor to ponder.

Why would Bitcoin users want just about anybody to know where and what they buy, how much they earn or how much money they have? There have already been kidnapping cases where criminals demanded a hefty ransom in exchange for the liberation of crypto millionaires, like the case of Pavel Lerner, the CEO of a UK cryptoexchange, Exmo Finance, who was kidnapped in Kiev, Ukraine and was only released after paying a ransom of $1 million in bitcoins.[248]

Also, not only individuals but businesses too generally prefer privacy, to avoid leaking money related details to competitors, so privacy and criminality do not necessary go hand in hand.[249]

Having privacy can actually protect you in more ways than you would think. On the Bitcoin network, for example, there have been specific coins blacklisted because they were identified to have been involved in illegal activities *in the past*. You could have received a bitcoin payment from A who received it from B who received it from C who received it from D, and there is a chance that D might have used bitcoins for selling drugs or weapons or for human trafficking. But is what B, C or D had used their bitcoins for really your responsibility?

If individual coins can be found "tainted" (the mere fact of having been involved in illicit activities means that such a coin is "tainted") and, as a consequence, can be taken out of circulation and blacklisted, it means that Bitcoin is not fungible. Of course, you would not be recompensated for the tainted bitcoins they would confiscate from you, which is just not right. We cannot be expected to pay for the crimes of others.

Fiat money is fungible because any of the coins or bank notes with the same value indicated on them is worth the same. There is no way to distinguish a "clean" one dollar bill from a "dirty" one dollar bill because it is not possible to trace its journey from transaction to transaction. So if you want to pay with a one dollar bill, everybody has to accept it (barring the case when the bill is obviously false).

However, with a public ledger where all transactions are public and traceable, there is no real fungibility. It is possible to trace the specific bitcoin you just received back to its point of origin (when it was mined) and find out if it had ever been used to pay for something illegal or if it was stolen from an exchange.

This is due to the fact that bitcoins do not exist as some special code that is somehow created by virtue of such code and can be found independently on the network. Instead, bitcoins are just individual packets of information. Each one of them is different from the rest because they were all created by putting together different transactions into blocks.

Each and every bitcoin is distinguishable from the rest, because this distinct and traceable origin is like a fingerprint. The immutability of the public ledger is what makes it possible to trace the entire history of a specific bitcoin, uncovering all the transactions it had ever been involved in. A bitcoin is not only a unit of account but also the ledger history of itself (the history of owners it has had and the transactions it has been involved in, up until the present).[250] That's why bitcoins and satoshis cannot be interchanged with each other because their histories are different.

There are already many Bitcoin companies and even government agencies that monitor blacklisted coins and use blockchain analytics companies for such purposes. It is not possible to do it with fiat currency, but anybody can track the public Bitcoin blockchain and follow transactions.

There are various methods that strip the anonymity of the transactions on the Bitcoin network which give free passage to not only regulators and law enforcement agencies but also to analytics companies and even technically savvy criminals to link Bitcoin addresses to the identities of the users.[251]

Bitcoin privacy is often quite limited because all the above organizations and individuals can analyze public blockchains, cluster addresses of the Bitcoin network and tie them to IP addresses or other identifying information. If a third party (a Bitcoin service, an exchange, an internet service provider or an online store) is able to attach your identity to a specific address it should not be very difficult to connect the dots and identify the rest of your transactions and balances.[252] "Monitoring the unencrypted peer-to-peer network, analysis of the public blockchain, and Know Your Customer (KYC) policy or Anti-Money Laundering (AML) regulation can reveal a lot about who's using Bitcoin, and for what."[253]

This means that although each bitcoin within the Bitcoin network is distinct, for users they are fungible because if there is no double spending each bitcoin can be used in the same way. The Bitcoin network does not single out coins with a shady past, but external entities can, and will, apply "tainting" information to the individual coins, which makes Bitcoin non-fungible. This also means that you can only sell bitcoins as a fungible asset on a peer-to-peer level, outside of an exchange or an official vendor, but for this very reason the risk that the bitcoins you buy "in private" will turn out to be tainted or blacklisted is high.[254]

As a first step of transferring bitcoins you have to broadcast the transaction to the network, and your identity could be found out already at this stage. "A clever and observant node, doing analysis on the movement of transactions through peers, can often pinpoint the originating IP address, and therefore, the likely owner of the coins."[255]

This lack of privacy could mean that you lose your money if it turns out that you bought bitcoin outside of a cryptoexchange, say from a private individual, in which case you cannot check if the bitcoins he offers had a dubious history or not. Many exchanges routinely perform risk assessment on coin deposits. If they find that the coins you bought outside of the exchange and want to deposit on the exchange have been involved in illegal activities, there is a high chance that they will backlist your coins and even close your account.[256]

This is why the lack of privacy could also result in a loss of fungibility, and why fungibility is an essential requirement for any currency in a free society. Ian Miers, co-founder of Zcash, which is a privacy coin (a cryptocurrency which puts special emphasis on privacy) cloned off Bitcoin with added privacy, was not far from the truth when he said that "Bitcoin is Twitter for your bank account."[257] Everything is public to everyone and instead of true anonymity you get pseudo-anonymity.

Even if complete privacy might only be an ideal which is nearly impossible to achieve when operating on the internet, it is possible to maintain a high enough level of privacy. However, it is always associated either with a high cost or some other inconvenience.[258] The vast majority of people for this reason simply choose to act as if privacy were not needed and as if there was nothing that they could do about it, just taking the loss of privacy for granted "because it comes with the territory" of the digital age.

There have been various technologies proposed to enhance the privacy of the Bitcoin network. According to one proposal, introducing confidential transactions could get Bitcoin closer to fungibility. With confidential transactions the amounts involved in a transaction could be hidden, and it seems that "known amounts are the root of all evil in most Bitcoin privacy techniques"[259]. Such confidential transactions would, however, cost more and also, authorities would not be happy about people not only trying to hide, but succeeding in hiding, the data of their transactions.

While the idea that Bitcoin is anonymous has been widely propagated, it is really just pseudo-anonymity. With the right knowledge everyone can find out to whom an "anonymous" Bitcoin address belongs. Derek Moore, who is currently working on a project to beat social media censorship using blockchain technology by storing multimedia and hypermedia content in Bitcoin Satoshi Vision transactions said that "Bitcoin is a mass surveillance system."[260]

According to Moore, "it's perfectly traceable, it's absolutely transparent. So when you're using a mass surveillance system...you actually have to go out of your way to regain some sentiments of privacy and you can do that with the crypto system that's built into Bitcoin...You could put your trade secrets on the chain, you could use those in your court proceedings as evidence, you could have the cryptographic keys that secure that data so only you can decrypt it. There's really an endless amount of use cases for this, I think one of the most important...is the censorship resistance of Bitcoin. If we can scale the blockchain, allow massive on-chain data, then people who are at risk of censorship in a kind of corporatocracy like we are in or in oppressive regimes like other people are in, then we can actually get that data out there."[261]

Derek Moore is working on developing Bitcoin into a secure data storage system (while maintaining its primary digital cash function), and believes that if people started to buy Bitcoin to be able to afford storing information on Bitcoin, it would also stabilize its price as opposed to the current store of value and speculative uses.[262] (The work is carried out on Bitcoin Satoshi Vision, but for its developers BSV is the real Bitcoin, and anyway, they believe that all Bitcoin versions could be merged later on. This is the reason why Moore is talking about Bitcoin and not Bitcoin SV specifically.)

Enhanced, not to mention near-perfect, privacy could make Bitcoin lose its relatively favored position as government agencies and regulators would likely change the regulations, banning confidential transactions on the Bitcoin network. Currently, all privacy coins are frowned upon by the establishment and should Bitcoin ever become a successful privacy coin itself, it is possible that the tides would turn and it could fall out of favor as number one cryptocurrency of the world.

Instead of adding confidentiality as a feature to the main chain, another possibility is to enhance Bitcoin by adding a specialized second layer code on top of the first layer (which is the original main blockchain layer). One such project is the Lightning Network which has been developed as a scaling solution to make payments faster and cheaper, and also to increase privacy. However, the already dubious privacy of Bitcoin may actually suffer from its implementation. Let's see why.

The Lightning Network and its effects on Bitcoin privacy

The Lightning Network is the most successful second layer protocol designed for Bitcoin to date. Its potential benefits were one of the most important factors that united a big part of the Bitcoin community to accept and implement the SegWit fork[263], although this could be due to the fact that it has become obvious that Bitcoin will be unfeasible for mass adoption as an exchange of value, a form of payment, unless the developers manage to integrate second layer solutions into it which make Bitcoin scalable without losing decentralization, privacy, and security.

The idea for Lightning Network came from Joseph Poon and Thaddeus Dryja in 2015, but its development is currently carried out by Blockstream, Lightning Labs and ACINQ. These three companies are developing the Lightning Network protocol for three different programming languages, but according to tests these three implementations can work together seamlessly.[264]

Blockstream is the corporation behind Bitcoin Core, which is said to have hijacked Bitcoin from 2015 to gain control over its development by dumbing it down and to keep it dumbed down to profit from selling related side chain products and hardware to enterprises.

According to the Bitcoin Core narrative, the Lightning Network, similarly to the layered architecture of Ethereum which has been developed step by step, adds another layer to the Bitcoin blockchain instead of wanting to solve its scaling issues by modifying the software code for the blockchain (layer one) itself.[265] However, from an "anti-leech" point of view the dumbing down of the original Bitcoin protocol prepared the conditions in which layer two protocols could thrive and companies building them could make money leeching the Bitcoin network.

The Lightning Network was designed for Bitcoin, but several other projects including Litecoin, Zcash, Stellar, Ripple and Decred have also announced their intention to integrate the Lightning Network with their networks since. Even though it was not adopted as is by Ethereum, its main developer and Vitalik Buterin started a common project to create a similar second layer protocol for Ethereum.

Monero developers have also been working with Litecoin to integrate the atomic swaps functionality of the Lightning Network in the hopes that the ability to directly exchange Monero to Bitcoin will increase the coin's relevance. Monero has an inbuilt scaling mechanism, so it doesn't otherwise need the Lightning Network, and clearly, adopting it for other than atomic swaps would be a fatal error and would cause a massive loss of privacy.[266]

It is just speculation, but a probable reason why Bitcoin ABC developers who are at war with Craig Wright's and nChain's Bitcoin Satoshi Vision wanted to incorporate the Lightning Network into Bitcoin ABC might have been because of the open "till-the-other-chain-dies" hostility between the two new currencies since the splitting up of Bitcoin Cash.

This move was really interesting because the Bitcoin Cash community believed that the original Bitcoin blockchain was scalable without the need to include second layer solutions that would lead to decentralization. However, after the hard fork which split Bitcoin Cash into two blockchains Roger Ver offered $1.25 million to OpenNode, a Lightning Network company for the implementation of the Lightning Network. But they refused to build on Bitcoin ABC for ideological reasons, stating that their "vision of a better, more open financial system is only possible with Bitcoin"[267] (meaning the dumbed down, side-chain dependent BTC). Which is, of course, a logical thing to do for a side chain development company.

On the Lightning Network any user can set up a direct payment channel with another user and until it is closed these two users can execute as many transactions as they like, sending money back and forth via this channel. The novelty is that these transactions do not get registered on the main blockchain, so there is no need for validation of the transactions. The result is very fast, almost instantaneous and very low fee transactions on the Lightning Network.[268]

As opposed to the seven transactions per second which the Bitcoin network was processing without this second layer solution and the block size increase envisioned by Satoshi, the Lightning Network is presented to be capable of processing millions of transactions per second for a ridiculously low cost. The capacity of processing transactions grows as the number of channels grows.[269] Compared to this potential velocity, Visa's maximum capacity seems deplorable.

The secret to this high velocity is using payment channels that are created by two parties who set up a multi-signature wallet on the blockchain. In a standard wallet only the sender has to sign the transactions, but "multisig" wallet transactions are only valid if both the sender and the receiver sign them. If you want to send money on the Lightning Network, first you have to open a payment channel between you and the recipient.[270]

You set up your payment channel between you and the person you want to send money to by making a ledger entry and depositing money into it. The recipient can either also deposit money or just deposit the minimum to cover the processing fees of the Lightning Network. Both parties involved in the payment channel have their own private keys and a transaction becomes valid only once both parties have signed it. This initial setting up of the payment channel takes the time any other transaction would take on the main blockchain to be validated.

The payment channel is bidirectional; both the sender and the receiver can send money back and forth to each other through it. Once the payment channel is established and validated, the two parties can make almost instantaneous transactions between each other using the funds that were allocated initially in that channel. This means that if you deposited 1 btc while your partner only deposited the minimum to pay the Lightning Network fees, the maximum amount you can send via this payment channel with the first transaction will be 1 btc. If you both deposited 1 btc, the maximum amount that can be sent in your payment channel in one transaction will be 2 btc.

As none of these transactions are recorded on the blockchain and no transaction validation is needed, the channel will keep tabs. These instantaneous transactions are made by passing signed transactions through the channel back and forth. When you decide to close this channel down because you no longer want to transact with the other person, the actual balance will be recorded on the blockchain and the final settlement of the total deposited 2 btc will be paid in your respective wallets.[271]

You can create as many direct channels as you like, but if you want to send money to a person with whom you have not set up a payment channel and you will likely pay them only once, opening a channel for just this one transaction and then closing it will not be cost effective. You can instead make the payment via a *routed payment channel*.[272] The Lightning Network will find a route from one of your existing payment channels to another channel all the way until it reaches your intended recipient. Just like the Kevin Bacon game where everybody is connected by various degrees of separation, the protocol creates a network out of these payment channels. This also ensures that the network stays decentralized.

So for example, if you only have a payment channel set up with Bob and you want to send money to George, the network will find payment channels that connect you through Bob to George. Maybe there will be only one other payment channel between Bob and George (if they happen to know each other and have set up their own payment channel), but it is also possible that your transaction will travel from several payment channels from Bob to Cindy, from Cindy to Dan, and from Dan to George.[273]

The more nodes there are that adopt the Lightning Network and set up payment channels, the faster and cheaper transactions can become. If for whatever reason the transaction could not be executed because one actor of any of the involved channels is malicious, the money sent is returned to the sender and it will not get stuck somewhere on its way from the sender to the receiver in one of the payment channels.

The advantage of the Lightning Network is that it makes micropayments feasible because transaction fees are so low. It also supports payments with cell phones. However, its adoption on the Bitcoin network is quite slow because nobody can be forced to use the Lightning Network. But whether the desired scalability can be reached depends on the number of people who set up payment channels. At the time of writing there are approximately 4,800 Lightning Network nodes which is not too many.[274]

The channel network is still too small to handle larger payments (the total capacity in May 2019 reached just a little over 1.1 million btc but dropped to 830,000 btc by September 2019)[275], and there is a high possibility that the network becomes centralized. In Januar 2019 for example an entity called Lnbig.com had 25 nodes which was enough for it to control 70% of the total capacity of the Lightning Network, although this disproportionality is at least partially due to the fact that the implementors were the ones who started to set up payment channels first, and obviously were more invested in creating as many connections as possible.

Another issue is that cell phones are not the best candidates for operating as Lightning Network nodes because nodes must be online in order for the channel to work. The lack of offline payment possibility and the fact that closing a payment channel once you no longer want to transact with a particular person takes too much time, are also issues. The fact that certain individual nodes could be easily attacked creates a bigger safety risk for the network.

Many people also think that the fact that Lightning Network transactions with their details take place on the second layer and do not get recorded on the main blockchain means that privacy will increase for Bitcoin users. Unfortunately, this is not the case and there are people who are adamant on emphasizing that the Lightning Network will actually degrade Bitcoin privacy.

The Lightning Network by design cannot provide free transactions. Lightning transactions are very cheap, but to open and close a transaction channel you will have to pay a regular Bitcoin fee which is relatively high. Although this will change as the Lightning Network becomes more extended, in September 2018 one had to make sixteen transactions before the Lightning Network became cheaper to use than Bitcoin Cash.[276] This means that very small payments are not yet worth making with the Lightning Network, unless a user is determined to use it repeatedly in many transactions, or if he transacts with the same people over and over.

However, transactions of large amounts are not safe either. Since the network is being enlarged slowly and organically, there is a maximum transaction value of 0.042 btc, compared to the maximum channel funding value of 0.168 btc, for security reasons. At this phase there is an intentional difficulty built into the system for safety reasons, which later on, when the security of the system will have been tested, can be changed.[277]

This transaction size restriction is a clear sign that even the developers themselves are not certain whether Lightning Network channels are secure. Consequently, they are not optimal for large volume operations either. The individual nodes can be attacked to steal the money stored in the channels, so it is simply not safe to use the Lightning Network for larger payments. You would not lose much if you have twenty dollars' worth of bitcoin on it to pay for coffee, but if you have hundreds or thousands, that is too big a risk, said even Andreas Antonopoulos who has been one of the most important advocates of the Lightning Network. For this very reason channels currently do not normally enable payments above 59 dollars.[278]

"At present, Bitcoin is not a great solution for medium-sized or infrequent transactions."[279] The Lightning Network launched on Bitcoin in March 2018, and at that time Bitcoin fees were around a dollar, while Litecoin average fees were 0.21 cents. Unless somebody wants to use the Lightning Network on Bitcoin very frequently, a rational user will not spend a dollar to open and close a Lightning channel. That is why Litecoin has a good chance to "fill up all the holes in the crypto-economy: not only for macro- and micro-transactions, but also everyday expenses."[280]

Having transactions off the blockchain and relegated to the second layer does not bring more privacy and security to Bitcoin for various reasons. The Lightning Network team indeed has been working on ways to add more privacy to the system, but the question is whether those are efficient. Ian Miers believes that Lightning Network will make privacy "much worse from an average consumer's perspective"[281]. Craig Wright went as far as to say (not disappointing his avid fans) that "Lightning is shit squared"[282].

The most advanced privacy feature is called *Onion routing*, which is part of protocols called the Basics of Lightning Technology (BOLT) used to make multiple iterations of the Lightning Network (those of Blockstream, Lightning Labs and ACINQ) interoperable. The onion name refers to the various layers of security added with each individual channel that the payment is passed through from the sender to the recipient because only the minimum amount of data about the payment is exposed to the multiple channels it passes through. A node can only know from which node it received the payment and to which node it should be sent to.[283]

Onion routing was first developed by the U.S. Naval Research Lab in the 1990's and later its code was released into the public domain. *Tor* is the largest and best known implementation of onion routing[284], its name is the acronym of the original name of the software project called *The Onion Router*.[285] Tor ensures anonymity by directing "internet traffic through a free, worldwide, volunteer overlay network consisting of more than seven thousand relays to conceal a user's location and usage from anyone conducting network surveillance or traffic analysis"[286].

Tor is one of the most well-known tools to navigate the deep web (or darkweb) anonymously. Tor was developed to enable anonymous communication and it "protects you by bouncing your communications around a distributed network of relays run by volunteers all around the world: it prevents somebody watching your Internet connection from learning what sites you visit, and it prevents the sites you visit from learning your physical location. This set of volunteer relays is called the Tor network. The way most people use Tor is with Tor Browser, which is a version of Firefox that fixes many privacy issues."[287]

However, it is well known that Tor has its weaknesses and cannot provide perfect privacy protection. Anybody can monitor the traffic entering and exiting the Tor network, so for example somebody who can observe your computer and the destination website or your Tor exit node could correlate the timings of your entering the Tor network and your Tor exit node. This way they could verify the suspicion that you are in communication with the exit node.[288]

"Tor cannot and does not attempt to protect against monitoring of traffic at the boundaries of the Tor network (i.e. the traffic entering and exiting the network). While Tor does provide protection against traffic analysis, it cannot prevent traffic confirmation."[289]

If we take into consideration that it took years for experts to understand all the threats against privacy when using Tor, despite all the academic analysis and technical development[290], it makes sense to think that the use of onion routing by the Lightning Network could have similar consequences to the privacy of users. Even Olaoluwa Osuntokun who first introduced the Lightning Network admitted that "similar to Tor, there exist known possibilities of timing leaks, and also unknown active attacks that may be viable."[291]

The onion routing does not provide perfect protection of information on the Lightning Network because the last node of a route has access to the transaction information and the identity of the sender. There is a risk that nodes that participated in the relaying of the transaction from the sender to the recipient could collude to break privacy.[292] On top of that, as admitted by Osuntokun, the Lightning Network does not provide a solution to beat off attacks by a "global adversary which is able to instantaneously monitor all channels on the network"[293]. Could such a global adversary exist? From what we know, Palantir for example might very well have the capabilities needed.

Fixed identifiers are the cause of another privacy defect. Payments on the Lightning Network are given a fixed identifier which does not change as the transaction is moving along on its route from sender to receiver. So if an attacker knows two non-contiguous nodes of the route, it is not impossible for them to link a payment flow. According to Osuntokun, the easiest solution would be to replace this fixed identifier with random numbers as a transaction hops from one channel to the next.[294]

Another potential risk to privacy is that the Lightning Network could become highly centralized. For the traffic of transactions in the Lightning Network to work seamlessly it is necessary that the total of the money deposited by all those users who opened up payment channels be at least equal to the total transaction volume. The amount of money that is needed to operate the network is very high. This definitely points to a tendency to create centralization ingrained into the architecture of the Lightning Network. If there are one million users with an average monthly transaction volume of $10,000, the Lightning Network will need to keep $10 billion tied up as collateral just to be able to stay operational.[295]

Blockstream even announced that they plan to broadcast Bitcoin transactions via satellite from space. While it could lead to centralization, Bitcoin developer Gavin Andresen said he has no issues with it as anybody else could emulate Blockstream and put up their own satellites to participate in the Bitcoin Lightning Network. Charlie Lee, the creator of Litecoin commented on this opinion saying that "it could potentially lead to central hubs being the most connected. For smaller payments, a bit of centralization is no big deal."[296]

There is another potential risk which comes from the fact that the Lightning Network is capable of hiding the transaction history of the individual bitcoins that are used in Lightning transactions. In theory, the longer the route through the various payment channels from the sender to the recipient, the more difficult it is to track the transaction. As soon as the bitcoin enters the second layer ecosystem of the Lightning Network, it can be passed on from the original owner (who may be aware of the tainted history of a specific coin) to many other people and this specific bitcoin would only appear on the main blockchain again if the payment channel of its latest owner is ever closed. There is no way to track the history of this bitcoin from the time it entered the Lightning Network until it exited with the closing of the payment channel. So in theory, the Lightning Network could provide a way for people to launder their tainted bitcoins.[297]

Currently, there are some features being developed that could further increase the privacy of the Lightning Network. One of these is called *Atomic Multipath Payments*. This means that the transactions are split up and parts of them are sent via different routes, which makes it easier to send large amounts on the Lightning Network. Because you can pass only as much money through a payment channel as the money initially deposited into it by the two parties of the channel, sending any amount bigger than the initial deposit can only be done by sending it in many smaller transactions. With Atomic Multipath Payments you could, however, initiate one transaction, and the protocol would split it up into as many smaller amount transactions as needed for the network to be able to handle it.[298]

The Atomic Multipath Payments feature could definitely increase privacy because otherwise without this feature it would make more sense to just use the bigger hubs with the most money deposited to avoid having to initiate several transactions. If users would have to send transactions of large amounts through the bigger hubs, it would definitely increase centralization and with that the possibility of attackers violating the privacy of users. The development of such a channel system with relatively new, large centralized hubs and many individual channels connecting to them is called the hub-and-spokes model and it would definitely mean more centralization. It could bring the appearance of such centralized hubs that do not want to take part in transactions but only will provide a lightning node as a service.[299]

Running a lightning node will obviously require people to lock up a considerable amount of money when opening the channel. This and the costs of running nodes will lead to centralization which then eliminates privacy.[300] Blockstream is working on solutions to counter the forming of hubs by programming the network to open channels at random, which would avoid hubs that could get more information about transaction traffic. This randomization would make the payment paths less predictable and safer, but at the same time would likely raise transaction fees.[301]

Although there is no public Lightning Network ledger for users to consult each and every transaction, nor are those transactions recorded on the main blockchain, payments still have to be broadcast across nodes. Users could potentially choose to be very picky and only transact if specific nodes that they trust are online and available, and could refuse to transact with unknown nodes, but not everybody will do that. To ensure that routing is always available for new transactions, users of payment channels have to have blind faith in other users of the Lightning Network.

Theoretically, Lightning Network users could pry on a transaction and even sell the information to authorities or advertisers. If the network evolves into a centralized hub-and-spokes structure, the risk of third parties using and abusing private information of the transactions of the users will be even greater.[302]

Atomic Cross Chain Swaps are another new development which have recently been successfully tested. An atomic swap is a smart contract technology that enables the exchange of different cryptocurrencies without a third party. The word "atomic" means that a trade happens as an indivisible whole as opposed to a normal trade on a centralized exchange. On a centralized exchange if you want to sell say 1 btc to Bob for 100 ltc, there is a chance that while you send your 1 btc to Bob, something happens during the process, either the exchange gets hacked, or your trading partner grabs your bitcoin and without sending you the corresponding amount of litecoins, runs away with your money.

An atomic swap, however, incorporates hash time-locked contracts (HTLCs) which will only release your money to Bob if he is able to generate a cryptographic proof of payment within a determined limited time frame.

This proof of payment acknowledges that he received the payment. If he cannot provide the proof of payment within the given time frame, your 1 btc will be sent back to you automatically. However, for you to receive the 100 ltc in exchange for your 1 btc from Bob, you will also have to generate a cryptographic proof of payment within a given time frame. If you are unable to do so, Bob will get his 100 ltc back.[303]

Atomic swaps are expected to disrupt the crypto space and could cause the extinction of centralized exchanges. Centralized exchanges can be hacked and they can go out of business and disappear without advising their clients. There have been quite a lot of exchange hacks up until now during the short history of cryptocurrencies (even the number one, Binance got hacked in May 2019 and the hacker got away with 41 million dollars' worth of bitcoins). Taking into account that when you deposit money in an exchange you do not have the private key but the exchange does, keeping your cryptos on a centralized exchange indeed seems quite risky. Although centralized exchanges could team up with government and be completely compliant with everything they require in exchange for being able to provide insurance against hackers etc., the result would be that centralized and decentralized exchanges would cater to different types of customers.

Atomic cross chain swaps could result in the appearance of decentralized exchanges not only because they are more secure while giving total control to users over their funds. They can also be virtually free because there are no exchange service fees, and very fast because the trading happens directly from wallet to wallet. Besides, atomic swaps eliminate the need for regulation because the transaction is only controlled by the people participating in it.[304]

Atomic swaps could significantly change the crypto economy and make it self-governing if old fashioned centralized exchanges that can be regulated die out. The Lightning Network can allow users to trade anonymously in a decentralized manner and trusting that their privacy will be undisturbed.

The narrative of Lightning Network proponents is that one of the most important reasons for adopting the Lightning Network is that atomic swaps can only be conducted via Lightning payment channels. To be able to conduct atomic cross chain swaps, the cryptocurrencies that you and your trading partner want to exchange also have to use the same cryptographic protocol. For example when Charlie Lee, the creator of Litecoin conducted the first successful atomic swap exchanging Litecoin for Bitcoin, and Vertcoin for Decred, he could execute those swaps because all these cryptocurrencies use the same SHA-256 cryptographic hash function.[305] If you wanted to exchange bitcoins for example for ethers, that would not be possible because Ethereum has a different hashing protocol called Ethash.[306]

Andrew DeSantis, the creator of the decentralized operating system called DeOS (http://deos.ai) has a very different view on the value of the Lightning Network atomic swaps. He claims that Bitcoin works according to the rules of quantum mechanics. In an interview he said that the Lightning Network is nothing more than a bug in Bitcoin because it leaks value off Bitcoin into Litecoin (when doing atomic swaps). He also said that "we have always been able to do atomic swaps and we have always been able to do instant atomic swaps via transactions because we have always been able to use payment channels. And so Lightning just lets us have payment channels that are open for different amounts of time and payment channels that work in a different way. It's just a different configuration of payment channels and on a network on top of it."[307]

According to DeSantis, Bitcoin had privacy before SegWit and now it doesn't, so it has to rely on sidechain solutions to achieve the privacy that was stripped off it.[308] This opinion ties in with the view that certain corporations including Blockstream have made sure to remove some of the important features of Bitcoin so that they could build their own value-extracting money machines in the form of sidechain products. To DeSantis the Lightning Network is just such a money machine because "it doesn't build Bitcoin up into becoming a more valuable system."[309]

To be able to conduct a transaction with an atomic cross chain swap, the user first has to download the blockchains of both currencies that he would like to exchange. This is a limiting factor as it is not very convenient for the average user. Also, there is some programming knowledge needed to set up an atomic cross chain swap, which is further limiting the number of users who can take advantage of this feature.[310]

There are already some works in the process to eliminate the need for downloading the entire blockchains for users to be able to conduct atomic swaps. One of the most promising projects is being developed by the *Komodo* team who are building a decentralized exchange called BarterDEX. They already successfully completed an atomic swap using an Electrum server which allows users to conduct atomic swaps without having to download the blockchains of the cryptocurrencies they wish to exchange.[311]

The Komodo website describes how before the atomic swap technology "each blockchain was like an island with only one bridge off: to either Bitcoin (for BTC-protocol coins) or Ether (for Ethereum-based ERC-20 tokens). Once on the larger islands of Bitcoin and Ethereum, traders had more bridges to choose from. However, every other bridge just led to another isolated island with only one exit option. Komodo's atomic swap technology builds bridges between 95% of all the coins and tokens in existence. As a result, traders will never be stranded on a small blockchain island ever again. This is the first stage of blockchain interoperability."[312]

The second stage of blockchain interoperability is achieving cross-chain transaction proofs and fungibility. With Komodo's new cross-chain smart contract technology exchanges can take place between two chains without a swap or trade occurring.[313]

Komodo is definitely one project worth watching as in June 2018 they ran a successful test in which Komodo outperformed Visa in terms of the number of transactions.[314] Komodo itself is a blockchain platform with its cryptocurrency token also called Komodo. This token is transparent, anonymous, private and fungible. Komodo achieves security by a delayed proof of work protocol which creates backup of its own blockchain data and "notarizes" it to the Bitcoin blockchain. By adding update information to the Bitcoin blockchain Komodo achieves a Bitcoin-level security. Moreover, users can choose to integrate zero-knowledge proofs for privacy protection.[315]

The Lightning Network is not "forced" on the users of the Bitcoin network, so we cannot really tell when its adoption will be completed because it is at the sole discretion of each node to adopt it. Unless Bitcoin will be adopted relatively quickly as a day-to-day payment tool instead of the current situation of being rather only a tool of speculation and a store of value, it is likely that the adoption of the Lightning Network will be relatively slow.[316] However, if we take into account the positive features of atomic cross chain swaps, maybe this adoption will happen sooner than we would think.

Probably because of the way so much of our time is tied up in activities that we do not want to do, like going to work and doing things that add no real value to the world or serve only a few and are detrimental to the rest, and because on top of it we are taxed and abused in numerous ways, we have become a society of seekers of the least resistance. We do not really care about privacy breaches or potential negative consequences of willingly (and many times unknowingly) handing over our valuable private data and personal information in exchange for more convenience. For example, we use credit cards when we could use cash, even if we know that we give away valuable information about our purchasing habits or our location at the moment of making the payment.

So it is sensible to say that the privacy of cryptocurrencies and other related systems will largely depend on what consumers demand. If the Lightning Network somehow manages to lure ten times as many new users into using Bitcoin than the current number of users and these new users will be more interested in having low transaction fees and fast transactions than in having privacy, the companies who are developing the various iterations of the Lightning Network will focus on speed and low transaction costs and will not care much about privacy either.[317]

Unfortunately, it seems that both for Bitcoin and for digital currencies in general the demand for privacy by the public is quite low. People generally do not think about possible long-term consequences, and that is not a good thing. Because of the current protocol decisions that make Bitcoin costly and slow, there is a chance that the Lightning Network will become widely used at one point in time. As it is expensive to operate a routing node, there is a high likelihood that the system will develop a hub-and-spokes structure. The small number of hubs may make it easy for attackers to overcome privacy protection measures. Besides, because everything happens off the blockchain, users would have little information to find out how much of their privacy is actually lost. The hubs would become information-sucking havens to privacy attackers and financial censors, including the official ones, which would mean that the privacy of Bitcoin users would be very low.[318]

There is a real centralization risk that comes from forcing everyone to use a second layer to conduct transactions due to the slowness and costliness of the Bitcoin blockchain. You can only send a transaction through a payment channel if that has equal or more money deposited into it by its two creators than your transaction amount. This obviously leads to centralization of the Lightning Network because the more money the creators of a channel had deposited, the more larger transactions can use it in their routing to reach the destination of the transaction. This tendency can already be seen today.[319]

The Lightning Network while solving many privacy problems also introduces new ones. The anonymity provided by the Lightning Network is similar to that of the traditional banking system: it keeps information of users hidden from other users and non-users, but the hubs, just like the banks, have access to user information. Its use of onion routing does help privacy, and another benefit is that the hubs do not request personal data from users to be able to operate. But the downside is that some public information, including the sizes of the payment channels, is available to all nodes, and the opening and closing transactions are also public.[320]

"It seems there is a consensus in all parts of the crypto sphere that Layer 2 is needed and needs to mature more, whereas Layer 1, the blockchain, should be considered as a distributed database reserved to only long/medium-term storage of larger values where you can wait for blockchain confirmations."[321] At the time of writing this book, the implementation of the Lightning Network has already started on the Bitcoin network and it is also being launched by other cryptocurrencies such as Litecoin, Stellar and Zcash (and even the non-crypto cuckoo's egg, Ripple).

Other privacy enhancing protocols for Bitcoin

Apart from the Lightning Network various other projects are worth mention-ing that are geared toward making sure that the Bitcoin network protects the privacy of its users. "Bitcoin gives you a choice to be your own bank. This way of using it requires a more privacy aware approach than using traditional institutes because they provide you privacy against your neighbors and your stalker ex-husband. If we do not improve Bitcoin's fungibility you can start practicing to live a perfect life, where you not only comply with the rules of your government but with the expectations of every other human being as well you ever get contact with during your time on this world."[322]

Currently, 99% of all Bitcoin users (meaning those who pay with it, not the traders and hodlers) who use a privacy feature opt for using Bitcoin mixers to regain their privacy and they more heavily rely on the centralized ones, which is ironic. For whatever reason, there are only a few coin-mixing projects that came out of research and are not centralized, these being TumbleBit, JoinMarket and Zero Link/Chaumian Coin Join.[323]

TumbleBit

While the Lightning Network is primarily aimed at providing portability to Bitcoin so that it can be used in practice in everyday situations, *TumbleBit* wants to provide fungibility to Bitcoin by making each transaction anonymous, while at the same time also increasing transaction velocity. The payment hub of TumbleBit called the *tumbler* cannot steal bitcoins from users. TumbleBit users enjoy anonimity even against the TumbleBit service due to the unlinkability of users and payments.[324]

TumbleBit is a protocol built on top of the Bitcoin main chain that creates payment channels between users using a centralized tumbler to obscure the relationship between users and their payments. The payment channels are off the blockchain, just like in the case of the Lightning Network. TumbleBit hides the sender and the receiver of a transaction using a trustless intermediary called a tumbler to enhance anonimity. TumbleBit has all participants send coins and receive the same amount of different coins in return at the same time. This breaks the trail of ownership of the coins and the tumbler has no way to figure out who participated in which transaction. This way the tumbler of TumbleBit cannot steal bitcoins or undermine the anonimity of the participants of the transactions.[325]

Similarly to the Lightning Network, users have to open a payment channel by depositing money in a first layer blockchain transaction. Once the payment channel is set up, users can send payments via the tumbler. As payments are made off-chain, TumbleBit can handle a high volume of transactions fast because there is no need for miner validation of the transactions. The TumbleBit payment hub provides anonimity to its users and fungibility to the coins involved in those transactions, while maintaining the same level of security as transactions made on the blockchain.[326]

The final balance after all transactions conducted on TumbleBit only gets recorded on the main chain after the user decides to close his payment channel and broadcasts this as a transaction on the blockchain. Similarly to the Lightning Network, the on-blockchain channel opening and closing transactions are relatively slow (as slow as the Bitcoin network), but the off-chain transactions, the actual TumbleBit payments, may take only seconds to complete. By adding only two transactions on the blockchain (the payment channel opening and closing transactions) TumbleBit processes many transactions, allowing Bitcoin to increase its maximum transaction volume.[327]

TumbleBit has two modes, the first is a classic Bitcoin tumbler which is a mixing service used to mix potentially identifiable funds so that the individual coins of various transactions in the tumbler cannot be traced back to their senders. The second one is the unlinkable Bitcoin payment hub mode. The main innovation of TumbleBit is *unlinkability* which ensures that nobody can tell which of the payers paid to which of the receivers in the payment phase. The only information that is available to others is the amount a user deposited to open the payment channel and the amount he withdrew once the channel was closed.

To achieve unlinkability, the probability of any of the possible transactions has to be equal. The more compatible possible transactions there are, the more anonymity TumbleBit can provide. If there are two payers and two recipients, the probability to find the recipient who received the payment from the first payer is 50%, but if there are ten payers and ten recipients, the probability goes down to 10%. To avoid decreasing the security of Bitcoin payments, this unlinkability is achieved by a puzzle-promise-protocol and the RSA-puzzle-solver protocol.

If Alice wants to pay Bob using TumbleBit, after both of them having set up a payment channel between the tumbler and themselves (unlike Lightning Network, these channels are not peer-to-peer but peer-to-hub), Alice has to provide Bob with a solution to a puzzle. The puzzle is generated through interaction between Bob and the tumbler, and solved through interaction between Alice and the tumbler. Each time a puzzle is solved, 1 bitcoin is transferred from Alice to the tumbler and each time Bob learns a solution 1 bitcoin is transferred from the tumbler to Bob[328].

So technically, Alice does not pay to Bob but instead pays the tumbler for solutions to the puzzle of Bob using the puzzle-solver protocol where 1 bitcoin is exchanged for 1 puzzle solution. Bob then receives 1 bitcoin from the tumbler each time he learns the solution to his puzzle.

The tumbler would know that it is Alice who is paying Bob if Alice gave the same puzzle to the tumbler that the tumbler gave to Bob. In such a case attackers would only have to somehow get that information from the tumbler to have access to the information of the transactions. To avoid this, Bob has to blind the puzzle by multiplying it with a randomly chosen number.[329] "This allows Alice to pay Bob by paying the Tumbler for a solution to a blinded RSA puzzle without revealing to the Tumbler which puzzle is being solved. All the Tumbler observes is Alice buying solutions to random puzzles that the Tumbler never issued. Thus, the Tumbler cannot link the solution to any puzzle to an issued puzzle."[330]

The TumbleBit project is still in development. For the moment a payment channel only works in one direction (either from the sender to the tumbler, or from the tumbler to the receiver). So if you want to be able to both send and receive payments with TumbleBit, you will have to set up two appropriate payment channels.[331]

Another current limitation is that all the payments must be of the same denomination. For example, if the denomination is set to 0.01 btc, then if you wanted to pay 0.1 btc via Tumblebit you would have to make ten 0.01 btc payments. The developer team is working on finding a way that would allow TumbleBit to use arbitrary denominations without losing its unlinkability.[332]

In the second half of 2018 the mainnet beta of the *Breeze Wallet* was released by Stratis Group Ltd. The Breeze Wallet is a decentralized in-wallet implementation of TumbleBit. Breeze is open-source so anybody can verify if it is as safe as Stratis says. The tumbling is performed by Stratis Masternodes which were released on the Bitcoin mainnet earlier. Masternodes provide a discoverable and trustless service on the blockchain, removing the need to trust a third party. So unlike with centralized mixing services, the funds of the users cannot be stolen by an attacker during the tumbling.[333]

When you want to send money with privacy using TumbleBit in your Breeze wallet, Breeze will inform the Masternode server which will select the Masternodes that meet the requirements of your transaction and randomly choose a Masternode to perform the tumbling. Because the election of the Masternode happens randomly, the tumbler and the users participating in the tumbling cannot collude to breach anonymity.[334]

The level of anonymity of each tumbling cycle is equal to the number of participants. If there are 100 people tumbling, including you, your anonymity set will be 100. This is better than most privacy solutions for Bitcoin and it even beats Monero, which is one of the most important privacy coins. Monero only achieves an anonymity set of between 2 and 10.[335]

An anonymity set is a pattern used to create privacy by aggregating multiple entities into a set to make them indistinguishable so that third parties cannot track the location of users, analyze their behavior or infringe on their privacy in other ways.[336] It is generally accepted that an anonymity set above 50 could provide sufficient anonymity.

CoinJoin

CoinJoin is another popular Bitcoin privacy protocol which has been around since 2013. Its name is a reference to the way the protocol mixes the bitcoins of the sender of a payment with bitcoins of other users on a joint payment platform before sending them to the intended recipient. This makes the transaction untraceable, but blockchain analysis can easily show that CoinJoin was used for a transaction.[337]

CoinJoin pairs up two transactions and makes a joint payment, so that while each recipient receives the exact amount their payer wanted to send them, observers cannot relate inputs and outputs within the same bitcoin transactionaa so third parties cannot know who exactly received payment from whom. This increases fungibility because the joint payment obfuscates from which sender to which recipient a particular bitcoin is moving.[338]

CoinJoin type mixing is a proposal of Adam Gibson, one of the main CoinJoin developers, meant to address the fungibility issue of Bitcoin. He believes that adding a Lightning Network payment channel to the anonymity process of CoinJoin will make it nearly impossible to identify the sender of a particular bitcoin. A proof of concept has been released in mid-2018 and Gibson stated that although the technology to achieve the goals of his proposal exists, a phase of research and development is necessary to achieve it.[339]

CoinJoin type mixing increases privacy for all users, including those who do not use mixing because not all inputs will always come from a single wallet, so third parties cannot reliably associate inputs with a single user. However, there is a weakness of CoinJoin. If several people create a transaction to send money back to themselves, they can use addresses to avoid being identified. If all senders participating in the transaction send the same amount, a third party cannot find out which new addresses belong to whom. But somebody has to construct this mixing transaction and for that he has to know both the old and the new addresses of each sender. There is no way for the senders to know if the person who constructs this mixing transaction is trustworthy or not. If he were a spy, the privacy of the transaction would be easily broken.[340]

The *Wasabi wallet* created by Ádám Ficsór seems to offer a way to successfully overcome this weakness of CoinJoin. Ficsór used a solution called *Chaumian CoinJoin*. This earlier, neglected proposal by David Chaum proposed to prevent spying with the help of a blind signature scheme. To prevent third parties from spying on the participants in a CoinJoin transaction, the senders have to connect to a central Chaumian CoinJoin server which can be operated by a wallet provider. They provide their old addresses and blinded (cryptographically scrambled) receiving addresses to the server and the server signs those. The participants then disconnect from the server and reconnect using a hidden connection like Tor and only provide their unblinded addresses.[341]

The server can verify if an unblinded address matches with a blinded address, so the server learns that the provided addresses indeed belong to the participants without knowing which address belongs to whom.

The Wasabi wallet is an open-source Bitcoin wallet for desktop which can be run on Linux, OSX, and Windows as well. Wasabi was released on the tenth anniversary of the Bitcoin whitepaper, on October 31, 2018.[342]

According to its creator, Wasabi is the "only truly light wallet that is already deployed and that does not fail against network analysis, thus protects your privacy against network observers."[343] The wallet uses Tor anonymity network and complies with the ZeroLink wallet fungibility framework.

The implementation of the Chaumian CoinJoin is said to enforce a constant 100 anonymity set which is the highest value used today. In Chaumian CoinJoin the coordinator of the mix, the mixing server cannot steal the participants' money, neither can it deanonymize the participants. The wallet is operated by a company called zkSNACKs which takes 0.3% mixing fees.[344]

Just to have a basis of comparison for how the Chaumian CoinJoin implementation by Wasabi wallet provides the best available anonymity, while cash has an anonymity set in the millions because there are millions and millions of banknotes in circulation, Monero, the most popular privacy coin has an anonymity set of 2-10. Zcash, another very popular privacy coin does not enforce any anonymity set by default, though its users can opt for enabling its privacy features which can seriously increase anonymity.

In contrast, Wasabi constantly provides an anonymity set of 100.[345] The downside is that it is a centralized service provided by a company.

The Lightning Network is not fully anonymous because while it provides anonymity toward other users, the user does not have privacy towards the hub he is connected to. One of the aspects of using the Lightning Network that decreases privacy is the opening and closing transactions that are broadcast to the blockchain. The developers of the Wasabi wallet are planning to provide users with a service to do such on-blockchain Lightning Network opening and closing transactions with coinjoin technology to increase privacy for Bitcoin users.[346]

The Wasabi wallet, however, has some weaknesses, for example that it is round based and transactions will not execute until there is enough liquidity to do the next round, so mixing can take a long time. Also, currently rounds have a common denomination, which is 0.1 btc. Having many coins means that you will have to participate in many mixing rounds while those users who have only a few coins will not be able to participate.[347]

JoinMarket

JoinMarket is the most interesting implementation of CoinJoin. JoinMarket is not a software or a service, but a market where makers (senders) and takers (receivers) can make CoinJoin transactions. JoinMarket arranges the right amount of coins because transactions are of random size, so participants do not have to wait for somebody who wants to transact with the same amount of coins as they do.[348]

A taker will pay a fee to the maker for mixing his coins. There is no need to use a centralized service, and the private keys are always controlled by the users. Despite its potential, JoinMarket is not very popular because its installation requires significant technical knowledge and time.

The Dandelion protocol

The *Dandelion* protocol has been developed by various people at Carnegie Mellon, MIT and the University of Illinois. Peer-to-peer analysis by research companies and authorities has been very important in breaking the privacy of the Bitcoin network and one of the main promises of Dandelion is to make this peer-to-peer analysis worthless so that user identity can no longer be compromised.[349] The May 2018 research paper titled *Dandelion++ Lightweight Cryptocurrency Networking with Formal Anonymity Guarantees* proposes some improvements to the original Dandelion protocol.

The Dandelion++ propagation protocol aims at providing privacy guarantees for broadcasting a transaction to the blockchain without the use of encryption. Dandelion promises transaction privacy even if there is a widely connected supernode that can monitor the network. It is cheap, uses no encryption and can be seamlessly integrated into the Bitcoin network without having to change implementation or consensus rules.[350]

Dandelion provides privacy to the process of broadcasting a transaction to the network only. It cannot hide or obscure connections between new coins and old addresses, it cannot obscure addresses or balances, or mix transactions. Enhancing the privacy of the transaction broadcasting process is important because currently a highly connected node can relatively easily establish a connection between the sender of a transaction and his IP address. The node only has to correlate the times a transaction was received to the nodes they were received from. The Bitcoin blockchain anonymity is quite weak and allows third parties to link transactions to IP addresses with over 30% accuracy.[351]

Now taking into account the fact that all transactions are recorded on the blockchain till eternity, a highly connected node could easily get information about all the transactions you ever made, find out your IP address and from that your physical location. How is that for safety? Before you say you have nothing to hide if you behave and play according to the rules, think how legal and illegal entities could use this information against you. Criminals might use this information to rob you.

Privacy "isn't necessarily about protecting against corporations that would sell your data, governments who want to use or control your financial activity, making 'nefarious' purchases on the darkweb [obligatory scary voice], or evading taxes. The Bitcoin network is a global and open network built from entirely open source software. This is about simply rebuilding the most basic privacy barriers between yourself and literally anyone on the internet."[352]

The weakness in privacy comes from how transactions are broadcast simultaneously to the network by diffusion, meaning that a node broadcasts the transaction to all the nodes it is connected to and then those nodes will broadcast it further to other nodes that are directly connected to them, until the transaction reaches every node of the network. This broadcasting process is called diffusion. The issue with diffusion on the Bitcoin blockchain is that the IP address of the source node (the sender's node) can be identified because "collaborating spy nodes" can conduct network analysis together and trace the transaction back to its origin.[353]

Dandelion deals with this weakness by making it more difficult to trace transactions back to their senders. Before starting to propagate the transaction to the network (before the actual broadcasting), the protocol sends it randomly through a variable number of nodes. This is where Dandelion got its name from because the random path is similar to a singular stem, while the diffusion phase, in which the transaction is broadcast to multiple nodes simultaneously, resembles the "fluff" of a dandelion.[354]

Basically, Dandelion hides the original node that initiated the transaction. The anonymity phase of the protocol is the stem phase in which the transaction is passed on to randomly selected nodes in a linear fashion. To make it more difficult to trace the transaction back to its originator, each node that receives the transaction during the stem phase has to "flip a coin" to decide whether the node will continue the stem phase or will start the propagation phase. That is why the number of nodes making up the stem phase is random.[355]

Each node in the stem phase has a 90% chance to continue with the stem phase and send the transaction on to one node. To make the process more unpredictable, the propagation or fluff phase starts when a node rolls a "fluff" and immediately broadcasts the transaction publicly (thus starting the diffusion phase), or a time delay expires which is determined by each stem node individually. The time delay is determined probabilistically which makes sure to avoid any patterns regarding which stem node will expire first. It prevents the first node that receives the transaction from always being the first to broadcast the transaction.

Due to the 90% probability, the average stem consists of 10 hops. This is a high enough degree of separation that can ensure that no matter which node initiates a transaction, it could end up being broadcast from any other node, due to the principle of 6 degrees of separation (or the Kevin Bacon game) and the high interconnectivity of the Bitcoin network.[356]

Also, in the stem phase the transaction is handled as private and is not available for query by other nodes and it is kept separate from other transactions even in the mempool. The transaction is only visible to those nodes that receive it, i.e. the nodes that are part of the stem phase.[357]

For any new transactions the Dandelion protocol randomly picks a set of nodes (the anonymity set) that will set up the *stem phase*. Meanwhile this group of nodes is active, the same paths are reused. By creating uniform patterns that all transactions follow while using this set of nodes, any data that could be used to distinguish a transaction from another is eliminated.[358]

When the transaction enters the *fluff phase*, it returns to normal Bitcoin diffusion and the transaction is broadcast to many nodes simultaneously. At this stage the transaction appears as public and visible in the mempool, however, it is not possible to see the path through which it got there. To complicate the propagation even more, each node of the stem phase is checking continuously if the transaction has been released publicly. When the stem nodes see that the transaction went public, every stem node immediately broadcasts their copy to their own peer nodes. For an outside observer it appears that the transaction is suddenly being propagated from multiple nodes at different locations in the network simultaneously.[359]

Dandelion could potentially become a widespread propagation protocol for not only Bitcoin but for other blockchains as well because the stem phase only takes a few seconds, so it does not affect negatively the user experience regarding speed. It is also very lightweight and can be implemented without changes to the underlying Bitcoin protocol.

Dandelion provides near optimal privacy using the concept of hiding in the crowd, and due to the fact that the anonymity set is chosen at random, anybody who would try to spy on transactions would find it difficult to do it because it is difficult for a spy to insert himself into a randomly selected group.

Because of this difficulty, adversaries are likely to try to attack by running Dandelion nodes, but if such a node behaves abnormally, the stem will end prematurely while still maintaining higher anonymity than what standard Bitcoin propagation provides. So even if only a part of the users of the network participate in Dandelion or during its adoption phase, Dandelion will provide heightened privacy to its users.[360]

The developers of the cryptocurrency *Zcoin* have already realized the usefulness of Dandelion in providing anonymity. Zcoin became the first cryptocurrency to adopt the Dandelion protocol in October 2018.[361] In comparison, Monero which is one of the most successful privacy coins has been working on implementing a Tor type onion routing protocol since 2014 to achieve anonymity. This developmental process is quite slow because routing over the Tor network can only be successful if you have access to global, up-to-date information about the network.[362]

In contrast, Dandelion was first introduced only in 2017 and was revised in May 2018 as Dandelion++. It is highly likely that in the near future Dandelion will be implemented in a Bitcoin Core update, especially because it does not involve having to mess with the main Bitcoin code.[363] In 2019 a test has been conducted on a smaller version of the Bitcoin network and the developers reported no software incompatibilities between Bitcoin and Dandelion.[364]

As we have seen, privacy, anonymity (and not the pseudonymity of Bitcoin), and untraceability are necessary for a digital currency to be truly fungible. If a digital currency is not fungible, especially if it is blockchain based, it is less desirable, as you can never know when a coin you just received as a payment was involved in something shady which may result in that coin being taken away from you due to its tainted history.

Also, Western governments and authorities, for example the Europol, the police force of the European Union, have already started to monitor bitcoin transactions. The Spanish tax authority for example announced that they obtained information from banks and exchanges (legally or not, is another question) in order to monitor people who have bought bitcoin. A blockchain based digital currency without the necessary privacy, anonymity, and fungibility features just makes it easier for governments to control "their" people.

The Dutch authorities in collaboration with the Europol started to investigate one of the biggest tumbler services called Bestmixer (bestmixer.io) which they finally shut down in May 2019 because of money laundering. Bestmixer had a turnover of $200 million since its launch in May 2018. It is worth mentioning that the investigations started in June 2018 already. This was the first procedure of its kind against a tumbler service.[365]

If you visit the website of Bestmixer, you can read the following message: "This service has been seized by the Dutch Financial Criminal Investigation Service (FIOD) under the authority of the Dutch Prosecutor's Office. Dutch law enforcement have started an investigation on Bestmixer.io in June 2018. In this investigation we have collected information about transactions, letters of guarantee and support messages. You are not anonymous."[366]

Will Bestmixer be the only mixing service investigated by the authorities? That would be very unlikely. What is more probable is that all of them will be outlawed at one point in time.

Any digital currency that cannot ensure fungibility and sufficient privacy via its protocols is either not optimal for everyday use (to say the least), or if such a digital currency will be used in everyday life, I suspect that means that the dystopian world of Orwell's 1984 has arrived. There are a couple of cryptocurrencies among the most popular ones that are privacy coins, so it would be sensible to prefer those in your transactions.

We have seen the same old tactic used in the mass media: they never tire of repeating that criminals love to use Bitcoin to get away from law enforcement and go about their illegal activities undetected. They somehow forget to mention that criminals have been using fiat currencies as well for hundreds of years. That has never seemed to be a reason for authorities and governments to clamp down on fiat currencies (which, of course, is one of the main reasons for why they want to eliminate cash).

The blockchain analysis firm, Chainalysis in its recent webinar revealed some very interesting findings. It turns out that, contrary to what is being propagated by the media, only a relatively small percentage of all coins sent through mixing services have been used for illicit purposes and that the majority of people who opt for using mixing services simply choose to do so for privacy. However, illicit funds obtained on the dark web also get sent to coin mixers. Their findings showed that 8.1 percent of all mixed coins were stolen and only 2.7 percent of the coins had been used on darknet markets.[367] The large majority has nothing to do with illicit activities.

Criminals will always try to use ways that are less monitored, but it is not a good enough reason for law enforcement and the state to rob people in general of more of their freedoms and liberties. After all, most of the time "they" do know who the drug dealers, the human traffickers, the illegal weapon dealers are. There are technologies to catch all of them in a coordinated fashion. It is not everyday criminals that are the real problem.

The real problem may just as well be that the real, top level criminals are also the ones who are behind the systems that control humanity. That is why there has been a silent push to eliminate cash and bring down Bitcoin which may be the only current chance of people to escape total digital surveillance and control in the very near future if the controllers manage to fulfill their plans of creating a world government with one world currency. Such a world currency will likely be based on the blockchain, but will be as centralized and monitored as it gets.

They cannot grab total control over Bitcoin if people who already own some bitcoin decide to act on their principles and either hold on to their coins or choose to use them to pay so as to avoid the necessity of using a fully traceable and fully traced one world digital currency when society will become completely cashless in the very near future (unless we do something about it).

Getting rid of cash has been under way for quite some time. In Italy (one of the founding member states of the EU) for example it is already illegal to carry more than 500 euros in cash, and the reasoning behind it is that you would only do that for illegal activities. The European Union has planned out the step-by-step elimination of cash (but it is happening everywhere, not just in the EU).

The banks are slowly shutting down their ATM machines and bank branches to force all their clients to use only digital services, while communicating to their customers that they are turning away from cash as a response to the changed habits of their customers and because there is a need for going digital.

Banks basically force people into abandoning the use of cash more and more in favor of digital services by making it more difficult to use cash. This is the best strategy called "nudging" to make people choose the option the banks prefer.[368] The fact that they then communicate this as a change demanded by customers is quite disturbing though because the real motives behind it are more corporate profit (at least on the level of the banks) and total control (by the establishment). While it is all just to save costs on the banks' end and will likely result in more costs (card fees etc.) for the customers.

And then there is the serious issue of the billions of people who currently do not have access to banking and their only way to participate in the economy is to use cash and who will be completely cut off access to financial services once cash is abolished.

As Andreas Antonopoulous brilliantly stated in his talk of June 12, 2019 at the CryptoCompare Digital Asset Summit in London, "Surveillance never stopped crime. Surveillance is the license given to the people who are on the top of that to control our lives. *They* will commit crimes. *They* will commit the worst of crimes, what I call mega-crimes. And I know Britain doesn't use the metric system, so mega is the prefix we use for millions. A mega-crime is one where for example you foreclose on a million home owners and don't go to jail. That's a mega-crime. We're doing surveillance and analytics to catch a petty drug dealer who sells pot for bitcoin. Who's doing surveillance and analytics on Lockheed Martin[369], who's doing surveillance and analytics on the money laundering banks? Nobody. Do you know why? None of them will ever go to jail; the regulators are completely captured, and the very system of controlling finance from above by having levers of power over the lives of millions and billions of people, of having the audacity to cut off entire countries and say: well, they're under sanctions, they're not privileged enough, they're not people enough to gain financial services. Guess who that attracts. If you build levers of power like that, the very worst sociopaths in our society are attracted like flies to shit to grab hold of those levers of power and destroy all of your freedoms as quickly as they can. We are building societies in which one bad election is the last election."[370]

Not to mention what would happen if the Chinese social credit system were implemented worldwide (you can bet they have planned for it to happen all over the world not much further down the road) and all of a sudden you were unable to pay with cash, and the government (or the AI operating the social credit system) could deny accepting your credit or debit card if you did not behave as the government wants you to. Because, obviously, the banks and the controllers work hand in hand, benefiting from every move they can while the controllers are tightening the noose around the neck of the population.

Computer technology and the giant internet related tech corporations pose a further, newer threat to our freedom. The likes of Google, Facebook, Microsoft, and Amazon have already gained too much control over huge chunks of our lives and have managed to become ubiquitous and quasi-essential for our day-to-day routine.

Microsoft for example announced in May 2019 that they had been working for a year to launch *Ion*, a decentralized identity tool built on the Bitcoin blockchain. Microsoft is the first major technology company to use the Bitcoin blockchain for a decentralized infrastructure implementation. While currently they are using a testnet, Microsoft is planning to use the Bitcoin mainnet for the Ion project later in 2019.[371]

Facebook has announced around the same time their plans to launch what they first called Global Coin (insert evil laugh) and then renamed

Libra, which would essentially be a payment platform based on the Libra stable coin backed by planned US dollar investments of 100 hand picked corporate entities. However, after a two-day exhaustive hearing about Facebook's plans in July 2019 the US Congress "asked" Facebook to refrain from developing the Libra project. They obviously feel such a corporate project to be a threat to their own power and monetary system.

Amazon has already launched its blockchain-as-a-service product on its cloud computing subsidiary, Amazon Web Services in April 2019. The *Amazon Managed Blockchain* (AMB) is built on Ethereum and Hyperledger and will allow customers to create their own blockchain networks. They announced that the network can scale to millions of transactions.[372] Of course, when your blockchain is not decentralized it's not such an impressive achievement.

Besides AMB, Amazon has managed to patent a process of generating Merkle trees as a solution to the proof of work algorithm in May 2019. Merkle trees are used as a verification tool to constitute the work in the proof of work protocol.[373] While it is not clear how Amazon plans to use Merkle trees, it very well could be that they have been planning to create their own corporate coin first for AMB, and later for the entire Amazon platform. Even Changpeng Zhao, the CEO of Binance claimed that Amazon would eventually have to create its own digital currency.[374]

Those who were hoping to witness Google losing power due to the blockchain revolution will be disappointed to learn that the tech giant is not planning to go down the route of dinosaurs anytime soon. Google has already released blockchain transaction history datasets for Bitcoin and Ethereum in 2018, and in February 2019 they released further datasets for Bitcoin Cash, Dogecoin, Dash, Litecoin, Zcash and Ethereum Classic. Google's new software called *Blockchain ETL* (which stands for extract, transform, load) integrates with their machine learning/data analytics platform called Big Query ML. So as Michael Del Castillo put it, "Google is now in the blockchain search business".[375]

They obviously intend to monetize their new blockchain analytics and research tool which will be free only for the first terabyte of information[376] (which may sound like a lot today, but we could get to a point where it will not be considered much sooner than you may think). At the same time, Google's popular Keyword Planner tool apparently has stopped showing historical data for "blockchain" related keywords, at least that is what Irina Tsumarava alleges in her Medium blog and the embedded video in it.[377]

It looks like some of the tech giants are tirelessly working to use the information, data, and power they have amassed to integrate blockchain technology into their operations to spread their influence and monopolistic power to finance and finally to governance. The scary thing about this development is that none of these corporations are famous for their altruistic behavior and are definitely not the right actors to define the new rules for how society and the economy should work.

Another reason why it is a bad thing to give control of money to private corporations motivated by profit instead of treating money as a utility, just like electricity and water. And in lack of a currency which is treated only as a utility and not as a tool for speculation, hoarding or controlling others, the best shot we have is using a digital currency that cannot be controlled by anybody, instead of giving in to convenience and propaganda, and adopting a centrally run and controlled blockchain based digital currency.

Or we can be even more radical, step up to the plate and create a new, alternative, likely local currency system or set up a local gifting economy, and drop money completely in our day-to-day life and only use fiat or even cryptocurrencies when absolutely necessary. Of course, this would require building a resilient, small community based lifestyle, but that is for another book. It is always an option though.

11

Privacy First: Privacy Coins

M any developers and crypto anarchists realized the need for privacy from the beginning and developed their own coins which concentrate on providing as much privacy as possible as their main feature. These coins are called privacy coins. In this book we will only look at a couple of the most important ones and compare them to Bitcoin, but if you value your privacy, I recommend that you investigate further and look at other privacy coins so that you have a full picture.

Whether or not Satoshi Nakamoto intended for Bitcoin to have privacy in the long run, Bitcoin as it is today does not provide the necessary privacy for users who want to fly under the radar. From Satoshi's online communications it seems likely that he envisioned the future of Bitcoin with added second layer functionalities being developed to achieve specific goals. However, he likely did not expect these second layer solutions to be developed as projects of private corporations that work to keep the Bitcoin main chain dumbed down for their own interests. Or maybe he did.

Anyway, this wouldn't be the first time an open source software was later picked up and changed by corporate entities once they had found a way to extract profit from its alteration and development. Linux, for example, was developed as an open source software against what developers thought was a distorted situation where companies like Microsoft, Oracle, SAP etc. were "extracting monopoly-like 'rents' for software"[378]. However, later on several companies like Dell, IBM, Hewlett-Packard, Red Hat and SUSE decided to develop specialized products related to Linux for profit.[379]

In contrast to Bitcoin, privacy coins have all been created with privacy features incorporated into their base protocol and with privacy as their top priority. The question is then whether these coins are superior in terms of privacy as well as other basic tenets, especially if they are decentralized or not.

Monero

Monero (XMR) is the number one privacy coin today. It is considered to be the most secure and most anonymous cryptocurrency. Its aim is to provide complete privacy and anonymity to users. Monero hides the sender, the receiver, and the amount of money involved in a transaction, as well as the balance of the wallets of users. The Bitcoin Market Journal in its listing of private coins gives it 4.5 points out of 5 which is the highest rating to date.[380]

Monero achieves this high level of privacy and anonymity by incorporating five features.

To hide the sender, Monero uses *ring confidential addresses*. When sending money, the Monero protocol will randomly choose various other wallets that will form a virtual ring. It is impossible for a third party to find out which wallet in the ring actually sent money to the recipient.

Ring signatures are digital signatures that can be performed by any member of a group so that no matter who signs a transaction, it is accepted as endorsed by all the members of the group. In Monero, because of the use of ring signatures, third parties are unable to tell which member of the group of ring confidential addresses signed a given transaction. This obscures the account keys and public keys of users, making it impossible to link transactions to specific users. Monero also provides fungibility this way because the network has no information on which specific coin came from whom, so the history of a coin cannot be traced back without a doubt to its origin of birth.[381]

Using ring signatures means that each signer of the group has the same chance to actually have been the real signer. There are a list of possible signers, but without any evidence of which of them actually signed a given transaction.[382] On top of that, for each new transaction a new, arbitrary group is picked, so the real participants of any transaction can "hide in the crowd".

To hide the recipient, *stealth addresses* are used. A stealth address is similar to a virtual post office box that has no information about the identity of the recipient. The recipient can find the stealth address meant for him and open it using a special key. To send the money deposited in a stealth address, the recipient will generate a new ring of arbitrary addresses when starting the transaction.

However, Monero uses other smart features too to further obscure the participants of transactions. Besides arbitrarily picking signers for the ring, the protocol intentionally picks signers of earlier transactions which appear on the blockchain to use their signatures as decoys. Such signers of earlier transactions are called *mixins*. As a result, the real signer who is actually sending money is mixed with signers of past transactions in an indistinguishable way.

Whether a user achieves sufficient privacy will depend on the number of mixins a user will add to a transaction because this feature is based on dissociating the sender from a transaction and the more potential signers there are, the less likely it is to associate the actual sender with his transaction. Currently, the standard mixin size is 7, but users can choose to add more signers to rings.[383]

The combined use of ring confidential addresses and stealth addresses provide the users of Monero with private transactions where the identity of users of any specific transaction is not recorded on the blockchain. In comparison, Bitcoin users (both senders and recipients) need to reveal their "home address", while Monero users always use the equivalent of virtual post office boxes.[384]

The Monero team has also been working to find a way to implement broadcasting transactions over the Tor network, which is the most well known privacy focused routing protocol of the darkweb. They are trying to implement Tor routing into their core protocol, which would give additional privacy to Monero, however, it is a very time intensive quest because up-to-date information about the network is needed to be able to route over Tor. The Monero team has been trying to find a way to achieve Tor routing integration since 2014. Integrating with Tor or other alternatives would have their own limitations and extra costs, and the question remains whether they will ever be able to make it work.

Monero executed a hard fork on October 18, 2018 with two major objectives. One was to make Monero ASIC resistant by changing its proof of work algorithm in a way that deters miners from using ASIC mining equipment.[385] Similarly to the cases of Bitcoin and Ethereum, the use of ASIC miners have threatened Monero with centralization when Bitmain launched earlier in 2018 an ASIC miner specifically developed for mining Monero. Many believed that Bitmain had secretly been using ASIC miners to dominate Monero mining for several months.[386]

The other major objective of the hard fork was to integrate the *Bulletproof* protocol into the privacy functions of Monero to ensure a stronger protection and faster blockchain validation while lowering fees. Bulletproof is a zero-knowledge protocol developed by people at Stanford's Applied Cryptography Group which helps hide transaction amounts. Bulletproof does not hide sender and receiver addresses though. Zero-knowledge proofs can prove to the verifier that the prover actually knows a value without having to reveal what that value is.[387]

Bulletproof adds further privacy without having to use additional computational power. It reduces transaction size by 80% and makes the process of transaction verification easier. This can reduce transaction fees and increase the speed of the Monero network. Bulletproof is based on zk-SNARK technology which maintains privacy while making transactions considerably faster. Zk-SNARKs were first implemented by Zcash, the second most successful privacy coin which can attribute much of its success to this specific privacy protocol.[388]

A further peculiarity of Monero is that it does not have a block size limit. Instead, the network automatically adjusts the block size based on previous transactions and transaction volume. This solution makes Monero completely scalable. Also, Monero has a set supply of coins with programmed inflation. In the following eight years 18.4 million moneros will be mined (that is the set supply), after this initial period a 0.86% annual inflation rate will be applied, which will be used for miner compensation to maintain the network.[389]

Interestingly, researchers from Princeton University have recently developed a tool that is able to analyze Zcash transactions to a limited extent, however, admittedly, they have not been able to crack Monero. It is no surprise that blockchain analysis companies already mark 100% of Monero coins as "suspicious" because, according to them, there is no way to prove whether any Monero coins came from illegitimate sources or not.[390]

Especially since authorities have openly started using software tools to monitor people who use Bitcoin, privacy coins including Monero became more popular. According to a recent report of the Europol, the law enforcement agency of the European Union, Monero is one of the favorite cryptos of criminals.[391]

However, according to Monero core developer Riccardo Spagni, the users of Monero do not necessarily behave badly or do illegitimate things with their coins. Monero users value their privacy above all, and they do not want others to know "whether they're buying a coffee or a car"[392]. Again, we bump into the dichotomy of the state spying on its citizens and the inherent right of people to privacy, which is not only a right, but a basic human need. (And to make things even worse, in case of the EU we are talking about a supra-national entity that was created according to a sinister plan by methodically chipping away the supposed powers and rights to self-determination of the people of Europe.)

However, despite Monero boasting this rather convincing mix of privacy features which have earned it first place among privacy coins, rather disturbingly one of its features can actually neutralize all the privacy, anonymity, untraceability, and fungibility of Monero. There is a *public view key* that users can choose to share with other people. This public view key enables others to be able to see your transactions.[393]

The silver lining though is that while regulators in the future could indeed try to force users to provide them with their public view key (which means that Monero is auditable), such auditors would not have a complete picture. "By giving your public view key to an auditor, he would be able to see all your incoming transactions. However, to know the correct balance he would also need to know if you spent any of those (which he can't just with the view key). For this, you'd have to compute a key image for your every incoming transaction, and send those to the auditor. With this, the auditor could establish your current balance. Nice part is, that if you receive something new, the auditor can't know if you spent this new output without kindly asking for the matching key image. This gives the user certain control over how he's being audited and who can know what."[394]

So, if you want to take back your power from banks, governments, and other organizations usurping your natural rights, Monero may not be the right cryptocurrency for you after all. Why? You can transact completely privately, but should the regulators manage to force you to provide them with your public view key, they would have access to all of your transaction history and the balance of your account. How is that for privacy coin? The question maybe is whether they can force users to give away their public view keys if there is no way for them to be identified.

As an example, Binance, the China based cryptocurrency exchange giant does not request much personal data if you want to register to operate on their exchange. Up until you decide to transfer some Monero into your Binance account. In that case they do want you to provide all sorts of identification. This may be a common occurrence, especially later on, as the regulation of the crypto space becomes more and more solidified. Not only that, but now various exchanges decided to stop supporting privacy coins on their platforms. Monero users would eventually likely have to stay away from centralized exchanges and only operate peer-to-peer if they wanted to stay under the radar.

Zcash

Zcash (ZEC) was launched on October 28, 2016 as a *clone of Bitcoin* by developers and investors who set up the Zerocash Electric Coin Company LLC.[395] Its developers forked the Bitcoin codebase 0.11 and the difference between the two coins is that Zcash was created with privacy as its main goal. Its added functionalities are supposed to provide complete privacy to Zcash users.[396]

The identities of the sender and the recipients, as well as the transaction amount are protected from third parties by the *Zerocoin protocol* and a relatively rare zero-knowledge proof cryptography called *zero-knowledge Succinct Non-interactive ARgument of Knowledge* (or zk-SNARKs). With the use of zk-SNARKs transactions are not recorded on the blockchain, only a cryptographic proof which confirms that the transaction made was valid. No information about the amount, the sender, and the receiver are recorded on the blockchain.

It is called a zero-knowledge protocol because the verifier does not have to know the details of the transaction to be able to verify it. By using this protocol the sender can prove to the verifier that something is true without having to reveal any further information. The sender can validate something as true without having to reveal how he knows that truth and without having to reveal the content of this truth to the verifier.[397]

The sender receives a publicly generated key which he has to combine with the sender address, the recipient address and the transaction amount with a special prover key. The system analyzes the sender's response using a verifying key. If the transaction is valid, the verifying key will be true.

Because the sender does not disclose any specific information regarding the transaction itself, the verifier cannot be sure if the sender was just lucky to be able to give a "true" answer. So to eliminate the probability of giving the correct answer based on sheer luck, the system will propose a few of these tests with different generated keys. The sender will have to combine the transaction information and the special prover key with every publicly generated key. This means that the sender will not be able to consistently answer correctly, unless his transaction is valid. With each consecutive round the probability of being able to just get lucky is diminished.[398]

One of the most important novelties of zk-SNARKs is that they reduce the size of the proofs, and consequently, the effort it takes to verify them.[399] However, in order to hide the details of a transaction from third persons on the Zcash blockchain, a user has to opt to hide the sender, the recipient or both. The default setting of Zcash is to not hide the details of transactions. It could actually be quite a security flaw because the private transactions do not reach 15% of the total transaction traffic of Zcash. This means that users have to constantly change between the public and the private version of the blockchain when they want to. This in turn can possibly leak metadata that weakens anonymity.[400]

While Monero seems to have solved earlier issues found with the privacy of ring signatures, Zcash still has not provided a sufficient solution to avoid privacy breaches the likes of which it suffered in the past. A study in May 2018 found that "69 percent of shielded transactions could be linked to either founders or miners. This problem continues to hurt Zcash, mainly because of how few users are using stealth transactions on the network."[401] The Zcash team is working to be able to eliminate this issue.

Besides the above issues, it is also important to mention that the launch of Zcash was highly publicized as it was backed by some influential investors, which likely has something to do with the fact that there is a 20% "genius tax" that miners have to pay to the Zcash team during the first four years of the lifespan of Zcash.[402] This percentage is disproportionately high compared to incentives awarded to the developer teams of other cryptocurrencies. Also, there is no way to know whether the developers will institute further taxes once the initial four years expire.[403]

On the surface the genius tax contradicts the official description of Zcash on its website where it is tauted as "a decentralized and open source currency that provides financial privacy enabled by the *Zerocoin protocol*"[404]. Edward Snowden, the famous NSA whistleblower, however, believes that this genius tax indeed has a fundamental purpose. According to him, this "tax funds a quality team that catches and kills serious bugs in-house, before they get exploited. Some other projects learn about bugs like this only *after* people have lost money."[405] Sounds reasonable.

"Proven cryptography and auditability" are also publicized as core values of Zcash. It is understandable on part of the developers that they would want to placate the suspicions of the authorities by making their cryptocurrencies auditable and thus hopefully avoiding banning, but it does not take much thinking to come to a conclusion whether such coins are really private or not, especially knowing the low number of transactions for which users have opted to apply the optional privacy settings. Now couple this with the generous 20% "genius tax" paid to the developer team to see why there has been some controversy around Zcash.

Those who seek privacy generally would prefer decentralization, but this case appears to be a cash cow for the developers and investors of the Zcash team. Even so, Zcash has been one of the most popular privacy coins. Despite all the above, The Bitcoin Market Journal gave an overall 4.5 score to Zcash and 5 points for reputation, exactly the same as the scores of Monero. Meanwhile, as mentioned earlier, Monero has proved uncrackable to date to the researchers of Princeton University, while Zcash showed some weaknesses. This, combined with Monero having been around longer, is the reason why the first place among privacy coins should probably go to Monero.[406]

The latest news is that the Korean branch of the cryptoexchange OKEX announced that as of October 10, 2019 it will delist all five privacy coins it supported (namely, Monero, Dash, Zcash, Horizen and super bitcoin). Their reasoning was that these privacy coins "violate the Financial Action Task Force's (FATF) travel rule[407]. The FATF is not even an official institution, it's just a "global money laundering watchdog" which recently has issued crypto guidelines that "require exchanges to collect and transfer customer information during transactions".[408] The required details include the name and location of the sender and the name and account number of the receiver.

OKEx finally decided to keep supporting Zcash and Dash for the time being, but to still go ahead with delisting Monero, Horizen and super bitcoin.[409] Earlier, in August 2019 the UK based crypto exchange CEX.io announced that it will delist Zcash and Dash for the same reasons. Coinbase UK also delisted Zcash.[410] It is very likely that this tendency will continue.

Several of the highly regarded cryptocurrency projects, those that have maintained leading position on the market with the highest market capitalization throughout the bear market of 2018 and 2019, are working toward adding privacy features in one form or another. Both Monero and Zcash are holding up well in market capitalization, showing that there is a definite demand for privacy coins. As Riccardo Spagni from the team of Monero said, "privacy isn't a thing you achieve, it's a constant cat-and-mouse battle"[411], but it is definitely something worth fighting for.

12

Pages from the Crypto Bestiarium

T his book cannot include all the cryptocurrency developments and projects which bring novelty or which are noteworthy for various reasons. However, there are two projects, two "specimens" I want to touch upon with the aim of motivating the reader to further research for himself. This section is only a short introduction to two of the most weird species of the crypto bestiarium, and is far from comprehensive.

Ripple, the cuckoo's egg

Ripple (XRP) is the token used for paying transaction fees among users of the Ripple network services. Ripple was created in 2012 and has been in the top five on the cryptocurrency market charts for a very long time in terms of market capitalization, and recently took second place for a short time before Ethereum. Currently it ranks as number three based on market capitalization.

However, Ripple is a cuckoo's egg in that it is not a cryptocurrency, even though it is sold and traded on cryptocurrency exchanges. Nor is it a decentralized project. It is a creation of a private company and it was developed specifically to cater to banking clients, working for the banking system, providing them with faster and cheaper digital ways of money transfers between banks and other payment processor companies.[412]

Ripple is a blockchain based platform which has its own "currency" (also called Ripple) but allows its users to create their own tokens on the platform. Its Ripple (XRP) token is centrally issued and used by banks and payment processors to make and accept payments. The XRP tokens are not transferred in transactions of Ripple clients, instead they "were designed as a way for many market makers to make a paring with — thus allowing for many transactions to occur with only one hop: Currency 1 → XRP → Currency 2."[413]

The Ripple token has a (theoretically) fixed amount, and there are no miners in its ecosystem. Although the Ripple company says that the blockchain is completely independent from the company itself and that it would stay operational if the company happened to shut down, there is nothing that prevents the company from creating more tokens whenever they decide. At its launch 100 billion tokens were created, of which the Ripple company keeps 20% and has been distributing the rest, however, currently it has still in escrow around half of the total Ripple tokens.[414] There is also nothing stopping the Ripple company from releasing or withholding the rest of the tokens as they see fit.

Besides, due to the fact that it works in cooperation with current financial institutions, Ripple just does not seem like a decentralized cryptocurrency or a true crypto project developed in the spirit of what cryptocurrencies were meant to be at all. Transaction validation is performed by way of its specialized Ripple consensus algorithm, and instead of miners there are validators. Ripple clients have to create a list of identified, trusted participants and can only use those to validate their transactions.[415] Obviously, this is completely opposite to the decentralized nature of the transaction validation of Bitcoin. Jeff Berwick of *The Dollar Vigilante* calls Ripple a banker coin, and with good reason.

Currently, there are only 25 validator nodes in the network, and as the Ripple website states, they "intentionally haven't rushed the process"[416] of decentralization, although they are working on it. The actual Ripple blockchain may technically be decentralized, however, it is the Ripple company who grants validator status, and what's more, it is likely that all those validators, including all the nodes of the Ripple system, belong to the fan club of the controllers.

Even Ben Bernanke, former chairman of the Federal Reserve backs Ripple. When he was invited to a Ripple conference as a speaker, he stated that governments will squash Bitcoin if it becomes too important.[417] "Bitcoin is an attempt to replace fiat currency and evade regulation and government intervention. I don't think that's going to be a success", said Bernanke at a Ripple conference in Toronto.[418]

The Ripple company has three software products: *xCurrent*, which is a platform for banks for faster and cheaper international transactions; *xRapid* which allows banks to use Ripple tokens to settle funds more quickly for transactions in emerging markets. The newest product, *xVia* launched in 2018 is geared towards non-bank customers enabling them to conduct financial transactions as well.

The Ripple token is not necessary to use the Ripple blockchain software. Only xRapid uses XRP tokens.

Banks are currently using Ripple as a test. It is, however, more likely that banks will choose to develop their own proprietary blockchains instead of allowing an external company access to their data.

The Ripple network is just a transfer vehicle, helping banks to transact from fiat to Ripple and back to fiat. Moreover, Ripple is not a public company and banks do not have to use the XRP tokens to transact at all. As the XRP tokens are not shares, their owners cannot perceive profits after them from the company either, which means that XRP tokens have little value after all. But there is a clever marketing behind Ripple and its XRP tokens which blurs the lines.

We do not hear about the fact that the more than one hundred banks that use Ripple products are all using xCurrent which does not use XRP. There is only one bank that uses XRP as a digital currency and one small non-bank financial institution from Mexico that uses xRapid (and XRP). All this means that XRP, the token (which is, let me repeat, not a cryptocurrency) is not really gaining adoption as the marketing would make us believe. In terms of digital currency usage, it's really nothing to write home about.

It is sitting on the third spot on the list of top cryptocurrencies because most people who are in the crypto space think that the fact that Ripple caters to banks and financial institutions gives it more legitimacy and better chances for it to survive and grow.

The latest announcement of Ripple was that they will rebrand their products. They will stop using the confusing names of xRapid,xVia, and xCurrent, and opt for the much less complicated *Ripple Network* name.

IOTA, the Trojan Horse

Many people, especially those technically oriented, can hardly wait for all our electrical appliances to be integrated into one giant data streaming network. The idea is that all technical devices will eventually become "smart", meaning that they will be connected to a global internet of machines called the Internet of Things (IOT) with the aim to function as an interconnected network of intelligent appliances exchanging micropayments with other appliances in their daily automated functioning.

Well, those people must certainly feel euphoric because of *IOTA*, the *Internet Of Things Application*. IOTA is the first cryptocurrency that is *not based on blockchain technology*. It is a public distributed ledger which was developed in December 2015 for machine to machine payments.

The idea is that IOTA will provide an infrastructure for smart devices (which will include anything from sensors, smart locks, cameras, printers, fridges, even bread toasters and basically any machine you have around you that works with electricity). Those smart appliances would be continuously connected to the internet to be able to communicate any time to buy or sell resources, autonomously making micropayments. The token of IOTA is called *MIOTA*. While it is traded as a regular cryptocurrency, it was invented for machine to machine payments only for the internet of things.[419]

IOTA provides free transactions, has no scalability issues, and actually the bigger the number of smart appliances that use the network, the quicker transactions become. IOTA can achieve scalability and free micropayments because instead of blockchain it is based on a new protocol called *Tangle*. The Tangle is a new distributed ledger based on *directed acyclic graph* (DAG).[420]

The basic idea behind the Tangle is that each transaction "forms a brand new block and essentially verifies itself. In order for one to successfully complete a transaction on the Tangle, one must first verify two other pending transactions, allowing for an extremely simple version of proof of work to take place."[421]

IOTA is supported by the CEO of Fujitsu and the company has already incorporated IOTA for its internal operations and is working on a test product for the manufacturing and automotive industries. The automotive supplier Bosch is already collaborating with IOTA, while Audi started negotiations with IOTA about its potential use in their vehicles. Volkswagen also collaborates with IOTA and has launched a concept of use about using Tangle for secure software transfer.[422] Volkswagen also plans to release blockchain cars already in 2019 in collaboration with IOTA.[423]

IOTA wanted to create its own decentralized Internet of Things data marketplace, partnering with various major companies. In November 2018 Bosch, the engineering and electronic manufacturer company announced that it is working on a "universal programmable sensor device" which will be essential for the economy of IOTA's data marketplace. The sensors will "simultaneously collect, upload, and sell data".[424]

It is clear that major corporations have been investing and working along the lines of moving toward the Internet of Things, which is tauted as the bringer of a new dawn of connectivity, automation, optimization, and efficiency into our lives.

Initially, it may seem as a fantastic development, but do we really need an Internet of Things with the technical parameters and infrastructure we have now? It may be convenient for companies and the individual to some extent, but will it be beneficial for us as individuals and as a species in the grand scheme of things?

Do we really have to have an intelligent fridge to buy our food on our behalf? Would that be the ultimate happiness or efficiency? Will the negative effects of the increased level of electromagnetic frequency (EMF) radiation be worth it as a trade-off for automating basic actions, like restocking our fridge or detecting when the detergent runs out and buying new supply?

If all our appliances will turn into smart devices connected via wifi to the internet continuously, what will that mean in terms of liveability? How will that impact the human biology and psyche? We already are exposed to way more electromagnetic radiation than what is healthy. It has been widely documented by scientists and medical doctors that electromagnetic radiation caused by the wireless phone system is detrimental to human health, causing a plethora of diseases, including "altered gene expression, altered metabolism, altered stem cell development, cancers, cardiovascular disease, cognitive impairment, DNA damage, impacts on general well-being, increased free radicals, learning and memory deficits, impaired sperm function and quality, miscarriage, neurological damage, obesity and diabetes, oxidative stress".[425]

While constantly creating all sorts of petty drama for the masses to focus on instead, the controllers are now silently implementing the 5G telecommunication system which in order for it to work properly needs the installation of smaller, local antennas every few hundred feet away or so, instead of the giant cell towers we are currently used to. While with earlier generation mobile networks (up to 4G) we still can escape from the source of radiation by moving away from cell towers and turning off the wifi, at least at night, it will not be possible to opt out and escape once 5G is implemented in the area you live in because it will be there everywhere, beaming you and your loved ones 24 hours a day.

5G refers to "5th generational" but it is important to know that there is a *qualitative difference* between the frequencies used by 4G and 5G. The current 4G system utilizes frequencies up to 6 gigahertz (6GHz). This newest, 5th generation of cell towers received authorization without health safety studies to operate between 6 GHz and 100 GHz and even above, utilizing sub-millimeter and millimeter waves.[426] You may be "lucky" to have one of those 5G small-range antennas installed outside your house and be exposed to extremely disturbing and harmful millimeter range frequencies non-stop.

There has been enough evidence that these frequencies harm living organisms, and especially harm humans, causing infertility, brain tumors and various other ailments. Why do you think the workers who are installing these 5G towers wear protective clothing against radiation? It is very concerning that this system is being rolled out without prior study into its public health implications and that governments are auctioning these frequencies to any company that wants to pay for them. In contrast, not everybody can buy the right to utilize radio frequencies which radio stations use to emit their programs, which is quite weird.

German scientist Harald Kautz Vella says that 5G will likely not be lethal in the sense that it will not kill the current population, however, it has been tested on some unfortunate rats and was proven that after being irradiated with 5G frequencies, those frequencies prevented the healthy development of the ovaries in the fetuses of the rats, and the offspring of the irradiated rats became infertile and, logically, there was no third generation.[427]

Either the people in governments are all ignorant about the dangers of the 5G technology which by the way Harald Kautz Vella classifies as a *down-scaled version of military use laser technology*, or they are well aware of them and are happy to go ahead with its implementation anyway as a relatively painful way of culling the population if not in the present, surely in the decades to come. Not to mention the push of the telecom companies that have already invested billions of dollars in the development of the 5G infrastructure and want to make a profit no matter what.

According to the people behind the www.5gSpaceAppeal.org website where people can sign the *International Appeal to Stop 5G on Earth and in Space,* the regulators simply did not pay attention to already existing scientific evidence of harm caused by EMF, and specifically 5G radiation. "Stakeholders thus far in the development of 5G have been industry and governments, while renowned international EMF scientists who have documented biological effects on humans, animals, insects and plants, and alarming effects on health and the environment in thousands of peer-reviewed studies have been excluded. The reason for the current inadequate safety guidelines is that conflict of interest of standard-setting bodies 'due to their relationships with telecommunications or electric companies undermine the impartiality that should govern the regulation of Public Exposure Standards for non-ionizing radiation'."[428]

Dr. Ellis Evans, an environmental scientist specializing in radiochemistry and atmospheric sciences states in his article titled *5G Telecomm Radiation the Perfect Tool to Mass Modify Human Brain Waves* that "it is clear that the latency period for adverse biological effects from devices using microwave frequencies from say 1 GHz to 5 GHz is approximately 10 – 20 years. In 2016 there are now many thousands of peer-reviewed medical and epidemiological studies that show, illustrate or correlate, adverse biological effects with use of mobile phone technology or WIFI. Using frequencies even higher than 5 GHz (and up to 100 GHz) will compress the time frame in which cancers and other biological effects show themselves within society. It is anyone's guess on what might happen in terms of biological safety yet it is clear to see that the pulsed nature of these high frequency, high signal intensity signals do not harbour good news for humanity, particularly in relation to the functioning of our DNA."[429]

As these millimeter waves are unable to travel to long distances and are absorbed by solid bodies like trees and buildings, in many cities they have been ruthlessly cutting down old trees to be able to install their fantastic 5G towers. Call it killing two birds with one stone; while they are giving a good dose of harmful radiation to the general population, they also make sure that trees are removed, further degrading the quality of life.

And not only do they plan to create a frequency prison around us on Earth, the US senate has already given green light to SpaceX, the company of Elon Musk to launch 12,000 5G satellites into the atmosphere. Beside SpaceX there are other corporations like OneWeb, Boeing, and Spire Global which have been authorized to launch further 8,000 5G satellites into the atmosphere worldwide.[430] All in the name of technological advancement.

The European Space Agency is also involved in the development of an all-encompassing 5G cage on Earth and in space. As they state in the description of their promotional video titled *Satellite for 5G*, "space has an invaluable role to play in the 5G ecosystem. Satellites can extend, enhance, and provide reliability and security to 5G like no other, helping to deliver its promise of global, ubiquitous connectivity, with no noticeable difference to the end-user. ESA's Satellite for 5G (S45G) programme aims to promote the value-added benefits of space to 5G, by developing and demonstrating integrated satellite- and terrestrial-based 5G services, across multiple markets and use cases."[431] The European Space Agency is planning to launch a test nanosatellite in 2019 into space to test the use of the 75GHz frequency band.[432]

This is a serious threat to life on Earth as we know it because while we still can choose to not use mobile phones with the current 4G system or choose an internet provider that does not yet have 5G and opt for using the internet only via cable, there will be no escape from an arsenal of satellites beaming down from space indiscriminately, covering every square inch of the planet.

The question is why they need all those satellites when 5G requires miniantennas every few hundred feet. Could it be an attempt to militarize space or to create a more robust surveillance system under the guise of providing seamless 5G telecommonunication worldwide?

Some say that satellites will not be an issue, however, even if they will not, those who live in cities and have nowhere to move, no rural areas they could go to, will be trapped in the frequency soup of thousands of micro antennae planted every few hundred feet apart.

One of the main reasons why it is so difficult for normal people to believe that there is an elite consciously and deliberately working toward the destruction of a large part of the population, not caring about how many plant and animal species or natural habitats go up in literal or figurative fire in this process, is that the majority of these elites believe that human beings are despicable, stupid and weak.

They are not like normal human beings who can't fathom the extent of evil these psychopaths are capable of. They want to attain physical immortality and are hoping to download their consciousness into some supercomputer, or that they will be able to merge with machines and interface on a biological level with artificial intelligence.

They are working on creating a "space suit" for their consciousness that does not expire as easily as physical bodies and which would make it possible for them to attain immortality. For such people pollution of the environment by heavy metals or harmful frequencies is not an issue because they are planning to turn themselves into transhumanist bio-machines or become part of a computer mind, living in a machine with a much longer lifespan than the commoner, or they may get access to secret advanced medical treatment capable of neutralizing the negative physical effects of their mass control agenda.

A further danger of ramping up electromagnetic frequencies in our environment is related to the disappearance of insects. If you were born in the 20th century, you can still remember how many insects the windscreen of your car collected on longer trips. There was no way to avoid collisions with at least a couple of unfortunate insects that found their death on your car.

Compare that to the number of insects your windscreen collects today. I can tell you my experiential data: two insects in a whole month with daily trips. Insects have been rapidly disappearing, likely due to a combination of various factors. The increased use of insecticides and UVC radiation which has increased in the past few years, as well as elements that shouldn't appear off ground; strontium, barium, aluminum, and titanium, now "miraculously" found in the atmosphere. The official narrative being pushed by NGOs and the like is that the culprit for the disappearance of insects is the use of insecticides. Yes, that is partly true...but what they are not telling you is what they are trying to hide.

A huge side of the story is that insects, due to their size, are impacted hundreds of times more severely by EMF radiation than humans, so their sudden decline in numbers should give us a clue to the "radiant" future we are facing if the 5G rollout keeps happening and they manage to inundate the planet with these extremely dangerous frequencies. Another factor in insect decline is aluminum which is now found in outrageously high amounts in the soil due to geoengineerings. By the way, NASA announced that it uses trimethyl-aluminum, lithium, and barium "for atmospheric observation of wind patterns" since the 1950's. What a joke. They even mentioned the word "trails". [433] According to the geoengineering.org website what "they" have been doing is weather modifications that has been ongoing for many years.[434]

Compared to the possibility of 5G neutering humanity and reducing the population in a "non-violent", "non-lethal" way (insert evil laughter), the second important issue could seem almost irrelevant. However, it is very much relevant.

The implementation of the Internet of Things and the full operation of the 5G network worldwide could bring forward the possibility of full monitoring of people by corporations and/or governments via such a widespread, all-encompassing system.

Will the Internet of Things and 5G increase your freedom? Will you be freer or more enslaved when your fridge, your toaster, your cell phone or your car can spy on you and transmit everything you say to a global cloud from where it can potentially be extracted to be analyzed and used against you? Couple this with the Chinese social credit "experiment" and you don't have to be pessimistic to see that there really is a dangerous, dark side to all this technology as it is being implemented.

Rejecting 5G "just because" is not enough though, if we want real solutions, we have to request those who are responsible for its implementation and who are ignoring the mounting scientific evidence of its dangers, to be personally accountable and provide evidence, clear, repeatable studies and testimony under their personal responsibility that these technologies are not harmful. Appealing to the personal responsibility of people in positions to make or affect decisions regarding 5G could prevent these people from saying they were just following orders, or something similar that takes away their personal responsibility.

Why would you want to use a technology which is more harmful than the one we currently use? Especially taking into account that there is more than enough scientific evidence that the current telecommunication system is already very harmful and causes illness. Who benefits? Think about that...

Will you be able to opt out of the 5G system which needs millions of micro towers everywhere to work? If you are lucky and will have moved in time to a remote, low population area in a village or to the mountains, away from cities, you will be able to get away from the worst of the land system of the millimeter towers (although in the US they are planning to cover the whole area, rural or not).

There have already been towns where 5G was banned due to public dissent. Curiously, Brussels, the capital of Belgium will not get 5G either. Why is that interesting? Well, Brussels just happens to be the seat of the European Parliament. Could it be that all those technocrates do not want to get fried by this technology which is after all meant for the ignorant masses?

However, if the space satellite program is seen through and every square inch of the Earth will be covered by these 5G related satellites, where will you be able to hide from them if you do not want to participate in the 5G telecommunication system? Do we really need thousands and thousands more satellites beaming down on us (even if they do not transmit 5G frequencies but maybe will be part of some scalar wave military technology installation)? Will you be able to opt out and stay unaffected? If not, that will be imposition, not freedom.

Will you be able to opt out of having your household appliances or the supermarkets and other public places you visit monitor you 24/7? If not, that is not freedom. That is not a direction you want to go. Unless you prefer to be enslaved even more. Then good luck to you and welcome to a Brave New World.

Remember, technology is not inherently good or bad (well, there is an exception: nuclear energy goes against natural law, should never be used and it is a crime against all life to use it), it is the use we give to technology that is good or bad. We must act responsibly. If having less and less freedom and a more degraded environment does not bother you, go ahead, and support IOTA with your energy.

But if you do not want these outcomes for yourself and your loved ones, stay away from it. The 5G rollout is under way and we have so little time left until the system would be turned on. Please research what 5G really entails and do what you can to stop this insanity from happening.

13

One Coin to Rule Them All?

We saw that since the introduction of the blockchain technology developers have been trying to tackle the issues with creating optimally working cryptocurrencies that are fast, cheap, reliable, safe, fungible, and that require no trust from users. Each one of these initiatives has its own strengths and weaknesses.

The goal for cryptocurrency developers seems to have been to come up with a perfectly functional cryptocurrency which could easily stay decentralized due to its qualities and functioning (in case that is really what people want) and hold the level of manipulation of the markets to a minimum. Though we cannot see the ultimate motives of the creators of each and every cryptocurrency or blockchain platform, I think it is safe to say that the majority of the developers of these projects had an altruistic vision in mind, desiring to do away with the centrally controlled nature of our economy and our society, and to create a better life for all.

The ethos of cryptocurrencies is to find a better, more just way to opt out of the abusive privilege based system ruled by banks and central authorities which has been rigged on purpose and by design. However, where the rubber really meets the road is in how these noble initiatives have been able to fare amongst a hoard of old world beneficiaries and in an environment primed to make individuals greedy and think mostly in short term selfish benefits as opposed to a grander scale vision that includes prosperity for themselves and a better life for others too in the long run.

It must be obvious to anybody that banks and financial institutions do not want to lose their monopoly on money, nor do the controllers who are behind these institutions plan to ever retire from their lucrative world domination game. The governments are not planning to delegate their power to the people any time soon either. This coupled with the greed of the majority of individuals who entered the crypto world to get rich resulted in a Wild West situation where everything goes. Darwin would be crying with joy if he could witness the developments of the crypto space.

In general, there seems to be a tendency by the controllers to steer people away from alt coins. It seems easier to grab control of the crypto space if people lose interest in other projects and flock to Bitcoin which then could be used as a single point of failure within the space. The focus of the media is mostly kept on Bitcoin, Ethereum, and the cuckoo's egg Ripple. As we saw, Ripple is not actually a cryptocurrency and openly serves the current system. The fact that it caters to banks deters crypto anarchists and visionary type people, but those who are in crypto only for the profit and do not care about how the consequences of their actions could influence the future of society are happy to invest in Ripple because they see its association with the banks as a big plus. No wonder it could become the third, and for shorter periods the second among cryptocurrencies in terms of market capitalization, due to its affiliation with the current banking system which legitimates them in the eyes of the public.

However, many investors who are into cryptocurrencies not only because of the potential quick buck they could gain from trading or just investing at a relatively early stage, but those who really want a better future for everybody, a more just and more humane world, stay away from Ripple.

As for Ethereum, well, at first glance there is not much for the establish-ment to like about Ethereum because it makes possible for anybody with the sufficient programming knowledge to create their own decentralized applications and smart contracts and just leave the control system out of their day-to-day operations. On the other hand, we must remember that it was the Thiel Foundation that awarded $100,000 to Vitalik Buterin to write the Ethereum code. So what really goes on in the background, and whether Ethereum is safe to buy, hold and build on, is not entirely clear.

Also, it is important to mention that one of the big bad wolves, J.P. Morgan has created its own blockchain platform on Ethereum earlier. As it turns out, that must have been just a test run for their own "cryptocurrency", the ingeniously named *JPM Coin* the launch of which they announced in mid-February 2019. The JPM Coin "will run on a private blockchain developed by the company with help from the Ethereum Enterprise Alliance, and coins will be issued by the bank."[435]

JP Morgan announced that the JPM Coin is a cryptocurrency, but accordingly to Jerry Brito, the executive director at Coin Center, a nonprofit research and advocacy center focused on cryptocurrency and decentralized technology, it is clearly just an "in-house-built payments system"[436]. As to why the JPM Coin is not a cryptocurrency, Brito stated that "a cryptocurrency is one that is open and permissionless, if you want to download it, you don't need permission; you just need some software"[437], which is not the case with the JPM Coin.

At the same time, most media outlets including the New York Times[438], CNN[439], CNBC[440] and many others described the JPM Coin as the first US dollar-pegged "cryptocurrency" which in the test phase will be used for payments between corporations only. To go even further, an article published in the Investor's Business Daily states in its title and the first paragraph that the "*JPM Coin, new JP Morgan cryptocurrency*" is the opposite of Bitcoin.[441] Wow. This is similar to saying that fire is a new type of water. It is the opposite of what ordinary water is, it's not wet, it's hot, it burns, but still, let's just call it bankers' water, shall we?

You may think that this is just a question of using the term "cryptocurrency" out of convenience for all digital currencies because people are already familiar with it, but what if all this is done on purpose, to blur the definition of what a cryptocurrency is? The fact that a digital currency uses blockchain technology does not make it a cryptocurrency. It also must be decentralized (at least if we take the definition of Satoshi as a basis).

Also, using a blockchain based digital currency for something that is clearly meant to combat whatever a real cryptocurrency could do to strip power from the controllers might just be one of those apparently innocent wordings that eventually steer the thinking of the masses in a certain direction. Do not fall for the trick, the JPM Coin will be a banker coin. Calling private, centralized digital currency projects cryptocurrencies will eventually blur the line between a true decentralized cryptocurrency and a possible future globally imposed controller currency.

The picture is not black and white though. While there is a likelihood that corporations and banks will keep trying to use already existing platforms like Ethereum for their benefit just like JP Morgan, governments and financial institutions are obviously interested in pulling independent ICOs down. Using the parts that can benefit them, and trying to destroy or ban those parts that could hurt them seems like a pretty predictable behavior of the establishment. Besides this, it doesn't help Ethereum and the crypto space in general that greed and lack of morals seem to be rampant everywhere.

Unfortunately, there has been a large number of ICOs which turned out to be nothing (or only little) more than scams set up to squeeze a quick buck out of naive investors who were enticed by the promises of making easy money. This phenomenon gives a good reasoning for the establishment to say ICOs need to be regulated, because of the danger they suppose for investors. Come on, folks, as if governments and banks had ever really been interested whether the investments of the common people tanked or not. It is an argument which is easy to sell.

There is indeed much uncertainty and ICOs can tank easily. And there seems to be a way higher failure rate among startups that launch ICOs than the conventionally operated average new company. In contrast to the popular notion that 80% of new businesses fail in their first year, the reality has constantly been that 80% of new businesses actually survive their first year in business and around half of the businesses survive the first five years. In this sense you are really at greater risk if you invest in an ICO because the chances that a blockchain project tanks is greater than those in conventional business.

From one side we have seen attempts to dethrone Bitcoin and obliterate it if possible, or if killing it is not possible then to make it unavailable for the general public and turn it into some type of digital gold which would enrich the rich even more and strip the rest of us from another possibility to thrive, while being an excellent segue way towards a cashless society and the centrally controlled, blockchain based transparency of the monetary system.

Jerome Powell, the chairman of the Federal Reserve said on July 11, 2019 testifying before the US Senate Banking Committee that Bitcoin is "a store of value like gold" and that "almost no one uses it for payments". The aim of the hearing was to determine whether cryptocurrencies, once adopted on a mass scale, could threaten the existence of the current monetary status quo, rendering so called anchor currencies like the dollar unnecessary.[442]

Meanwhile, a large percentage of the population of Venezuela has already adopted Bitcoin (together with Dash and Zcash) for various types of transactions to somehow weather the mind boggling 1.3 million percent inflation the official currency of the country has endured during the past year.[443] Bitcoin is already accepted by one of the most important shopping chains of the country and many people are exchanging their dollars to bitcoins.

Of course, the ideal situation for adopting Bitcoin or other trustworthy cryptocurrencies is not a hyper-inflationary chaos like in the case of Venezuela, but the possibility to use cryptos can be a blessing in that situation. Although for the moment it seems that Bitcoin is mostly used as a means to get access to US dollars which many people then stack away on bank accounts outside of Venezuela, Bitcoin could also slowly be adopted as a real peer-to-peer currency once people familiarize themselves with cryptocurrencies, their benefits, and understand how they work.[444]

However, Venezuela has also issued its own state-sanctioned digital currency called Petro which the establishment obviously prefers to the use of Bitcoin.

Japan has already accepted Bitcoin as an official means of payment as well as Australia. In contrast, the Central Bank of Spain has declared that Bitcoin is inefficient to be used as a means of payment.[445]

If we take into account that according to a poll run by the Official Monetary and Financial Institutions Forum and IBM, 38% of the central banks confirmed that they are working on creating some form of digital currency. The poll even dares to say they are "building on the Bitcoin foundation".[446] Just another of those examples of when the establishment is trying to steer mass thinking according to their liking.

There may be several factors that could propel one specific cryptocurrency to be the "chosen one", the one that will ultimately prevail and get massively adopted (but that doesn't necessarily mean that such a cryptocurrency is adopted because the establishment approves of it). The fact that Ethereum is above all a platform designed to create thousands and thousands of new applications and potentially thousands of private or community created and owned cryptocurrencies (and digital currencies just like the ominous JPM Coin) probably is a negative attribute in the eyes of those who would like to keep control over the economy. So this could be a factor why Ethereum may not be the ideal candidate for the powers that be to replace current fiat currencies and create a digital worldwide cryptocurrency.

The obvious question is whether Bitcoin could be the one cryptocurrency that rules them all, and if at all, will there be at one point one single cryptocurrency, or will we end up with a government issued worldwide digital currency.

The front cover of The Economist, the financial magazine of the powers that be, is well known for foreshadowing what the so called elite is up to. Well, in 1988 one of its covers showed a prediction that by 2018 a global currency will be used to solve the economic problems of the world. Seriously, the only problem they saw in the world was the existence of exchange rates between various currencies...? Anyway, it is clear that the globalists had been planning to create a world government and a single global currency further down the road, the more traceable the better, so for that reason a digital currency based on blockchain technology would be ideal.

It is not very likely, although not impossible either, that Bitcoin was created insidiously and deceptively for this purpose while Satoshi declared it was meant to get away from central control over people's money. We just simply do not know who planned what, who wants to do what. But Craig Wright's book may give a hint of what actually was behind the creation of

Bitcoin. He wrote that "Bitcoin was created to be a means to allow the world both to commoditise information and to create sound money. Bitcoin is the balancing point between what is just able to be totally legal and stop crime and what is acceptable. It's the neutral knife point. It can't be a state tool for oppression. It can't be an anarchist thing. It has to be right down the middle."[447]

To have a hint of what is really going on, we have to look behind the curtain where we are not dazzled by the smoke and mirror tricks of these wizards of Oz. If we observe the actions of some important actors in the financial field as opposed to what they say, we can see that in 2018, especially since the second half of the year, there have been new Bitcoin wallets appearing loaded with huge amounts of bitcoins.

Somebody has silently started to buy up bitcoins, while this increased demand has not been reflected in the price of Bitcoin on cryptocurrency exchanges. In fact, the price of Bitcoin fell to $3,500-4,000 by the end of 2018 and in early 2019 it was still lingering in that region.

At the same time, we know that several major crypto related establishments including Coinbase, Binance, Bittrex, Genesis Trading, and Circle[448], have been offering their clients the possibility to buy bitcoins over the counter (OTC), normally starting from a transaction size of $100,000. It is clear that big institutional investors like Wall Street traders have been buying ever larger amounts of bitcoins over the counter, thus avoiding the increase of the price of Bitcoin on crypto exchanges.[449]

Over the counter trading desks can provide a quoted price for large transactions, and what is more important, these trades are not included in the total market capitalization figures of the crypto exchanges. As these trades happen outside of normal crypto trading, the large transactions that otherwise would trigger a price increase on the exchanges do not move the price. Imagine what would happen if these large volume traders wanted to buy say 1000 bitcoins on a normal exchange. They would have to make quite a lot of transactions to be able to buy up that many bitcoins because not many people are trading with such large quantities, which means that with every buying transaction the price would be increasing.

Buying those 1000 bitcoins over the counter for a quoted price, while staying outside of the awareness of the other traders of the exchanges makes sure that prices do not rise. As a result, the OTC trader can buy at a lower, better price.[450] This explains, at least partially, why cryptocurrency prices have been so low for almost one and a half years despite the large and growing volume of OTC trading.

The behavior of institutional investors does not necessarily mean that they know with certainty that Bitcoin will become some kind of digital gold (as the mainstream media has been hammering it into people lately) or that it will ever become a universally accepted currency. What we can know for sure at this point is that these investors, as they always had, are trying to profit from this new emerging "asset class".

We do not know who created Bitcoin, who Satoshi Nakamoto really is. There are even those who speculated that the Japanese meaning of this name could be loosely interpreted as the intelligence or wisdom of some central kingdom or central area and supposed that this might be an indication that the Satoshi Nakamoto name is a code for "central intelligence" from the name of the CIA. Well, for one it is true that Bitcoin uses the SHA256 hashing protocol which was invented by the NSA and made public as a standard. Also, we do not know whether the NSA has a backdoor to the Bitcoin protocol as some allege. However, Craig Wright's account in his book about how he came up with this pseudonym looks quite convincing.

If Bitcoin indeed had a backdoor, its inventor(s) would be able to change the blockchain, falsify or delete transactions. More importantly, whoever grabs the control of such information about the backdoor would get full access to the financial history of each Bitcoin user. We don't know if such backdoor exists. If there is such a backdoor, the game is over, and we can say good bye to our dreams and hopes of a decentralized untraceable money system. If there is no backdoor, the efforts to make Bitcoin stronger, unhackable, with true privacy for its users are very important.

There is then the question of criminals. What will happen if criminals start using cryptocurrencies? Drug cartels, weapons dealers, those involved in human trafficking, sex trade, child trafficking, and all sorts of dirty jobs have always used fiat currencies for their payments. What about money laundering? Well, they had been laundering money using fiat currencies and they still do. That is true. What if drugs were not illegal? There would be no need for anybody to buy them illegally, and drug cartels could not flourish. Also, the problem is not only the drug cartels and other crime organizations.

The real issue is that those criminals have strong ties to the existing power structure. Many people think, and have collected what they deem as sufficient evidence to say, that the CIA and its dark operations are at the helm of all kinds of illegal trades, including drugs, weapons, human trafficking, or stripping the Amazon basin from its trees. The deep state is the possible owner of the poppy fields in Afghanistan. It is a very clever operation: make drugs illegal, organize their sale yourself via drug cartels and criminal organizations, then use taxpayer money allocated by the government for "the war on drugs" to make control of the general population even stronger while making a bunch of money for your friends at the military industrial complex. But we digress.

Buterin recently said in an interview in 2019 that Bitcoin will likely be reduced to a digital asset with only one function: that of store of value[451], and there is certainly a push from the establishment in this direction. With the launching of Fidelity's and Bakkt's physical custody bitcoin futures products this seems more likely than ever. At the same time, whether Ethereum will be able to solve its issues of scalability, privacy, and usability, or whether it will be overtaken by newer projects and slowly forgotten, still remains to be seen.

A very different view to that of Bitcoin eventually being reduced to be a store of value, a type of digital gold is represented by Andrew DeSantis, the developer of the DeOS decentralized operating system. According to him, it is very likely that Bitcoin will be forked again and again into many new altcoins, similarly to how a tree grows from one trunk and separates into branches which then grow many individual leaves. However, once a bunch of variants of Bitcoin have been created, further down the road the most powerful version of the Bitcoin variants will absorb all the rest.

DeSantis does not care about Bitcoin as a cryptocurrency, and definitely not as a "store of value" in the money sense. He sees it more like an underlying system that will provide a trustless basis for all systems relating to everyday life based on its capacity to maintain a copy of the history of anything intact.[452] Wright talks about the creation of the *Metanet* as the ultimate goal of Bitcoin, which seems to be in line with the views of DeSantis: "people think that Bitcoin and blockchain is the big invention, but it's just a Lego block. It's a Lego block that was needed in the creation and that if not available, if not solved, and if not incentive-based, would not have led to solutions that will create the Metanet."[453]

14

Libra Hits the Fan

The current old-world rulers (the banksters included) may be pushing Bitcoin now specifically as a store of value, partly to be able to maintain their control (investing in Bitcoin itself and in blockchain related new corporate developments such as cryptocurrency exchanges, specialized financial products, and side chain applications), and certainly to regulate cryptos to grab hold of as much of the decentralized crypto sphere as possible. Probably in the hopes that eventually they will be able to regulate the inconvenient perks out of cryptocurrencies and that they could use this to maintain their power somehow.

At the same time, as we have seen so far, giant tech corporations have been working to carve out their own niche of the blockchain space. These developments have mostly been met with anticipation because they promised to bring the blockchain technology closer to mass adoption once these tech companies step behind it and improve usability.

However, when Facebook published a whitepaper on June 18, 2019 about a "cryptocurrency" they are planning to develop and launch, things went a bit crazy. Facebook first called this project Global Coin (which is either a bit over-confident wishful thinking, or just an example of how the controllers believe that they must inform us, lowly commoners of their evil plans of world domination to avoid karmic backlash).

The name of the coin was later changed to *Libra* which can be an allusion to not only "liberty" as in free, borderless payments, but also to balance, as if they wanted to convey that Libra could be the magic coin that brings the global economy into balance.

According to the whitepaper, Facebook would use the best features of Bitcoin, Ethereum, EOS and Ripple, but there is just one tiny little detail: they say it will be decentralized, proof of stake, permissionless *in the future*. But first they would implement it as not decentralized and needing permission from a central authority.

They intend to launch their own wallet for Libra called *Calibra*, and the semantic trick is that they say: not to worry, everybody, Libra will not be controlled by Facebook, but by an association of 100 corporate entities who all have an initial investment in the project, and Facebook will only be one of these companies that have a say in what goes on the Libra network. The whitepaper also promises that Facebook will not use the profile information of Facebook users for Libra and that user information will not be shared or used for surveillance.

Sounds good, but judging from historical evidence of how Facebook has been surveilling and censoring people and selling their data, it may not be prudent to trust that they will actually deliver what they promised instead of keeping the project as a centralized, corporate controlled coin. Not when Libra may become a very-very powerful money making machine. According to Andreas Antonopoulos, Facebook did the same with Whatsapp, the chat application which was free until Facebook acquired it, and started to use it for surveillance.[454]

Andreas Antonopoulous gave a speech the day after Facebook's announcement at the Scottish Blockchain Meetup at Craiglockhart Campus in Edinburgh, Scotland where he stated that this whitepaper changes everything. According to him, the announcement of Libra means that "Silicon Valley is coming for banking in a big way."[455] Big tech companies have already grasped such a large part of our lives (think of Facebook, Amazon, Netflix, Google, Airbnb, or Uber) and have amassed so much private data about billions of people that this new development is quite scary, says Antonopoulos.

These corporations hardly pay any taxes, they have been shamelessly using their influence on governments to tweak laws and policies to create an environment which allows them to take out more profit from the market, and follow their own rules when it comes to censoring voices (by banning, shadow-banning or demonetizing them) that do not stay between the political lines they prefer.[456]

The US Congress has reacted almost immediately; within one month Facebook already had to answer the questions of senators on the Senate Banking Committee. Interestingly, though not really surprisingly, the questions raised were related to the probability of "crooked developers" selling users' data and stealing user's money, or how Libra would handle money laundering by terrorist organizations. The committee also found it worrisome that Facebook does not intend to embed other cryptocurrency wallets into its Messenger and Whatsapp messaging applications, which means that the potentially 2 billion users would all use the Calibra wallet because of convenience, which would give an unfair advantage to Facebook.[457]

The following day Facebook was grilled by the US House Committee on Financial Services. The regulators definitely did not like Facebook's history of interference in elections, and its mismanagement of users' private data. All seemingly worries "for the good of the people".

However, the real cause of the urgency in citing Facebook to the congressional hearings must have been that the government is more than aware of the dangers Facebook's corporate coin would pose to their hegemony and ability to influence the economy of the country. "Steven Mnuchin, the US Treasury Secretary said he has 'very serious concerns' about Libra. Jerome Powell, chairman of the Federal Reserve, said he has 'many serious concerns regarding privacy, money laundering, consumer protection and financial stability'."[458]

Obviously, the most serious threat to the government is that of the potential disruption of financial stability, and Powell was not exaggerating. Andreas Antonopoulos calls this historical moment the rise of techno-neofeudalism. Due to its 2 billion users and all the information Facebook has about them, Libra could seriously undermine the ability of central banks to successfully execute inflationary policies. "Facebook is going to be effective at disrupting regulation in a way the banks have not been able to."[459]

In Antonopoulos's view, if governments let Libra take off, they will likely create a government issued alternative in the form of some stable coin based on a basket of currencies (the IMF's Special Drawing Rights or SDRs). These government issued stable coins will be stable only because their value is pegged to the value of the local currencies it is based on, meaning that a coin will always be worth say 1 dollar, independently of the change of the purchasing power of that dollar. If those local currencies lose value (which is inevitable due to the nature of debt money and the great level of indebtedness of most countries), their respective stable coins will also be worth less in purchasing power. In contrast, according to Antonopoulos, "what Facebook is planning to do is consumer retail level SDRs."[460] The danger this would pose to the financial system is that inflationary devaluation policies would not work anymore because the population could opt to buy Libra for the local currency and store their money in Libra which would be more stable and less affected by inflation than any singular fiat currency or their stable coin brothers.[461]

This relative stability would come from the fact that the value of Libra would be pegged not to one fiat currency, but to the overall value of all currencies of its users in the first place, a basket of currencies which Facebook users could exchange for Libra. If one particular fiat currency lost value, it wouldn't decrease the purchasing power of Libra in other countries.

If Facebook manages to launch Libra, that will be the beginning of the post-national era, according to Antonopoulos, and in the new era governments will lose their power to control money, partially because of Bitcoin, but mostly because of Facebook. If mega tech corporations will start creating their own money, they can transform their business models to generate huge amounts of money and will become so powerful that these amoral corporations will dictate to the governments, says Antonopoulos.[462]

For the above reasons Libra got a big fat no from the US Congress (at least for the moment), and this may even push the government to the direction of supporting Bitcoin, if not for other than their own self interest. One thing seems to be certain though: tech giants will not let the governments stop them so easily, and from now on we can count on a triangular game with legitimate cryptocurrencies, government created electronic cash or tokenized fiat coins, and the corporate coins of powerful private enterprises competing for survival and, ultimately, for the control of the economy and our society.

Mark Zuckerberg, the CEO of Facebook testified at a House of Financial Services Committee hearing on October 23, 2019 about how Facebook plans to market its platform with the help of Libra. The continued pressure on Facebook has already resulted in PayPal, eBay, Visa, Mastercard, and Stripe withdrawing from the Libra project.[463] It doesn't necessarily mean that Libra is destined to fail, just shows the amount of pressure generated as governmental and techno-feudalistic forces clash over the future control of the economy.

However, some think that the introduction of Libra could benefit Bitcoin and the entire crypto space as well. One of the reasons why not too many people use Bitcoin for day-to-day payments is that in various jurisdictions, including the US, the law categorizes Bitcoin as a digital asset and not as a digital currency. What this translates to in practice is that each and every time you want to buy a cup of coffee with Bitcoin, the transaction you make is a taxable event, so you would have to record these events (and track the "capital gains") for taxation purposes. This is obviously very inconvenient, and a major disadvantage compared to fiat currencies.[464]

It's more than just a question of inconvenience, it is the biggest tool the IRS has to prevent people from using Bitcoin as a currency, mainly for payments, and to encourage them to treat Bitcoin as an asset, something to invest in or to trade.

Even if somebody would like to pay for low value items with Bitcoin, currently there is no application capable of handling the capital gains tracking aspect of such transactions. Consequently, until the legislators decide to view Bitcoin as a legitimate digital currency and not as an asset, the majority of people will only want to use it as a store of value or for larger, one-off payments.[465]

One at least seemingly positive side effect of the appearance of Libra in the electronic cash market could be that Facebook would likely fight tooth and nail, sending its hordes of top notch lawyers into action to achieve digital currency status for Libra. Bitcoin might also benefit from such a development because for the government having Bitcoin (which does not have a central, profit based, power-hungry corporate entity behind it) could be less threatening than having to face a giant tech company which is too powerful to regulate or stop.[466]

This view certainly has some truth in it, especially if we take into consideration the lobbying efforts mega corporations usually take to stir legislation into the direction which is best for them. Bitcoin doesn't have a lobbying force behind it to tackle "unruly" regulators.

However, another take on the potential role Libra could have in the shaping of the relationship of real cryptocurrencies and governments is that it may accentuate the difference between a corporate coin like Libra and a decentralized cryptocurrency to the advantage of the former. Governments might, after their initial aversion, choose the ability to work with the lawyers of Facebook within an established framework instead of having to regulate or adopt Bitcoin which may feel like trying to grab mercury with bare hands, without owners or central authorities, and especially with the understanding that Bitcoin can rip power off the hands of the establishment.

Unless some top government officials have great insight into the end game of what going blockchain-digital really entails, it is more likely that governments would eventually choose to side with Facebook and Libra because those promise to operate within the boundaries of the current system.

On September 13, 2019 France and Germany declared that they will ban Libra in their countries saying that Libra could potentially threaten the financial stability and the monetary sovereignty of European countries. At the same time, they had this ingenious idea to create a "*public cryptocurrency*" which the European Central Bank is apparently already working on in the shadows. The idea seems to be "to use electronic currency that would be directly deposited into the ECB, eliminating the need for bank accounts, clearinghouses or intermediaries."[467] There goes your monetary sovereignty, dear EU nations.

It is quite a sinister plan to have all the money of individuals, companies and nations be controlled by the central bank of the EU. They aptly managed to overlook the issue that the supply of currency could of course be increased any time, as has always been the case with banks. Giving full control to a supranational central bank is just a stone's throw away from the birth of the New World Order.

The EU is not the only one with such plans at all. According to a study by Cambridge University, 80% of countries participating in the survey were researching or already developing their own digital currencies.[468] Dubai, Canada and India for example are also in the process of developing their own digital currencies, while Russia is still looking into having its digital currency as a project for the future.

The Chinese central bank, the People's Bank of China announced in August 2019 that they were ready to launch a blockchain based digital yuan anytime, which they started to develop based on their five-year research into existing cryptocurrencies and the crypto economy. It seems that the hasty announcement was caused by China's worries that if Facebook were allowed to go ahead with its dollar-centric "multinational basketcoin", it would undermine the monetary sovereignty of China and devalue its money.[469]

The People's Bank of China reacted to Facebook's June 2019 announcement to launch Libra by stating in August already that they could launch a digital yuan any time. But in September they retracted, saying that there is no exact launch date because they are still developing and testing the new digital currency. In October 2019 they planned to hire well known experts with a focus to potentially launch in 2020.[470]

The Chinese government must be serious about coming out with a digital state currency and adopting blockchain for its own purposes because they passed a law on cryptography on October 26, 2019 which will enter in force as of January 1, 2020. As the last proposal for the text of the law said, "clear guidelines and regulations are needed to evaluate commercial cryptography technologies used in the major fields related to the national interest as the current 'loose' system is not suitable for the industry anymore." Apparently, the law will focus on bringing cryptography closer to government employees, companies, and social groups and will encourage education in this field. The question is, in what form. At the same time, trading cryptocurrencies still remains illegal.[471]

Not surprisingly, the Federal Reserve too has started to develop its own digital currency. In October 2019 Philadelphia Federal Reserve Bank President Patrick Harker said that it is inevitable for the Fed and other central banks to develop their own digital currencies.[472] According to Doug Casey, the Fed will undoubtedly issue its own digital currency and will make sure that everyone in the US use it. Such a Fedcoin could become the anti-cash, with full transparency and complete lack of privacy[473]; heaven for the banksters, a nightmare for the people.

Meanwhile, *Line*, the Japanese Whatsapp-like messaging application has launched its cryptocurrency exchange for its 81 million users in Japan after receiving approval from local authorities in September 2019. The exchange is called Bitmax and operates in Bitcoin, Bitcoin Cash, Ethereum, Ripple, and Litecoin. This means that about half of Japan's population now can easily buy and sell cryptocurrencies within an app they are already accustomed to. Line already opened another crypto exchange called BitBox earlier in Singapore with services available to almost all countries except for Japan and the US.[474] Google is also looking into potentially launching its own digital currency.

The trend is clear; more and more tech companies will jump on the band-wagon and get involved with cryptocurrencies. Of course, launching a crypto exchange or adding the opportunity to buy established cryptocurrencies in Line's app does not pose a threat to the system the way Libra and its planned pegging to a basket of fiat currencies based on user location does to local monetary policies. Also, Facebook is in a priviliged position due to its size to become a disruptive blockchain giant that could potentially hurt real cryptos as well as, without a doubt, national currencies.

At the same time, the interest in Bitcoin and cryptocurrencies in general has already seen an increase since Facebook announced that it is planning to enter the crypto business. The majority of people are quite resistant to technical novelties and prefer to only consider adoption if major, already trusted companies launch products and services with the new technology. The upside is that all the articles and videos comparing Libra and Bitcoin will hopefully educate the public more on the differences between a corporate coin and a real, decentralized cryptocurrency.

However, as things stand at present, Libra might never see the light of day. As Jeff Berwick said, the central banks and governments "want to get all their currencies digital because we're moving towards negative interest rates. They wanna get everyone into the banks, and they can't do that if there is still physical cash. So there is a huge (...) war on cash. So they wanted to just create it so the dollar and the euro are all just digital, sort of like a digital currency. Sort of like what Libra wanted to do. And I think they want to make sure that they control it all so they don't want these corporations to have [as] a competitor.[475]

It would be foolish to think that the controllers will give up their plans. Now more than ever, governments and central banks are feeling the pressure to create government issued blockchain currencies, to push aside Libra and other similar corporate contenders, and to try to squash Bitcoin and the whole crypto space via regulations, taxation or outlawing.

The spirit of war for monetary control among these three paradigms has been unleashed; a war to be fought over our money, our time, and ultimately our life force.

15

The Financial Leeching of the Bitcoin Power

J ust as rats are the most dangerous when they are cornered, it will not come as a surprise that the controllers and their henchmen (bankers, financiers, and legislators) have been really busy in the past few years trying to milk Bitcoin as much as possible for themselves while at the same time doing their best to extend their control over it. In most cases overtly, but sometimes also covertly. It shouldn't come as a surprise either that they do everything they can to maintain their power while the world is changing operating systems.

We have already seen how corporations have been busy building second layer applications and ecosystems on the Bitcoin blockchain with the aim of diverting transaction fees from the main chain (and Bitcoin miners) to their own, proprietary products. Another way the controllers found to prevent common people (meaning everyone except the extra rich) from attaining financial freedom by investing and owning Bitcoin was the introduction of Bitcoin futures.

Bitcoin futures

Bitcoin futures contracts "allow traders to bet on the future value of Bitcoin without having to use exchanges. The trader who enters into a futures contract agrees to buy or sell Bitcoin in the future at a preagreed price at a certain given time in the future. What this means for Bitcoin is that future traders can influence the price of Bitcoin simply by betting its future price, while they do not have to actually own Bitcoin because the future contracts are settled in fiat currency."[476] Introducing derivative products is a less than subtle way of manipulating Bitcoin. It looks very probable that the huge bull run just before the first fiat exchanges received authorization to launch Bitcoin futures trading had been caused at least partly by the manipulation of some actors who later would benefit from shorting the market, meaning that they would bet on Bitcoin losing some of its value.

Bitcoin futures first appeared in December 2017, which, rather unsurprisingly, coincided with the greatest price spike and bull run of the history of cryptocurrencies followed by a precipitous fall both in exchange market capitalization and prices. To date, the market has not been able to recover from this long bearish tendency yet, though by the end of May 2019 it seemed that the tendency was starting to turn. The trading of cash-settled Bitcoin futures first started on December 10, 2017 by the Chicago Board Options Exchange (CBOE) and on December 17, 2017 by the Chicago Mercantile Exchange (CME). Just as a reminder, the historic maximum price of Bitcoin occurred on December 17, 2017 after which date the entire crypto market took a nose dive.

Because trading future contracts is an excellent way for investors to make money without actually having to deal with the negative consequences of the eventual price drops of the asset they buy and sell future contracts of, the price of gold has been controlled in the same way, by having people trade future contracts without actually having to own physical gold.

During the long bull run at the end of 2017 the rapidly rising cryptocurrency prices and the continuous, and likely orchestrated, media hype around Bitcoin caused many uninformed people to jump on the bandwagon and buy into cryptocurrencies just before everything went south. The majority of those people, unless they invested in cryptos out of conviction, so the ones belonging to the visionary-futurist-anarchist types or those who thought that cryptocurrencies will be the winners of the future, have already sold out with a huge loss and lost faith in cryptos. On the other hand, the institutional investors have silently increased their Bitcoin lot.

The introduction of Bitcoin futures made it possible for big players to manipulate the crypto market very heavily. When the first futures contract expired in January 2018, the price of Bitcoin plummeted by 40%. The possibility of trading Bitcoin futures could very well be the customary way for the big players to control Bitcoin prices, always betting for falling prices while they amass as much Bitcoin as they can in the subsequently opened over-the-counter markets too. The reason to follow this tactic would be to keep prices low and keep the interest in Bitcoin of institutional investors as much out of the sight of retail traders and the general public as possible.

Another plus of Bitcoin futures for the controllers is that their regulating bodies now can point the finger to the cryptocurrency market, insisting that cryptoexchanges need to be regulated because of the heavy manipulation that has been going on. So while they take as big a chunk of the crypto cake as they can playing with Bitcoin futures, they would also, ideally, get to control the cryptocurrency market, turning cryptocurrencies into another tool for mass surveillance and control instead of tools of at least some level of financial freedom. Of course, all "for the greater good, to protect investors".

It is clear that the current fiat currencies will not be able to survive for too long, so the controllers are trying to amass as much of the 21 million bitcoins as they can. How could they do it? Well, they are the ones who own and control the mass media, they can create fake news and propagate false information. They can label those who have opposing views as conspiracy theorist lunatics or spreaders of false news. They can make loud statements that go against their actual acts. They may say something that gets people react in a way which is beneficial for the controllers.

For example, what they were doing during the entire year of 2018 was lowering Bitcoin prices and with that the prices of all the altcoins, trying to shake out as many of the small investors who entered during the last quarter of 2017, when the prices were rising very quickly, as possible. Those people who entered the crypto market because of the hype, euphoria, and the fear of missing out, have subsequently suffered a great loss, in case of Bitcoin over 50%, in case of altcoins even more. With each wave of creating false hopes by the media that something "positive" was just around the corner (meaning something that would result in the prices rising again), the prices are driven down artificially.

This is possible not only because the cryptocurrency market is not regulated, but because the market is very small compared to the resources available to the market manipulators. They can use their billions of dollars to short the market and cause prices to fall. Basically, this has been the history of the entire year of 2018 and the first half of 2019 as well.

And it is not only about manipulating Bitcoin prices because the majority of cryptocurrencies have historically been tied to the price of Bitcoin (although we have seen this tendency break in 2019). Many altcoins are only available for purchase for Bitcoin or Ether and not for fiat currencies, and the majority of the coins are not interchangeable among them, but you have to exchange them for Bitcoin or Ether. So manipulating Bitcoin prices automatically moves the prices of other cryptocurrencies. Combining that with the high percentage of the capitalization of Bitcoin in the entire cryptomarket (which currently is 69% but this figure doesn't include the OTC market, so the Bitcoin dominance is likely even higher) it is clear that one only needs to control Bitcoin to have power over the entire crypto ecosystem.

Interestingly, we have seen a change in tendency since the beginning of 2019 in that the movement of the price of Bitcoin no longer seems to be as strongly related to the price movement of altcoins. This may be due to the fact that everybody's interest has mainly turned to Bitcoin, besides the smaller market capitalization of other cryptos makes it easier to keep their prices down.

Bitcoin ETFs

Another nail in the coffin of the chance for Bitcoin to become a decentralized currency that would benefit people in general instead of becoming another, way more easily controllable tool of the controllers could be the approval of Exchange Traded Funds (ETFs). An ETF is a security that tracks the price movements of an asset (in this case Bitcoin). A custodian (bank or financial entity) is safeguarding the assets. This means that instead of giving customers the bitcoins upon buying, they receive shares that represent the ownership of those bitcoins. These institutions would sell bitcoins without giving them to the buyers, and the buyers would instead just get a paper, a promise that the custodian will give them the bitcoins if their clients request it so.

They would like to do the same as they did with gold. Financial institutions keep the gold "in custody" and sell you promises that when you show the paper containing this promise, they will give you your gold. The only problem is that there is not as much gold as there supposed to be based on all the papers sold. Technically, we could mine much more gold because mining is now limited on purpose to keep the scarcity of gold, but if we ever did so, gold would quickly lose its advantage to other forms of money.

There is a push by the establishment to set up and solidify Bitcoin as a digital gold, as a store of value which is only valuable because of its scarcity. However, the big difference is that while gold is certainly beneficial and could have several industrial uses which make it a valuable raw material, Bitcoin can serve not only as a digital cash, but also as a digital registry which can hold the entire history of our culture in a way that makes the truth unbendable if we ever decide to use Bitcoin for it.

There are two basic types of Bitcoin ETFs for which old world entities have been seeking SEC approval. The one VanEck Securities and SolidX Management wanted to get approved would hold actual "physical" bitcoins, where they would store the bitcoins of clients in physical wallets. Another type of Bitcoin ETFs would buy Bitcoin derivatives only based on the typical speculative tools of financial institutions like futures and options, without actually storing real bitcoins in any way.

In 2018 nine requests have been made to the SEC for ETF approval by various companies, including the CBOE and the CME, but all of them have been declined. The final deadline for the SEC to make a decision on the latest joint physically backed Bitcoin ETF request by VanEck and SolidX expired in February 2019. While everybody thought that the SEC would finally give green light to this ETF, they postponed the decision until May 20, 2019. Then May came and the SEC once again declined to make a decision, this time postponing its deadline until August 2019.[477]

When the SEC postponed its decision once again until October 2019, VanEck and SolidX decided to circumvent the standard approval procedure by using a SEC exemption. Instead of real ETFs they decided to offer shares in the VanEck-SolidX trust to institutional investors only.[478] Less trusting readers might think this could have been a coordinated effort to exclude retail clients, because normal ETFs would allow retail clients too to buy them. Whatever was the reason behind the decision, this way VanEck and SolidX did not need to register their product with the SEC.

The Vaneck-SolidX trust shares "provide institutional investors access to a physically-backed bitcoin product that is tradeable through traditional and prime brokerage accounts", according to their press release. [479] This broker-traded fund called VanEck SolidX Bitcoin Trust 144 A Shares, however, started to trade with a surprisingly low volume in the first days after its launch of September 19, 2019. During its its first 25 days the total net assets purchased was only $532,200.[480] At this time it is unlikely that the SEC will approve the ETF request of VanEck and SolidX before 2020.[481]

Bakkt launched its Bitcoin futures product on September 13, 2019, as they had announced earlier, which could explain why VanEck and SolidX decided to go ahead with their "ETF-like" product to overtake Bakkt. Bakkt's Bitcoin futures are physically backed, hence the company name, so once the futures contract expires the buyer receives physical bitcoins that until then are stored by Bakkt in its warehouse backed by Intercontinental Exchange (ICE). Bakkt has two bitcoin futures products, a monthly and a daily, so buyers should receive their physical bitcoins on the second day after the date of a daily contract.[482]

What most people in the crypto space expected to happen was that once Bakkt has launched its bitcoin futures, institutional investors would jump in amd the price of Bitcoin would skyrocket. Instead of this, in the first few days since its launch hardly anybody bought Bakkt Bitcoin futures. The launch volume of Bakkt's Bitcoin futures (72 btc) was only 1.36% of the volume traded on the launch day of the CME's cash-settled Bitcoin futures product in December 2017 (5,298 btc). Moreover, only 1 btc's worth was traded on daily contract, which is surprising, as the daily contracts were the flagship offering of Bakkt which have been promoted since August 2018 as the instrument that could tame the volatility of Bitcoin price movements. [483]

As everyone knew that CME cash-settled Bitcoin futures caused the market to crash and created more volatility in the market, most people in the crypto space expected that once Bakkt launches its Bitcoin futures, institutional investors would jump in and the price of Bitcoin would skyrocket.

This especially seemed to make sense because, as Michael Moro, the CEO of Genesis Capital said, physically settled Bitcoin futures can give market-makers a hedge in the eye of the SEC which could make this type of contracts more useful to institutions than CME's cash-settled futures.[484]

Instead of this, there were practically crickets. It now seems that, unlike what most crypto retail investors had hoped, and as Mr. Kristof, a crypto influencer on YouTube said, "institutions do not care for Bitcoin. If you were to talk to a commodity trader who does this every single day on a trading desk about having one of their clients put in 2-5% of their portfolio into Bitcoin, they're gonna look at you like you have lobsters coming out of your ears."[485]

The efforts of the CBOE and the CME to have the SEC approve their ETFs for Bitcoin speaks for itself. As they say, if you can't beat your enemy, join him. This seems to be the strategy of the powers that be who own the majority of the major financial institutions including the Chicago Mercantile Exchange and the Chicago Board Options Exchange. Actually, the same companies are behind these two exchanges as the ones who have achieved the approval of Bitcoin futures and requested some of the Bitcoin ETF approvals. Just a coincidence?

So why has the SEC kept declining these ETF approval requests since 2016? The more conservative answer to this question would be the one suggested by the CME's chairmain, Terry Duffy who in a March 2019 interview said that the biggest issue regulators have with Bitcoin is its finite supply. (What a bummer, right?) That you cannot print more and more and more, that you cannot create more debt. It just cannot be used as a currency the way the system wants to operate. Duffy also stated that it is more likely for the SEC to approve dollar backed stablecoins than Bitcoin because those stablecoins are pegged to the value of the dollar. He added that it would be a dumb step for the SEC to approve something as radical as Bitcoin because it could undermine the current system.[486]

There are those, however, who think that sooner or later Bitcoin ETFs will be approved and that this seeming hesitation and the continued delays by the SEC is merely a tactic to gain time for institutional investors to accumulate as much of the existing Bitcoin supply as possible relatively unnoticed, largely via over-the-counter purchases. According to this logic, by the time the SEC would indeed approve Bitcoin ETFs, institutional investors will have accumulated a large enough chunk of the supply to be able to manipulate the markets in the future by their sheer size compared to the rest of the retail traders. They could lock Bitcoin down as a digital gold and nothing else, to save their banking system and debt based currencies. Or maybe by then the establishment would manage to pull off a centralized global "public" digital currency.

In fact, the way the price of Bitcoin took a nose dive right after Bakkt launched its ETF-like Bitcoin product and the surprisingly low interest in it shows that institutions are not interested in Bitcoin. At least not as much as retail investors would like them to be. It is true that in 2019 institutions got involved with Bitcoin, but most of their investment is in derivatives, in worthless paper bitcoin.

Moreover, institutional investors have already amassed a significant amount of OTC bitcoin and their transactions will also be OTC-style, which will not move the price up on crypto exchanges.[487]

When Bakkt launched, the price of Bitcoin fell from $10,000 to $8,000, and for a short time even below that, in a matter of a few days. As the Bitcoin crypto exchange market (currently below $200 billion excluding OTC volume) is so small, institutional investors now have another tool to play the market more easily, to manipulate it into more extreme volatility if they want to.

John Boyle made an interesting comment to the YouTube video of Mr. Kristof which may actually contain some truth: according to him, the "CME is the trading desk of the Federal Reserve, it's how they control the BTC price. They do the same thru the Comex to control the price of gold and silver, it is not in the best interest of the Fed to allow competitors to the dollar to gain value. That's why we don't have an ETF yet and they're approving these sh*#t derivatives left and right."[488]

Whichever of these two (or any other) possible explanations may be closer to the truth, we cannot say that Bitcoin ETFs would be beneficial for Bitcoin and cryptocurrencies. Besides the obvious issues with possible market manipulation in case ETFs for Bitcoin are approved, there are serious risks involved with keeping your bitcoins in the custody of a third entity. If such a custodian that holds your "physical" bitcoins goes bankrupt, it may no longer support the ETF. The actual value of Bitcoin would also be way more difficult to track, and much of the transparency of the current cryptoexchanges would be lost.

Investors would have to have faith that the companies selling derivative Bitcoin ETFs are able to track the performance of Bitcoin correctly. For this reason physically delivered Bitcoin ETFs could be safer, but it doesn't mean that Bitcoin ETFs would steer the use of Bitcoin and other cryptocurrencies toward their original, publicly declared intent.

Up to the present, all financial products launched involving Bitcoin have been futures related "where there is money to be made by having a collapse", says Mr. Kristof, which did nothing else but made it easier for Wall Street and friends to turn Bitcoin into a commodity, a type of digital gold. According to him, it is not by accident at all because institutional investors answer to the banking cartel, which does not want Bitcoin to gain popularity.

According to Mr. Kristof, there is, however, another possible scenario where Bitcoin reaches seemingly insane price levels, "where they take Bitcoin and it goes parabolic. They do that because that means: all of you out there, the idea of having one bitcoin is out of your reach. (...) If they bring bitcoin to a hundred thousand dollars, the conversation where we're trying to tell you: buy one, get one, own one is out the window. It goes to: hey, make sure you buy satoshis, get a few satoshis. That's the conversation we're gonna have. It's out of their reach, to where the small guys have no real impact, no real control."[489]

The actions of authorities like the Internal Revenue Service also heavily contribute to keeping Bitcoin from going into mass adoption as a currency which people are happy to use for making payments.

So many people in the crypto space had hoped that if Bitcoin ETFs are finally approved, the price of Bitcoin will rise due to the massive amount of institutional money that will enter the market. However, it could be the end of decentralization as institutional investors would enter to buy the regulated Bitcoin products and instead of people using their cryptocurrencies for decentralized and hopefully control-free transactions, more and more of the bitcoin supply would end up in the hands of entities of the old/new world order.

And the hits on Bitcoin haven't ended yet. Fidelity Digital Asset Services just announced on October 18, 2019 that after having operated since February with a limited pool of clients including hedge funds, "family offices" and financial advisors, they are now ready to open the shop up for "all qualified investors" (i.e. they exclude the small guy) offering digital asset custody and trading services.[490] Fidelity might bring more investors to cryptocurrencies, but it will only tilt the scales further towards the store of value narrative.

The CME is planning to launch Bitcoin options in early 2020, which means that, once again, they will get a chance to weaken Bitcoin by making the price more volatile and, consequently, reducing the probability that people will want to use Bitcoin as digital cash.

Bitcoin options will allow traders to bet on the future price of Bitcoin and give them the right to buy Bitcoin at a specific price on a predetermined day. But traders will not be obligated to actually buy.[491] It is likely that if the CME gets green light to launch Bitcoin options, we may expect another dip in the price of Bitcoin in early 2020.

Bakkt, however, just announced on October 24, 2019 that it will launch its bitcoin options contract on December 9, 2019, thus overtaking the CME. And, again, they happened to have self-certified the product with the CFTC.[492]

All these regulated products would naturally come hand in hand with the need of serious, all-encompassing regulation of Bitcoin, and that would eventually lead to the complete regulation of cryptocurrency exchanges and other venues of trade. What if you no longer could trade on your own on a cryptoexchange without involving an officially approved agency, just like in the case of Forex trading, which would of course be bound by strict regulations?

But the more important issue is that institutions have been setting up Bitcoin and other cryptocurrencies to be controlled by the establishment. They have already accumulated massive amounts of bitcoin and will undoubtedly use it to make as much money off Bitcoin as a tradeable digital asset as they can, while at the same time working for its regulation and on preventing it from being used as an alternative to fiat currencies.

There have been rumors spread for whatever obscure reason about an imminent worldwide adoption of Bitcoin. Rumors insisting that the US dollar is on the brink of collapse (which is true, of course) and that there are plans by the US government to substitute the dollar with Bitcoin (which does not sound realistic). Interestingly, when a US congressman threatened that the government will ban cryptocurrencies in May 2019, crypto prices jumped up immediately and kept rising for a while, largely due to a number of projects all related to the involvement of big corporations with Bitcoin. But also because many people did not want to be left out, should the US government indeed ban cryptos.

At the end of September 2019 the US rehipotecation market visibly started to struggle. Banks get most of their liquidity on the repo market, and now it seems that the financial system ran out of money. As a measure, not surprisingly, the Fed started to pump billions of dollars into Wall Street every single day. The problem is that on the repo market banks can act as if they had more treasury bonds than they actually do. Banks are very well aware of how bad the situation is, that is why liquidity dried up on the repo market. And the last time this happened, the tax payer had to bail out the banks. To make things even worse, since the last financial crisis the US has passed bail-in laws that allow banks to just take the money from your bank account in case of a financial meltdown, while only 1% of the money sitting on bank accounts is protected by the FDIC.[493]

If the US government adopted Bitcoin to save the economy amidst the fall of the dollar, its price would rise astronomically because there are only 21 million bitcoins versus trillions of dollars. But is that even likely to happen? It would undermine the entire system, which obviously wouldn't be that desirable for the government.

However, even if such a government adoption does not take place, with all the corporate projects going on that are being developed to start to use it, Bitcoin will eventually increase in value. Which is one reason why the controllers have tried to push crypto prices down throughout the whole of 2018 as well as the first quarter of 2019, in order for them to gather as many Bitcoins as possible before prices would start to rise.

Just business as usual in controller land? Not really. This time the system is fighting for its life by trying to control Bitcoin to derail it into being nothing but a digital asset. But would Bitcoin ever be the official substitute of a major fiat currency? The Central Bank of Venezuela, out of neccessity because of a US embargo, has just announced that it is considering holding Bitcoin and Ether. Venezuela has already sold oil for bitcoin[494], so there is precedent that under extreme duress countries may resort to adopting cryptocurrencies, even if only as a temporary measure.

Full adoption of Bitcoin by a government could only happen within the framework of the current governmental system if Bitcoin were changed drastically, stripped from all its characteristics that make it a totally different animal. I do not necessarily mean centralization, but total auditability, and its stripping of all kinds of fungibility and privacy. Such a Bitcoin adoption would mean that instead of people having a chance to keep their privacy by using cash which is fungible and untraceable by so called authorities, we would end up with a tracking nightmare. If your transactions are protected from third persons but are totally auditable and visible to the government and its various institutions, what we thought Bitcoin stands for would be totally distorted.

Others suggest that Bitcoin should be backed by gold to give it stability so that it can be more suitable for using it as a means of payment. Well, we know how gold has been fairing in the past few decades, giving great power to the controllers who have been doing everything to keep the gold supply limited, while it is a fact that gold is much more abundant than they would like us to believe. Actually, they have to keep the belief of people that gold is scarce, otherwise it would lose its value. Moreover, a large part of the registered gold supply of various countries has "evaporated" and no one knows where the gold is. Bitcoin's value is derived not only from its limited, uninflatable supply, but also from the transparency and immutability it provides as basic characteristics via a decentralized architecture.

It is important to note that the very actors of the system are the ones who have caused, and still are causing, the volatility of Bitcoin by creating financial products in order to profit off Bitcoin. Exchanges and monopolistic mining equipment manifacturers also cause Bitcoin volatility as far as its price goes, but the value of the Bitcoin network is in fact quite resistant to volatility because of the fix supply of coins, its decentralized nature, and its permanent ability to serve as a safe storage of truth not only regarding transactions but also by being able to act as an inmutable digital library of any file we can save inside transactions.

Once again, we see an example of the problem, reaction, solution method. They have been trying to distort Bitcoin into being volatile and, consequently, "not good enough" to be a currency. They then declare that Bitcoin cannot be used as a currency but that it is an excellent digital asset. The "solution" would likely come as a centralized, fully regulated "public currency".

As Caitlin Long wrote, "at a systemic level, the traditional financial system is as fragile as Bitcoin is anti-fragile."[495] According to her, an anti-fragile system becomes stronger with every shock it endures, and Bitcoin is like that because its natural security grows along with the growth of its processing power. It is also important to note that price volatility is not inherent to Bitcoin, but is the result of it being traded as a commodity. As a system, Bitcoin is way more stable by design than the fiat money system. Unlike the current financial system, Bitcoin does not have inbuilt instability with periodic bank runs because it's not debt based. That's why "Bitcoin is an insurance policy against financial market instability."[496]

What does all this mean to you, the individual? Up until now the majority of cryptocurrency investors bought into Bitcoin either because they are crypto-anarchists who believe that this new technology could bring a more just future for humanity (those guys have been into Bitcoin for many years and have seen quite some profit from the rising of prices), or those who tried to use cryptocurrencies as a means of payment to avoid the establishment because they believe that it is the way for the people to take their power back from the controllers.

Then there are those who entered the crypto market when prices started to go up, and the media was burning with Bitcoin fever, and fear of missing out (FOMO) were rampant. These people entered because they saw a good way to make a quick buck with no effort. Many of the latter have already given up on Bitcoin after the prices plummeted and suffered more price drops during 2018 and in the summer of 2019 as the price of Bitcoin has risen once more above $10,000, they may have started to show interest again. Too bad for those that Bitcoin fell briefly to $7,700 after the Bakkt launch.

As we saw, Bitcoin and other cryptocurrencies can best be controlled by speculative means. If governments ban them, people would just go underground with it and would keep using them for actual payments. Even if they are not banned, we would need to start using cryptocurrencies as means of payment in order to first stabilize and then slowly raise their value, but that requires that all their technical characteristics be optimal for such use.

Currently, it is not worth using Bitcoin for smaller payments. Also, why would anyone want to pay for goods and services in bitcoin when it is likely that the value of Bitcoin will increase over time (and likely exponentially) while it is certain that the value of fiat currencies will soon go down, slowly but surely tending towards zero? It is just rational behavior; if people have two currencies on hand, they will more likely spend first the one which they deem less valuable. Currently, for everyone with a little bit of future vision, between Bitcoin and the US dollar, Bitcoin seems to be the better contender to survive.

However, besides becoming less volatile, Bitcoin would need one more very important thing to be sorted out. The treatment the SEC, the IRS and the CFTC give to Bitcoin is certainly not by accident. None of these bodies want to see a world where Bitcoin is a winner.

"The CFTC sees Bitcoin as a commodity, the SEC as a currency, and the IRS as a property. (...) It makes no sense that they can't have a unanimous decision as to what Bitcoin is. This is not by accident,"[497] says Mr. Kristof who believes that if the IRS started to treat Bitcoin as a currency, it would mean the end of the dollar. People would buy bitcoin and dump their dollars, which would lead to the banks and the government losing control over the population.

The most effective move against Bitcoin was that the IRS categorized Bitcoin as a digital asset. Consequently, any time you exchange your bitcoins to fiat currency, or any time you pay with bitcoins, the IRS wants you to pay taxes on capital gains, even though the US Securities and Exchange Commission says Bitcoin is a currency.

With this move the IRS threw a monkey wrench into the adoption machine of Bitcoin. Not many people can, or are willing to, pay capital gains tax on each and every purchase they make with bitcoin. Also, as we saw earlier, there are no applications that can automatize the accounting of such a tax for Bitcoin purchases, so not only you are at a disadvantage if you want to use Bitcoin for payments, but to add insult to injury, you can spend time keeping track of your related tax obligations. Moreover, the IRS doesn't even have the right to determine what category Bitcoin belongs to. What they issue are guidelines, not laws. So it is also partly just a fear tactic on behalf of the tax collectors, but it is expected that many people will let themselves be intimidated by whatever the IRS says.

The attack on Bitcoin didn't stop there. On October 9, 2019 the IRS published its first cryptocurrency tax guidelines since 2014. According to the new guidelines, if you receive new coins from a hard fork or an airdrop, you have to pay capital gains tax. As Jerry Brito, executive director at Coin Center said, "one unfortunate consequence of this guidance is that third parties can now create tax reporting obligations for you by simply forking a network whose coins you own, or foisting on you an unwanted airdrop."[498]

The IRS also gave no concession to pay with cryptocurrencies for low value items. Even if you want to pay your coffe with bitcoin, you must report it as a capital loss.[499] Why on earth would the IRS treat Bitcoin as property? Essentially, the IRS is trying to make sure that Bitcoin and cryptocurrencies never get to be used as currencies. Not a surprising move at all.

Of course, nothing is 100% sure. Maybe the controllers will manage to pin Bitcoin down when ETFs will finally be approved, and regulate it into something it was not meant to be. Maybe instead of an increase in value Bitcoin will lose its value completely once the big players have made enough money while betting on its price movements. Why would they do that? For one, it is possible that those people who shorted the markets, those who are behind the manipulation of prices have already earned all they wanted with those operations and may prefer to introduce their own, centrally controlled "cryptocurrency" before Bitcoin could take strong enough roots among the population.

Or maybe they will want to issue something backed by gold or silver, both of which are completely manipulated and controlled. They may want the new world currency to be a new fiat currency with a gold standard, something along the lines of the IMF's Special Drawing Rights (SDRs). The same of the old, but this time fortified by the blockchain, making it completely traceable. Every one of your purchases, transactions recorded, forever open to whoever has the means to search for them.

It could turn out to be the worst thing in recorded history. But if we do not go (only) for the short term gains, if we do not care so much about trading and speculation but instead focus on the coins that actually have utility to society, maybe we could avoid such a sad future, if not for the whole of humanity, at least for those individuals who manage to shift their focus from greed to practical usage.

A very telling sign of the intention to grab what Bitcoin stands for and turn it into something that serves the system on behalf of the big players is what we have been seeing with the conscious obscuring of how the word "cryptocurrency" is being used indiscriminately. As we saw earlier, there are now various major banks which announced that they will issue their "own cryptocurrencies."

The proper thing would be to say that they issue their own digital currencies. Instead, by saying that for example a bank issued, bank controlled digital currency is a cryptocurrency, even if technically they are based on the blockchain and use cryptography to provide security to the system, the mental water gets muddied. And as a likely result, the majority of the masses will effectively be unable to see what the differences are, and why they would be better off investing in, and using, real decentralized cryptocurrencies.

Once the lines between government issued digital currencies, corporate coins, and real cryptocurrencies are blurred and cash is completely eliminated, it would be way easier to introduce a new, one world "cryptocurrency" as opposed to Bitcoin, saying that the latter demonstrably has not worked out and is difficult and impractical to use. Or think of any kind of reasoning the control system could come up with.

The problem is that we are all accustomed to instant gratification. We have been trained to want everything now, and also have been conditioned to be selfish, and because of the very nature of the kind of money we use (debt money), we all have a deeply ingrained tendency to opt for immediate benefits instead of looking out for future benefits not only for ourselves but for everyone else including future generations. Sadly, this is directly related to the fact that official currencies all tend to give interests over time, as we saw it when discussing demurrage currencies.

Unless the new currencies we will use stop encouraging the behavior of selling the future in exchange for present benefits in the form of interests, and until we stop hoarding money to at least keep our purchasing power as currencies are continuously devalued, there is little chance that people will stop speculation and will opt for using Bitcoin and other cryptocurrencies as mainly utilities that serve to exchange goods and services.

Recent signs have been indicating that it will be quite difficult to move society as a whole in a less selfish direction based on ideology only. One such sign has been the appearance of interest-yielding bitcoin deposit accounts which seem to be a success among investors. The majority of the bitcoins deposited are lent to institutional investors: something that a real crypto-anarchist would never do.

But in the current ecocultural environment where we are all being leeched from day one of our life till the grave, it is extremely difficult to convince people to choose not only based on self interest and convenience. Maybe the best way to tackle this issue is to ask yourself: is it creating a better future for all people or just for me?

From a governability point of view the logical step would be to try to squash all the potentially dangerous, bigger cryptocurrencies and crypto projects, any platforms that make it possible for anybody to build their own customized applications and crypto ecosystems. It would then make sense to create one worldwide digital currency (or declare an already existing digital currency to become "the one") and only let those altcoins survive which do not pose a threat to the system.

Well, ex-CFTC chair Christopher Giancarlo just happened to confirm on October 22, 2019 in an interview to CoinDesk that "the CFTC, the Treasury, the SEC and the [National Economic Council] director at the time, Gary Cohn, believed that the launch of bitcoin futures would have the impact of popping the bitcoin bubble. And it worked."[500]

Giancarlo stated that the steep Bitcoin price increase by the end of 2017 was the first bubble after the 2008 financial crisis, explaining that "coming out of the 2008 financial crisis, the legit criticism of regulators was along the lines of: Where were they during the expansion of the real estate mortgage bubble, and why didn't they take steps to pop that bubble when they could have?"[501] This is how he explained why they "allowed the market to imteract" with this bitcoin bubble.

Of course, the establishment didn't do anything to pop the real estate bubble because real estate does not threaten the status quo the way Bitcoin does. And now they try to paint it as if they had learned from a mistake and allowed Bitcoin futures to prevent another bubble. Ridiculous, taking into account the relatively low worth of the entire cryptocurrency market even at the end of 2017. The coordinated effort of the administration, the CME, the CBOE, Bakkt, Fidelity and friends in fact is benefitting the establishment and the banking cartel.

Just a week before Giancarlo admitted that the establishment purposefully weakened Bitcoin in 2017, he and Daniel Gorfine in their article in The Wall Street Journal proposed the creation of a dollar backed stablecoin to keep the dollar afloat.[502] During the October 23, 2019 Facebook Libra hearing anti-crypto congressman Brad Sherman said that Bitcoin is a threat to the dollar as it could weaken it or even displace it.[503] You see the pattern.

Speculating about a possible global adoption of Bitcoin really does not mean much either way. There is some chance that in specific cases they might want to use Bitcoin which is already functioning and proven to work, with a relatively large amount of money invested into it by over 25 million people (as there are approximately 25 million Bitcoin wallets, although you can have more than one wallet, so this number is not definitive). However, it looks more like the system is fighting against it to keep it small and relatively inert until they are ready to launch their government issued public coins.

Sometimes the best way to have the upper hand is to not squash a new invention or an enemy of the system completely and openly, but instead to let it live on while you shape it according to the needs of the system, in the hopes that the majority will not notice what has happened. If they manage to create a copycat of Bitcoin with comparative advantage like better taxing or ease of use, the majority of folks are guaranteed to go with the centralized coins. They wouldn't care much about the related economical and political issues.

We cannot really know what the future of Bitcoin will be, whether it will indeed be adopted by the system and used to squash freedom because each and every movement of everybody is registered and traceable forever (and as we saw, the identities of Bitcoin users are far from being untraceable).

Maybe the controllers will try to return to the gold standard and use gold to back the one world global "cryptocurrency". Which means that they could come up with more gold any time and make gold less valueable (because gold mining has been restricted on purpose to a certain amount to maintain the appearance of scarcity), or they could just reduce the ratio of gold required to back the currency. We would be back to square one, where the currency would be devalued, in both cases.

It seems that the phrase "use it or lose it" very much applies to Bitcoin too: either we use it as a digital cash despite what the establishment is throwing at us, or the chances that we will lose Bitcoin as a digital cash are high.

However, if we collectively choose a healthier society and a more just economic system, we can go with a few or many cryptocurrencies, using each of them for what they are best at. We may want to use one cryptocurrency (like Nano) for selling surplus solar energy to other homes as part of a decentralized network. We could use Dash or Pundi X for day-to-day transactions like paying at the grocery shop or at the hairdressers. Bitcoin may end up as a currency used to pay taxes and for purchases of larger value. The question always remains whether we can still opt out and use cash or create our own alternative or local currencies not controlled by any so called authority.

16

Ready or Not, Truth Goes Digital

S ince the introduction of Bitcoin many developers have been working to come up with new applications of the blockchain technology, and the number of people working in this field has been continuously growing. It is not sure whether the blockchain will be the ultimate technology that will be widely used or whether it is just a stepping stone destined to be left behind by some hitherto unknown, or even known, technology. Today there are already contenders to replace blockchain even at such an early state when we are only beginning to use it on mass scale. It is worth mentioning Leemond Baird[504] and his proprietary invention, a software called *Hashgraph* which claims to be way quicker than blockchain. Hashgraph is truly mind boggling and you may want to look into it. However, that is a theme for another book.

If done right, the application of blockchain could eliminate uncertainty, human error, and cheating by criminals or governmental and infrastructural systems. Of course, always given that we can eliminate the possibility of 51% attacks and other ways to hack the systems. If we manage to avoid the corruptibility of the blockchain, we saw that it could potentially be useful for many areas, for example healthcare for keeping records of patients or for integrated personal data management by governmental agencies (uniting registries related to births and deaths, tax information, police records, address and real estate registries). All official records of people could be stored on one central blockchain which would eliminate the need for a large percentage of public servants, and could shorten the time it takes to deal with authorities in official proceedings.

Sounds great, if you think that such increased efficiency would result in you having to pay less taxes. It could in theory, unless we keep pushing along the ever growing giant snowball of national debt most countries are stifled by. Even if national debts were annulled all over the globe, the question of personalized treatment would still be an issue. It is very difficult, if not impossible, to create algorithms and smart contracts based on compassion and empathy, and if we eliminate the human element from the handling of official matters, life will not be easier and certainly not more humane for the users of such systems. The result will then be technofascism just the way we can see it developing in China.

However, we could use blockchain solutions as a plus, without stripping people off their freedom in certain areas. Companies, for example, could keep all their internal information on some blockchain as well as use blockchain for trading with other companies. We could eliminate the piracy of copyrighted materials such as books, music, and other media by publishing works of art on blockchains where it would be impossible to copy a file unless its price has been duly paid. Creators, artists could finally eliminate the middlemen and earn what their art is worth instead of being milked by publishing houses and music labels and robbed by freebie seeking "fans", as has been the case for a very long time.

Blockchain could be used in any area of life, but the question is *whether we need to, and want to*, use it for everything. We could definitely benefit from leaner institutions with less public servants if governments were willing to use the leftover taxpayer money for things that actually benefit the population instead of pumping it into the war machine of a few, or into the health care (or rather death care) industry. But is it likely that governments as we know them, and the people who work for them, will actually be willing to change their psychopathic behavior and for once in history be dedicated to serve people instead of themselves? It would be naive to think so, unless we, the people take actions to eliminate the possibility of psychopaths controlling our lives. And this brings up some issues.

Where I am seriously opposed to using the blockchain is for the surveillance of people. It is not normal for a government or a state to subject their people to surveillance as a default procedure, or to spy on somebody. These establishments are said to be (ought to be) in place to serve the people and to manage infrastructures for the population, as Max Igan says. By people I mean the individuals who live in that society. Not a homogeneous mass. And serving people as individuals and as a society should never be done by preemptively watching everybody.

The big and only reasoning for such a surveillance state has been the "threat of terrorism" but anybody who has a bit of common sense can think why it was impossible for the steel columns of the Twin Towers in New York to vaporize and disappear into nothingness if they were indeed hit by airplanes. That goes against the laws of physics. Unless what really hit those towers were directed energy weapons. There is the first big question mark there.

Then the billions upon billions of dollars and all those years that have been spent to fight various wars (in fact the United States has fought some 300 wars during its existence, a number horrifyingly high to be casual). It has all been a setup to feed the war machine of the powers that be, those who have been making very good money from pitting nations against each other and selling their weapons to both sides.

Another, recent addition to the handful of reasons why the establishment has been clamping down more and more on our privacy is what they term "hate crimes". Unfortunately, hate crimes now include not only de facto acts of violence based on hatred against a specific nationality, minority or people of a specific skin color or sexual orientation, but also simply saying or writing your opinion if that does not match the current cultural trend of political correctness. In the UK saying something you think is deemed to be a hate crime if it offends the sensibilities of somebody else. How convenient for a corrupt system to shut dissenters up in the hopes that this way they can keep their empire going as always. Social media, especially Facebook and YouTube are now discriminating against people who have views that oppose those favored by the globalists. Twitter and the popular crowdfunding site, Patreon, as well as certain payment providers like PayPal and Stripe have recently closed down the accounts of various content creators, due to their rightist or radical opinions.

Independently of what your beliefs and political affiliations are, it is important to notice that there is something inherently wrong with large tech companies now censoring who and what gets disseminated on their platforms (and who gets banned, shadow-banned or demonetized). Of course, these platforms argue that they are against "hate speech", but in a free society everyone should be allowed to say whatever he wants. Freedom of speech as a basic human right, remember? The irony of this situation is that often it is politicians who practice hate speech, and nobody moves a finger. But if Joe Smith utters something out of anger, that is a hate crime. What this skewed and evil program to curb our freedom even more does not take into account is the level of influence a well known politician bashing certain groups of people has compared to what happens if Joe Smith happened to be swearing out of frustration. They use a distorted version of morality against the people in a very convoluted way.

The situation is even more dangerous if we take into account how these social media and internet platforms are intentionally trying to shut down those voices which are against the globalist massification agenda. Technological systemic control coupled with the state can result in a dangerous fascist system that squashes anybody who does not want to stay between the lines. Take that to the square and you will get a global government using the same technological control grid. Very bad.

If you think that big tech companies do not already manipulate public opinion and even political outcomes, watch the interview Greg Coppola, senior software engineer at Google gave to Project Veritas on July 24, 2019. He went on the record to say that Google is not politically neutral: *"I look at search and I look at Google News and I see what it's doing and I see Google executives go to Congress and say that it's not manipulated. It's not political. And I'm just so sure that's not true."*[505] By the way, after this interview Google placed Greg Coppola on administrative leave.[506] Censoring and editing out dissenting people's opinions on social media and search engines is just not ok when doing so can tip the scales towards those political powers which would grant more influence to these tech giants.

When talking about the adoption of blockchain in everyday life, a most alarming development needs to be mentioned which may come a country near you soon: China's citizen surveillance via cameras, the internet and other smart devices under a currently beta tested *social credit system*. This is not something most people want if they are aware what it really means. Do you really want to be given scores by a machine, or by your government for that matter, according to what you read, what you search on the internet, or what your opinion is about a politician or some world event? Do you want the government or the system to decide if you can have access to certain products and services? What if you do not think like the majority, and even though you are not planning to apply violence (which most people don't, despite what the government indoctrination outlets want you to believe), you still have "dissident thoughts" about how things are versus how they should be?

Do you think it would be ok and just for the system to punish you for your thoughts and opinions or for your "unhealthy" lifestyle choices by not letting you purchase international flight and train tickets? Because that is how the Chinese social credit system operates. What if you lost the right to rent a home because you do not have enough social credits?

Even if there are people who have no problem with being constantly watched and scored (you know, the typical reasoning of "I have nothing to hide"), governments do not have the right to push this onto anybody. If an individual wants to be watched, let them submit themselves to such vigilance voluntarily, but let everyone else have the right to decide about his own life. (Yes, I am using "his" on purpose, as a protest against the deliberate over-feminization of the language for the purpose of creating an even stronger division between men and women. If the linguistic over-corrective push to use the feminine forms was really about bringing balance between men and women, the solution would be to invent a *neutral* third person singular pronoun. The Hungarian language for example has only neutral pronouns for third person singular and plural. How about that?)

Unfortunately, this surveillance system is related to the Internet of Things as all smart devices would create an all-encompassing net around still organic human beings, which would provide the perfect infrastructure for full-on continuous surveillance. You should think twice before you invest your money into anything that could bring closer such a dehumanizing existence for yourself and your children.

17

Grab 'Em by the Bitcoins

In an ideal world we could happily go ahead and automate all the tedious processes necessary for the operation of society. We could eliminate surplus effort, unnecessary and inefficient work which sucks the life out of so many people. We could make sure that we respect the natural balance of Earth and never take more than we need, developing efficient recycling and production systems by redistributing all that we currently waste on the maintenance and feeding of criminal organizations masquerading as governments and monstrous corporations that are propagating sickness, war, pollution, suffering, and death. In an ideal world we could automate everything, putting everything that needs efficiency on the blockchain. But taking into account the reality we live in, should we just yet?

We could certainly create a decentralized monetary system that many hope will free us from the slavery of the parasitic economical system we have been suffering from for thousands of years. However, having everything supervised by algorithms and machines does not sound like an ideal world we would like to live in. Why not? Because it is based on the false, very detrimental belief that humans are intrinsically bad, evil creatures who need to be supervised, controlled and kept within the lines, lest we cheat, steal, destroy and kill without end. Living in such an automated society would mean that humanity would be kept under this false premise which would certainly cause more psychological harm to the individual and as a consequence to the entire species as we relinquish our power and inner responsibility to the algorithms.

Wouldn't it be better to use blockchain in a limited way for things that are best dealt with in a decentralized and trustless way, while leaving the more important things to organic, live human interactions?

Wouldn't it make much more sense if we simply went ahead and abolished the concept of usury, by making interests illegal? What if we decided that from now on we would use money as a utility just like we treat water and electricity, and we would simply use it for exchanging goods and services but not for hoarding to gain something by simply sitting on the money as we do now?

Demurrage currencies could definitely be at least part of the solution that could transform the way we live simply by the logical self interest of the individuals. But even if we are not yet ready to go that far, the debt money should disappear anyway, because as we have seen it, it is one of the root causes of all human problems in society.

As for the question of governance, there are now some governments and institutions that are working on adopting blockchain in their operations, but of course, those will be there for gaining more control over you, and not for the greater good and prosperity of the people. As they say, talking is free, so most likely governments will create a good enough sounding narrative for why exactly we need more surveillance and control instead of more freedom.

We could simply write off all accumulated public debt and not let millions of people suffer, and pay, for something their banks had done over their heads.

What blockchain could really be used for is for example securely managing direct democratic processes, keeping a record of direct votes of all citizens regarding issues. Instead of centralized governments and their institutions we could use the blockchain as a good infrastructure on which to build our direct democratic governance.

Direct democracy simply means that citizens get to vote on each and every question that directly affects them, as opposed to the bullshit system where you are brainwashed to believe that voting for some guy from a limited pool of candidates once in every four years is all you can do to make decisions about the kind of world you want to live in. Especially as politicians are not legally responsible for breaking their election promises during their time in office.

A real direct democracy system would be more than possible to implement with blockchain now technically, how come they never mention it in the mainstream media? Direct democracy would also mean that we would have way more say in the local questions than in nationwide or global questions, but that is ok, because once people really get to decide how they want to live locally, the global problems would start to slowly disappear.

Can you imagine letting the people decide by using blockchain based voting on say military spending or whether a country should build a nuclear power plant? Such a direct decision making process would quickly put an end to all war spending, you can be sure of that, because no sane person will ever want to go to war, and the ones who would benefit (the ones who now benefit) would be definitely outnumbered by the 99%.

In the real world though, various parts of the establishment are working to deform Bitcoin into something it is not, and to use the blockchain technology to subdue the population to a never hitherto seen extent. Governments have been desperately trying to catch up with the technology and are talking about the need to implement ways of control (meaning surveillance) into blockchain systems for taxation and "security" reasons.

There is a chance that the authorities will use the advances in blockchain technology to put the focus on how blockchain cannot be cheated, and how implementing blockchain technologies into official institutional operations will be the best thing for humanity since slice bread, finally eliminating corruption (and tax evasion).

When in fact what we should focus on now is, whether we really need central, elected (and like in the EU, in some cases unelected) people making decisions above our heads, based on some hundreds of years old tradition called government.

What we should focus on now is all the suffering and injustice the debt based money system had caused to billions of people throughout the ages (and is still causing today) and how we could eliminate the ever growing debt that weighs nations down and fuels all the wars on the planet.

Why is there nobody talking about the need for structural and conceptual change? All the emphasis on this great new technology, and nobody mentions the need to eliminate all accumulated public debt? Of course, until governments exist they would never want you to be free of government control. That is just simple logic. And this leads us back to the question of who is really behind the things that are happening on the planet right now. Is this technological development random and the fruit of human ingenuity, or is it something pre-planned and sinister in nature?

Just imagine for a moment if it was not a coincidence that for example Bitcoin was built using the SHA-256 protocol which was developed by the NSA. Why would the NSA release a supposedly unbreakable protocol to the public when they are in the business of breaking into systems and getting all kinds of information, most of the time obviously without the consent of the affected? It just does not make sense.

What if the SHA-256 protocol indeed has a back door only known to the NSA which makes it possible for them to snoop around the Bitcoin network as some people believe? Even Vitalik Buterin commented in 2011 on Bitcointalk, an online forum to a user called Brazil who wrote: "This is probably one of the major reasons Satoshi never let anyone know who he was. I wouldn't be surprised if he is actually an American working for the NSA specializing in cryptography. Then he got sick of the government's monetary policies and decided to create bitcoin." Vitalik Buterin replied to this saying: "Or the NSA itself decided to create Bitcoin. Things as big as megacorps and governments work against themselves all the time, I wouldn't be too surprised if the NSA has some part in at least supporting it."[507]

When this 2011 conversation resurfaced in June 2018, Buterin commented that since then his views have changed and that "would not be surprised" does not mean certainty, but a 10-50% chance.[508] Anyway, if he were certain that the NSA was involved, he would likely not tell it to anybody for personal safety reasons. Also, what if Ethereum were also related to the NSA or the

Deep State?

Why would the controllers set up such a weird trap, creating or participating in the creation of Bitcoin? The advantage to them would be that the
population would be duped once again: in our hopes to change the corrupt
and centralized current money system to something which we believe to be
decentralized, untraceable, uncontrollable. We would willingly give up the
last vestiges of our freedom within the current money system (which is the
ability to use cash that is fungible and the least controllable and traceable
form of currency by the government and its many institutions).

In a way we would willingly walk into the slaughterhouse where once
everybody is lined up inside, the controllers could just shut the gates and
come out of hiding.

While I am finishing the editing of this book, Edward Snowden just gave a
keynote speech at a Berlin conference via video-link from Moscow, where
he emphasized the importance of privacy coins and that *"a fundamentally
anonymous currency to be able to engage in private trade"* must be recognized
as a basic human right.[509] Freedom is really what makes us human, and we
must retain our freedom of choice, or we seize to be real human beings and
become like individual bodies of an insect colony.

Whether or not you believe that Craig Wright is Satoshi Nakamoto (or
has anything to do with the origins of Bitcoin), his comments during a BSV
meetup video conference with Singapore enthusiasts are worth considering
because they come from a different perspective which could be shocking
to many. Wright emphasized that opposite to what many people believe,
Bitcoin was not created to fight the government but instead to create an
"honest money" where corruption and cheating are not possible because
the algorithm does not allow them.[510] (When he talks about Bitcoin, he
means the original Bitcoin and Bitcoin SV into which the corrupted Bitcoin
"reincarnated".)

According to Wright, Bitcoin allows normal people to transact honestly,
but it is extremely unfriendly to illicit users. He also said that "decentralized"
means that it is a distributed database, but because of practical reasons it
was always foreseen that Bitcoin would be run by large mining clusters and

not that every single person could run it.[511] (Hence the importance of not having a low block size limit because that creates transaction speed issues and large mining pools get to charge urgency fees.)

Another interesting claim by Craig Wright worth considering is that "Bitcoin with a standard protocol takes away power. If no one can change the protocol, not me, not God, there's no power in money. Money is all about power. And this is one of the things Bitcoin has done, it's removed that power. It will remove that power globally."[512] For Wright, Bitcoin is an electronic cash system and not a cryptocurrency; an open, distributed "honest money" public ledger which does not intend to hide transaction information, but which *can be used for encrypting and storing data in the blockchain.*[513]

The difference in definition could refer to Wright's belief that substituting fiat currencies with Bitcoin will be enough to clear things up for humanity, to end all cheating and corruption. His vision is to provide an honest public ledger that makes crime and cheating impossible, while providing more transaction speed for the economy, and also providing the currently unbanked masses with a way to participate in the economy. However, it does not seem enough to be able to radically eliminate abuse of power by the ruling elite. And here we bump into the question of governance and societal structure again.

As far as the storage of encrypted data in the blockchain goes, which is one of the main projects the BSV team have been working on, their vision for Bitcoin is to become a "source of truth", a backbone of sorts on which all aspects and interactions of human society can be based. Wright expects the internet to one day become a sidechain of Bitcoin.

Because of the hash function of the Bitcoin code you can encrypt data of any size, even long videos, and embed them into one transaction information which then gets into a block, and thus the encrypted document, audio, or video is immutably saved in the blockchain forever. No censoring or tampering possible.

As for the future, Wright thinks that states will first not adopt Bitcoin as an official currency, but will use the capabilities of the Bitcoin blockchain to release their own tokenized fiat currencies on top of Bitcoin, which is certainly one option.[514]

Both from the communications of Craig Wright and Andrew DeSantis it sounds as if Bitcoin had the potential to become an all encompassing, underlying connective tissue or a sort of unified digital mycelial network that fuses with the various functionalities of specific systems to keep a safe, immutable record of everything that goes on in those systems.

In the meantime another large player, Binance just announced on August 19, 2019 its "plans to initiate an open blockchain project, Venus, an initiative to develop localized stablecoins and digital assets pegged to fiat currencies across the globe. Binance is looking to create new alliances and partner-ships with governments, corporations, technology companies, and other cryptocurrency companies and projects involved in the larger blockchain ecosystem, to empower developed and developing countries to spur new currencies."[515]

This is just an example of how large tech corporations as well as crypto giants are apparently aiming at the same goal, that of creating stablecoins pegged to existing fiat currencies, or providing platforms for states to create their own stablecoins. In such an environment Bitcoin will definitely not be the only contender, and we are yet to see how the new lines of power will be distributed on the global monetary map.

A possible outcome could be, especially because Bitcoin would eliminate cheating and shady dealings, that once it would reach a level of (grassroots style) mass adoption which the establishment deems to be dangerous, they could come out with the obvious, turning the focus on how it is not as private and anonymous as we all were told, maybe suggesting a "better", globalist version. You know, one which would be created by them, a nice government controlled public coin. Or a digital cash of a mega corporation that will have managed to seize the control of the government. Which even could be Libra, if it ever gets developed by Facebook and the corporatocracy manages to grab hold of more power over nations.

It is a possibility, especially if governments become more fearful of Bitcoin and other cryptocurrencies than of Libra and its corporate brothers that will undoubtedly surface. Some legislators might find it less threatening to deal with corporations with headquarters and official leaders than trying to regulate a crowd-sourced entity where decisions are not made in a top-down fashion.

Although at this moment it very much looks like the governments have already freaked out by the idea of Libra and its potential to undermine their control of the economy. It is not a coincidence that Facebook was kindly requested to not carry on with the plan to implement the Libra coin. However, they might be willing to team up with bigger crypto companies that are experienced in blockchain but are not too powerful to be able to overpower governments in the short run.

As for Facebook, IBM has recently announced that it is cooperating in the development of the Libra project, so obviously, for Facebook a no from the US, German and French governments is not a no forever.

What is clear at this point is that all the players who have a stake in the future of money and cryptocurrencies: the banksters, technology mega-corporations, governments, tech geeks and developers who would like to see a more just world, and the people who have already seen the potential of cryptocurrencies, will keep working towards their own version of an ideal future. It promises to be a race of ideologies, morality, and technologies, and who will end up as the winner is the most important question of our time. But because the controllers' skin is at stake, it does not promise to be a fair game, so buckle up.

If we think in terms of creating a real, positive change in the structure of the economy and society, the main problem with Bitcoin, Ethereum, and the rest of the crypto projects is that they do not have built in features that incentivize people for acting in a way that builds value for the future, that protects the environment (which is the sane and logical thing to do in a finite system) and that builds cooperation between humans instead of greed and hoarding for ourselves, not giving a rat's ass about what our actions related to money cause to the environment and other people, and staying in the mentality of Darwinian-style competition.

What if Bitcoin was indeed created by some letter soup agency or its secret arm to dazzle us with the promise of freedom, knowing that its features would seem like liberation to almost all humans as we have been shackled for thousands of years in the fiat money debt slave system? The end game then would be for the controllers to manage to transition us into our new, lighter shackles at a time when the old shackles are falling off naturally because the banking system and the control system are faltering and falling apart.

If Bitcoin indeed was created by (the team of) Craig Wright (remember, he stated that Bitcoin does not fight government), they may have thought that creating Bitcoin would be enough to "exorcise immorality" from people and corporations. However, that might just not be enough. No matter how we like to tell ourselves that the government is the cause of all the bad things happening to us and to the country, the truth is that we, individuals, always have the final say in what we do or not do.

We know that buying certain products directly causes the destruction of rainforests or the extermination of orangutans in Borneo, but as we are not directly, personally affected, most of the time we choose based on what is comfortable and easy, or what saves us a few bucks because money is such a hard-to-get resource.

With the appearance of cryptocurrencies the focus and thinking of humanity is actually being corralled in a way that blames the banking system only (and they really are to blame too), while we do not realize that our issues are not just centralization or that our economy is based on debt money.

The real issue is that money should support us as individuals and as a society and not enslave us, but it does enslave us because we are addicted to the debt money. If people understood how a demurrage currency can bring out the best in everyone, how it incentivizes people for taking actions that are responsible and that create real value for the future (like planting trees for the future versus cutting trees down to put the money into the bank for compound interest), it would mean the end of the imprisonment of the human spirit.

We could so much more easily go back to living a natural, creative life based on real human values instead of parasitic-vampiric economic "values". The natural, real human value game would be about who creates more beauty, harmony, knowledge, who contributes to the healing and thriving of people, society, and the environment, and not who can hoard more money at the expense of others.

Demurrage currencies could be at least part of the solution, but we would need to be able to pay taxes with them, or else such demurrage currencies would not survive. And that leads us to the question of government.

Realizing the intrinsic faults of the money system is just one piece of our hopeful liberation. Another, perhaps even more important issue we need to solve is the question of governance and freedom.

Who and why decides about how we should, and are allowed to, live our lives? Why do we have to conform to a system which we inherited from people who aren't even alive today? Why do we, as social beings, behave as if we were only cogs in a giant computer, programed to execute the same program? Where is freedom in all this? Everything the controllers are doing is to keep the belief systems which hold us hostage to their exploitative political and religious systems alive.

To illustrate how cultural programming influences what we believe to be even possible (and therefore achievable), and how even well-meaning people could be digging the grave of cryptocurrencies simply because we have been indoctrinated so well, let's see an excerpt from an article by Michael K. Spencer regarding the development of Ethereum:

"Ethereum as a ragtag community needs to crack a problem on human governance but how can we expect a bunch of bohemian engineers to do it? Failures of leadership are rife in nearly every industry and system of human society in 2018. We see it in corrupt politicians, greedy tech executives, unethical engineers and, of course, crypto profiteers who especially abused the ICO system. EOS is a perfect example of this. Ethereum might be more attractive to developers, but it may not have as bright a future as blockchain-as-a-service in the Cloud does, led by the likes of Alibaba and Amazon. The market necessitates centralized blockchains before we are ever near decentralization taking place. Crypto might have to die for its equivalent when it is ready to be born.

It might be painful to accept, but Ethereum might have to die for public blockchains to evolve. Ethereum won't be able to organize a scattered global network of contributors and stakeholders without sacrificing "decentralization".

It's just not realistic. It would be better if Amazon acquired it and funded it. You can't reinvent the wheel of how businesses and organizations can or should work. You need to strike a balance with reality."[516]

One of the main pullbacks we, human beings could experience regarding the developments around decentralization is our diminished capacity to break our mental limits about what is possible for us as individuals and as a society. Thinking that Amazon would be a better foster parent to Ethereum than a "scattered global network of contributors and stakeholders" means the author of this article has given up on our species. Something I do not intend to do. Looking at what humanity has become, it's not a pretty sight, but our creative potential is way beyond what we dare to dream of.

This is not to say that Ethereum would be "the solution"·to anything, but it is important to realize how we tend to discard collaborative, less formal projects due to our belief that collaboration that is not structured strictly pyramidally is doomed to fail. And Ethereum is not the best example here anyway, because of its quite strong central leadership.

Obviously, Mr. Spenser refers to all the issues that we can see everywhere: it is extremely difficult to make optimal, just decisions that will benefit everybody because of various personal factors. Humans have egos and those egos do not like to lose, especially the ones in leading positions (because they got to those positions by outsmarting, outwilling or outcheating the rest). Of course, corruption is rampant everywhere, and time and time again it seems as if the law does not judge equally the poor and the mega rich. If you polled people I bet over 90% would say that politicians and people in the various governmental institutions are corrupt, especially the leaders. A similar dynamic can be observed at any work place, where not always the best idea or the best candidate wins or where things are decided in skewed ways.

However, all the above is caused by the evil parasitic system we were born into which extracts time, life force, and money from everyone, and where everything is commoditized. The issue is the fact that we are "governed" by others who decide what we can and can't do and what we must do. The issue is that we are indoctrinated at school but also by all the propaganda in the media, movies, books etc. all trying to make us believe that we need government. That if we do not have somebody above our heads who tells us what is right and what is wrong and who makes the rules "for our own good" and "for the greater good" of the nation or the country, all hell will break loose and the entire country will fall into total chaos.

And by chaos they mean not something organic where everybody follows his or her own inner moral compass and acts according to it. They mean people perpetrating all kinds of abominable acts against each other. You know, that never ceasing argument that we need the rule of the law and we need people supervising the rest to prevent us from committing bad things. Back to Darwin, again...

Giving up "human governance" and handing authority or the right of supervision to algorithms is not going to lead us down the path of true freedom for humanity. Not at a time when artificial intelligence is already being introduced to the public, when merging with the machine is mentioned casually as the next goal of certain people, not when brain augmentation with chips is being developed that would save you from having to go to school, and surely prevent you from developing critical thinking skills (excellent idea, Google!), not when Elon Musk wants you to implant an artificial intelligence interface into your brain.

Not when the 5G telecommunication system is being rolled out without proper scientific studies when it is evident that the same technology had been developed and used by the US military for purposes of war already. Millimeter wave weapons, active denial. Please research these terms.

If the controllers manage to steer our attention towards the question of "lean, efficient and transparent governance" (which would stay centralized, or in their preferred scenario, globalized) and away from the question of how and why we could change to participatory democracy or local self governance without leaders and decisions made above our heads and often against our will, we could miss a unique opportunity to openly *question whether any central governing organizations are needed at all* now that we can achieve transparency through blockchain technology.

We could miss grabbing the momentum to create our own grassroots organizations based on natural, organic human interactions where each individual acts as a truly grownup spiritual being, instead of behaving like a spiritual infant in an adult body, and takes responsibility for the decisions pertaining to his or her own local community.

In this sense providing an external solution like the blockchain technology and its "trustless trust" can really be enticing for the disempowered individual who is riddled with fears accumulated throughout a lifetime of oppression, indoctrination, and negative programming. It takes a lot of courage for a person who is fearful (and rest assured, the human mind generally is very much steeped in the fear frequency) to take action and stand up for what he thinks and believes is right. The majority of people feel and understand that things are skewed and that injustice is rampant everywhere they look. However, the majority also feels a sense of impotence because most of us deep inside believe that going against the established norms, customs, and institutions is dangerous and could potentially bring negative consequences to the individual.

And here is where placing your hopes and trust in an amazing new technology comes in to provide the ultimate psychological crutch: *look, now with this amazing blockchain technology being developed we no longer have to stand up for ourselves and make things right and tell them that we think they're acting immorally. We will not have to brave up and stop being cowards. No, the technology will provide morality without me having to move a finger. I will just have to adopt it and wait for things to get better....*It is all about passivity, fear, and staying in our comfort zone.

It is power to the empowered, spiritually adult individual or power to the New World Order this time. Either we grab this once-in-a-lifetime opportunity, or we wait and passively watch how the controllers will grab us by the bitcoins to cement in their power, and use the very remedy we were hoping to liberate us to kill off yet another piece of the collective soul of mankind.

We are at the precipice of a never hitherto witnessed technological renaissance which has just started. It can go extremely well, catapulting us to a more just, more livable time when we are freed from the hurdles of the

40-hour work week (which only exists because of the extortions applied by the power structure) and can dedicate ourselves to activities that are truly human like art, creativity, true science, community building, play, the loving stewardship of our environment, and the cultivation of our capabilities to love and be love as individuals and as a society.

Or it can become our worst nightmare, thrusting humanity into an electronic frequency prison where we are quarantined by impersonal machines and protocols and the 5G frequencies, where our creative genius and the highest aspirations of our species are slowly killed off.

It all depends on whether we are capable of looking ahead and thinking critically, taking off the blindfold and discarding limiting beliefs and outright lies we were fed, whether we are able to choose not based on our apparent self-interest and short term gains according to the current parasitic system, but based on what would serve us as individuals, and by extension what would serve humanity in creating a better future, a life worth living.

May we choose, invest in, and use, the new technologies wisely.

Notes

INTERESTING TIMES

1 https://onlygold.com/gold-prices/all-the-gold-in-the-world/

2 Dobrica Blagojevic. How Many People Use Bitcoin? How Many Bitcoin Wallets are There? https://captainaltcoin.com/how-many-people-use-bitcoin/

3 Carlos Terenzi. Data ScientistSsuggests Bitcoin Has Reached Global Penetration. https://usethebitcoin.com/data-scientist-suggests-bitcoin-has-reached-global-penetration/

4 https://maven11.com/2019/01/16/top-5-adoption-trends-blockchain-in-2019/

WHAT THEY DID NOT TEACH YOU ABOUT THE ECONOMY AND SOCIETY

5 MJ DeMarco. Unscripted: Life, Liberty and the Pursuit of Entrepreneurship. Viperion Publishing Corporation, 2017

6 E.F. Schumacher. Small Is Beautiful: A Study of Economics As If People Mattered. Vintage, 2011, pp. 68-69

7 Kerri Smith. Brain Makes Decisions Before You Even Know It. https://www.nature.com/news/2008/080411/full/news.2008.751.html

IN DEBT WE TRUST

8 Margrit Kennedy, Stephanie Ehrenschwendner. Occupy Money: Creating an Economy Where Everybody Wins. New Society Publishers, 2012, p. 23

9 Margrit Kennedy, Stephanie Ehrenschwendner. Occupy Money: Creating an Economy Where Everybody Wins. New Society Publishers, 2012, p. 24

10 Margrit Kennedy, Stephanie Ehrenschwendner. Occupy Money: Creating an Economy Where Everybody Wins. New Society Publishers, 2012, p. 24

11 See www.lietaer.com. If you want to dive deeper, I suggest you read Creating Wealth: Growing Local Economies with Local Currencies by Gwendolyn Hallsmith & Bernard Lietaer (New Society Publishers, 2011)

12 https://en.wikipedia.org/wiki/Reserve_requirement

13 Bernard Lietaer. What is Money? http://www.lietaer.com/2010/09/what-is-money/ (highlighting by BK)

14 https://www.federalreserve.gov/faqs/about_14986.htm

15 https://www.stlouisfed.org/in-plain-english/who-owns-the-federal-reserve-banks

16 Statement of Michael Schuman delivered during a speech in Vermont in 2007, as quoted in Creating Wealth: Growing Local Economies with Local Currencies by Gwendolyn Hallsmith and Bernard Lietaer, New Society Publishers, 2011, p. 23.

17 Thomas D. Schauf. The Federal Reserve is Privately Owned. https://www.facts-are-facts.com/news/the-federal-reserve-is-privately-owned#.W7n9jNRLdjG

18 Mark Shepard. Restoration Agriculture: Real-World Permaculture for Farmers. Mark Shepard, 2013

CAN NEGATIVE INTEREST BE POSITIVE?

19 Silvio Gesell. The Natural Economic Order. http://www.appropriate-economics.org/ebooks/neo/preface.htm

20 Bernard A. Lietaer.   Community Currencies: A New Tool for the 21st Century. http://www.transaction.net/money/cc/cc04.html

21 If you want to research alternative local currencies, check out the ithaca dollar or the bristol pound as successful examples of creating a more vibrant local community.

22 Michael Albert. Parecon, Life After Capitalism. Verso, 2003

ENTER SATOSHI

23 https://bitcoin.org/bitcoin.pdf

24 Nolan Bauerle: What Is Blockchain Technology
    https://www.coindesk.com/information/what-is-blockchain-technology

25 Ledger Stuff: The Anatomy of a Bitcoin Address Commonly Confused by a Public Key – https://www.theopenledger.com/the-anatomy-of-a-bitcoin-address-which-is-not-a-public-key/

26 Ledger Stuff: The Anatomy of a Bitcoin Address Commonly Confused by a Public Key https://www.theopenledger.com/the-anatomy-of-a-bitcoin-address-which-is-not-a-public-key/

27 Jake Frankenfield: Bitcoin Wallet – https://www.investopedia.com/terms/b/bitcoin-wallet.asp

28 Yessi Bello Perez: The differences between a bitcoin wallet and an address – a secret guide for embarrassed crypto noobs – https://thenextweb.com/cryptocurrency/2019/06/21/the-differences-between-a-bitcoin-wallet-and-an-address/

29 Chris Pacia: Bitcoin mining explained like you're 5 – Part 2 - Mechanics - https://chrispacia.wordpress.com/2013/09/02/bitcoin-mining-explained-like-youre-five-part-2-mechanics

30 Bruno Skvorc: How to read Bitcoin blockchain data on Blockexplorer? - https://bitfalls.com/2017/10/03/read-bitcoin-blockchain-data-blockexplorer/

31 CryptoCompare: How is a block hash created? - https://www.cryptocompare.com/coins/guides/
    how-is-a-block-hash-created/

32 Sangeetha-prabhu and Arvind Padmanabhan: Blockchain – Summary - https://devopedia.org/blockchain

33 Shawn Dexter: How are blockchain transactions validated? Cons

34 Shawn Dexter: How are blockchain transactions validated? Cons

35 Shawn Dexter: How are blockchain transactions validated? Cons

36 Patrick Nohe based on the original written by Jay Thakkar. What is 256-bit Encryption? How safe is it? https://www.thesslstore.com/blog/what-is-256-bit-encryption/

37 IBM News Room. https://newsroom.ibm.com/2019-01-08-IBM-Unveils-Worlds-First-Integrated-Quantum-Computing-System-for-Commercial-Use

38 Jose Antonio Lanz. What Google's Quantum Computer Means for Bitcoin. https://decrypt.co/9642/what-google-quantum-computer-means-for-bitcoin

39 Jose Antonio Lanz. What Google's Quantum Computer Means for Bitcoin. https://decrypt.co/9642/what-google-quantum-computer-means-for-bitcoin

40 https://bitcoin.org/bitcoin.pdf p. 2

41 OP-ED. Segregated Witness Removes One of Bitcoin's Data Integrit Checks. https://news.bitcoin.com/segregated-witness-removes-one-of-bitcoins-data-integrity-checks/

42 Coindesk. How Do Bitcoin Transactions Work? https://www.coindesk.com/information/how-do-bitcoin-transactions-work/

43 John Carvalho. Bitcoin is Not Fungible, Should It Be? https://medium.com/@BitcoinError-Log/
    bitcoin-is-not-fungible-should-it-be-620a28f3f8b1

44 John Carvalho. Bitcoin is Not Fungible, Should It Be? https://medium.com/@BitcoinError-Log/
    bitcoin-is-not-fungible-should-it-be-620a28f3f8b1

45 Chris Pacia. Bitcoin Mining Explained Like You're Five: Part 1 – Incentives. https://chrispacia.wordpress.com/2013/09/02/bitcoin-mining-explained-like-youre-five-part-1-incentives/

46 Chris Pacia. Bitcoin Mining Explained Like You're Five: Part 1 – Incentives. https://chrispacia.wordpress.com/2013/09/02/bitcoin-mining-explained-like-youre-five-part-1-incentives

47 Chris Pacia. Bitcoin Mining Explained Like You're Five: Part 1 – Incentives
    https://chrispacia.wordpress.com/2013/09/02/bitcoin-mining-explained-like-youre-five-part-1-incentives/

48 Chris Pacia. Bitcoin Mining Explained Like You're Five: Part 1 – Incentives

https://chrispacia.wordpress.com/2013/09/02/bitcoin-mining-explained-like-youre-five-part-1-incentives/

49 Chris Pacia. Bitcoin Mining Explained Like You're Five: Part 1 – Incentives
     https://chrispacia.wordpress.com/2013/09/02/bitcoin-mining-explained-like-youre-five-part-1-incentives/

50 Chris Pacia. Bitcoin Mining Explained Like You're Five: Part 1 – Incentives
     https://chrispacia.wordpress.com/2013/09/02/bitcoin-mining-explained-like-youre-five-part-1-incentives/

BITCOIN TO THE RESCUE?

51 Bitcoin Exchange Guide News Team. Bitcoin Mining Energy Comparison: Global Banking Industry Uses 500 Times More Energy than Bitcoin. https://bitcoinex-changeguide.com/bitcoin-mining-energy-comparison-global-banking-industry-uses-500-times-more-energy-than-bitcoin/

52 Philip Poutintsev. What is the Next Big Thing in the CryptoWworld? https://hacker-noon.com/what-is-the-next-big-thing-in-crypto-world-c3c55146b931

53 Josiah Wilmoth.   Bitmain's Mining Pools Now Control Nearly 51 Percent of the Bitcoin Hashrate. https://www.ccn.com/bitmains-mining-pools-now-control-nearly-51-percent-of-the-bitcoin-hashrate/

54 David Hamilton: How Antminers became the best Bitcoin mining hardware in less than two years https://coincentral.com/how-antminer-became-the-best-bitcoin-mining-hardware-in-less-than-two-years/

55 Paddy Baker. Declining Bitmain Hash Rate Means BTC Is Safe And Decentralized. https://cryptobriefing.com/bitmain-hash-rate-falls-10/

56 David Hamilton. How Antminers Became the Best Bitcoin Mining Hardware in Less Than Two Years https://coincentral.com/how-antminer-became-the-best-bitcoin-mining-hardware-in-less-than-two-years/

57 David Hamilton. How Antminers Became the Best Bitcoin Mining Hardware in Less Than Two Years https://coincentral.com/how-antminer-became-the-best-bitcoin-mining-hardware-in-less-than-two-years/

58 https://cryptocoingrowth.com/2019/03/13/valued-at-1-billion-canaan-creative-is-encroaching-on-bitmains-dominance/

59 Paddy Baker: Declining Bitmain Hash Rate Means BTC Is Safe And Decentralized https://cryptobriefing.com/bitmain-hash-rate-falls-10/

60 M. Szmigiera. Number of Blockchain Wallet Users Worldwide from Second Quarter 2016 to 2nd Quarter 2019. https://www.statista.com/statistics/647374/worldwide-blockchain-wallet-users/

61 https://bitcoingold.org/

62 Josiah Wilmoth. Bitmain's Mining Pools Now Control Nearly 51 Percent of the Bitcoin Hashrate. https://www.ccn.com/bitmains-mining-pools-now-control-nearly-51-percent-of-the-bitcoin-hashrate/

63 https://btc.com/stats/pool?pool_mode=day3

64 Jordan Tuwiner. Bitcoin Mining Pools. https://www.buybitcoinworldwide.com/mining/pools/

65 Dmitry Laptev. Bitcoin: Transactions, Malleability, SegWit and Scaling. https://medium.com/lightningto-me/bitcoin-transactions-malleability-segwit-and-scaling-258af8ed9cbf

66 Dmitry Laptev. Bitcoin: Transactions, Malleability, SegWit and Scaling. https://medium.com/lightningto-me/bitcoin-transactions-malleability-segwit-and-scaling-258af8ed9cbf

67 Jonald Fyookball. Should We Fix Malleability in Bitcoin and Bitcoin Cash? If so, How? And When? https://news.bitcoin.com/should-we-fix-malleability-in-bitcoin-and-bitcoin-cash-if-so-how-and-when/

68 Jonald Fyookball. Should We Fix Malleability in Bitcoin and Bitcoin Cash? If so, How? And When? https://news.bitcoin.com/should-we-fix-malleability-in-bitcoin-and-bitcoin-cash-if-so-how-and-when/

69 Jonald Fyookball. Should We Fix Malleability in Bitcoin and Bitcoin Cash? If so, How? And When? https://news.bitcoin.com/should-we-fix-malleability-in-bitcoin-and-bitcoin-cash-if-so-how-and-when/

70 https://bitcoin.org/en/wallets/desktop/windows/bitcoincore/

71 Jonald Fyookball. Should We Fix Malleability in Bitcoin and Bitcoin Cash? If so, How? And When? https://news.bitcoin.com/should-we-fix-malleability-in-bitcoin-and-bitcoin-cash-if-so-how-and-when/

72 Jonald Fyookball. Should We Fix Malleability in Bitcoin and Bitcoin Cash? If so, How? And When? https://news.bitcoin.com/should-we-fix-malleability-in-bitcoin-and-bitcoin-cash-if-so-how-and-when/

73 Jonald Fyookball. Should We Fix Malleability in Bitcoin and Bitcoin Cash? If so, How? And When? https://news.bitcoin.com/should-we-fix-malleability-in-bitcoin-and-bitcoin-cash-if-so-how-and-when/

74 Jonald Fyookball. Should We Fix Malleability in Bitcoin and Bitcoin Cash? If so, How? And When? https://news.bitcoin.com/should-we-fix-malleability-in-bitcoin-and-bitcoin-cash-if-so-how-and-when/

75 Carlos Terenzi. Milestone: SegWit Payments Reach 50 Percent of Transactions. https://usethebitcoin.com/milestone-segwit-payments-50-percent-transactions/

76 https://p2sh.info/dashboard/db/segwit-usage?orgId=1&from=now-6M&to=now

77 Jonald Fyookball. Should We Fix Malleability in Bitcoin and Bitcoin Cash? If so, How? And When? https://news.bitcoin.com/should-we-fix-malleability-in-bitcoin-and-bitcoin-cash-if-so-how-and-when/

78 https://www.theice.com

79 Emilio Janus. BAKKT Bitcoin Futures Could See Green Light in Just 10 Days. http://bitcoin-ist.com/bakkt-bitcoin-futures-cftc-10-days

80 CryptoCredits News. What's So Bullish About Bakkt's Bitcoin Futures? https://www.cryptocredits.net/whats-so-bullish-about-bakkts-bitcoin-futures/

81 Nick Chong. Crypto Tidbits: ErisX Bitcoin Futures, Blockchain on Jeapardy, Proposed BitMEX Ban. https://www.newsbtc.com/2019/07/06/crypto-tidbits-erisx-bitcoin-futures-blockchain-on-jeopardy-proposed-bitmex-ban/

82 Isabel Woodford. Bakkt Confirms September Launch Date After Getting Green Light from Regulators. https://www.theblockcrypto.com/2019/08/16/bakkt-confirms-september-launch-date/

83 Binance Research. September Markets Overview. https://info.binance.com/en/research/marketresearch/Global-Markets-September-2019.html

FORKS IN THE BITCOIN ROAD

84 John Light. The Difference Between a Hard Fork, a Soft Fork and a Chain Split, and What They Mean for the Future of Bitcoin. https://medium.com/@lightcoin/the-differences-between-a-hard-fork-a-soft-fork-and-a-chain-split-and-what-they-mean-for-the-769273f358c9

85 Amy Castor. A Short Guide to Bitcoin Forks. https://www.coindesk.com/short-guide-bitcoin-forks-explained/

86 John Light. The Difference Between a Hard Fork, a Soft Fork and a Chain Split, and What They Mean for the Future of Bitcoin. https://medium.com/@lightcoin/the-differences-between-a-hard-fork-a-soft-fork-and-a-chain-split-and-what-they-mean-for-the-769273f358c9

87 Amy Castor. A Short Guide to Bitcoin Forks. https://www.coindesk.com/short-guide-bitcoin-forks-explained/

88 John Light. The Difference Between a Hard Fork, a Soft Fork and a Chain Split, and What They Mean for the Future of Bitcoin. https://medium.com/@lightcoin/the-differences-between-a-hard-fork-a-soft-fork-and-a-chain-split-and-what-they-mean-for-the-769273f358c9

89 John Light. The Difference Between a Hard Fork, a Soft Fork and a Chain Split, and What They Mean for the Future of Bitcoin. https://medium.com/@lightcoin/the-differences-between-a-hard-fork-a-soft-fork-and-a-chain-split-and-what-they-mean-for-the-769273f358c9

90 Timothy B. Lee. Major Glitch in Bitcoin Network Sparks Sell-Off; Price Temporarily Falls 23%. https://arstechnica.com/information-technology/2013/03/major-glitch-in-bitcoin-network-sparks-sell-off-price-temporarily-falls-23/

91 Litecoin versus Ethereum: Understanding the Differences. by Genesis Mining. https://www.genesis-mining.com/litecoin-vs-ethereum

92 Dany Bradburry. Scrypt-based Miners and the New Cryptocurrency Arms Race. https://www.coindesk.com/scrypt-miners-cryptocurrency-arms-race

93 Coins with Memory-Intensive Mining. https://bitcoin.stackexchange.com/questions/22752/coins-with-memory-intensive-mining

94 Coins with Memory-Intensive Mining. https://bitcoin.stackexchange.com/questions/22752/coins-with-memory-intensive-mining

95 Alex Meears. Back to Basics – The History of Litecoin. https://news.bitstarz.com/back-to-basics-the-history-of-litecoin

96 Rilcoin. Cryptocurrency Hash and the Difference Between SHA and Scrypt. https://medium.com/@rilcoin/cryptocurrency-hash-and-the-difference-between-sha-and-scrypt-1f2217eb5b89

97 Alex Meears. Back to Basics – The History of Litecoin. https://news.bitstarz.com/back-to-basics-the-history-of-litecoin

98 Alex Meears. Back to Basics – The History of Litecoin. https://news.bitstarz.com/back-to-basics-the-history-of-litecoin

99 Jonathan Chester. The Battle for Bitoin: What You Need to Know About Bitcoin and Bitcoin Cash. https://www.forbes.com/sites/jonathanchester/2017/11/27/the-battle-for-bitcoin-what-you-need-to-know-about-bitcoin-and-bitcoin-cash/#57422805331f

100 Wilma Woo. SegWit Now Comprises 50 Percent of Bitcoin Transactions. https://bitcoinist.com/segwit-now-comprises-50-percent-of-bitcoin-transactions/

101 Larry Cermak. SegWit Adoption Tapers Off After Rapid Early Growth. https://www.theblockcrypto.com/2019/01/11/segwit-adoption-tapers-off-after-rapid-early-growth/

102 Alex Moskov. Bitcoin Cash to Hard Fork: 32MB Block Size & Smart Contracts. https://coincentral.com/bitcoin-cash-hard-fork/

103 Jonald Fyookball. Segregated Witness Removes Bitcoin's Data Integrity Checks. https://news.bitcoin.com/segregated-witness-removes-one-of-bitcoins-data-integrity-checks/

104 Jonald Fyookball. Segregated Witness Removes Bitcoin's Data Integrity Checks. https://news.bitcoin.com/segregated-witness-removes-one-of-bitcoins-data-integrity-checks/

105 Jonald Fyookball. Segregated Witness Removes Bitcoin's Data Integrity Checks. https://news.bitcoin.com/segregated-witness-removes-one-of-bitcoins-data-integrity-checks/

106 Kerati Apilak. Bitcoins Substantive & Technical Road to $100K. https://hackernoon.com/bitcoins-substantive-technical-road-to-100k-2637b899ffc5

107 https://en.m.wikipedia.org/wiki/Bitcoin_Core

108 Laura Shin. Will This Battle for the Soul of Bitcoin Destroy It. https://www.forbes.com/sites/laurashin/2017/10/23/will-this-battle-for-the-soul-of-bitcoin-destroy-it/#9fe768e3d3c0

109 Laura Shin. Will This Battle for the Soul of Bitcoin Destroy It? https://www.forbes.com/sites/laurashin/2017/10/23/will-this-battle-for-the-soul-of-bitcoin-destroy-it/#9fe768e3d3c0

110 Decentralized Thought YouTube channel. Why Blockstream destroyed Bitcoin. https://www.youtube.com/watch?v=0BZoKH-hX_o

111 Jonald Fyookball. Jimmy Song Tries to Claim Bitcoin Cash is "Fiat Money"… Seriously? https://medium.com/@jonaldfyookball/jimmy-song-tries-to-claim-bitcoin-cash-is-fiat-money-seriously-e53a3706d41c

112 The Coin360 Editorial Team. Blockstream: Developing Bitcoin or Taking It Over? https://coin360.com/blog/blockstream-developing-bitcoin-or-taking-it-over

113 Decentralized Thought YouTube channel: Why Blockstream destroyed Bitcoin https://www.youtube.com/watch?v=0BZoKH-hX_o

114 The Coin360 Editorial Team. Blockstream: Developing Bitcoin or Taking It Over? https://coin360.com/blog/blockstream-developing-bitcoin-or-taking-it-over

115 The Coin360 Editorial Team. Blockstream: Developing Bitcoin or Taking It Over? https://coin360.com/blog/blockstream-developing-bitcoin-or-taking-it-over

116 Jimmy Song. BCH Is a Fiat Money. https://medium.com/@jimmysong/bitcoin-cash-is-a-fiat-money-39626c002f77

117 Jimmy Song. BCH Is a Fiat Money. https://medium.com/@jimmysong/bitcoin-cash-is-a-fiat-money-39626c002f77

118 Jimmy Song. BCH Is a Fiat Money. https://medium.com/@jimmysong/bitcoin-cash-is-a-fiat-money-39626c002f77

119 Jimmy Song. BCH Is a Fiat Money. https://medium.com/@jimmysong/bitcoin-cash-is-a-fiat-money-39626c002f77

120 Jimmy Song. BCH Is a Fiat Money. https://medium.com/@jimmysong/bitcoin-cash-is-a-fiat-money-39626c002f77

121 Jonald Fyookball. Jimmy Song Tries to Claim Bitcoin Cash is Fiat Money…Seriously? https://medium.com/@jonaldfyookball/jimmy-song-tries-to-claim-bitcoin-cash-is-fiat-money-seriously-e53a3706d41c

122 Jimmy Song. BCH Is a Fiat Money. https://medium.com/@jimmysong/bitcoin-cash-is-a-fiat-money-39626c002f77

123 Jimmy Song. BCH Is a Fiat Money. https://medium.com/@jimmysong/bitcoin-cash-is-a-fiat-money-39626c002f77

124 Jim btc Youtube channel. Gavin vs Vitalik, "Craig Wright Is Probably Not Satoshi" Mic Drop Moment. https://www.youtube.com/watch?v=2qLI3VIHuKU

125 Shaurya Malwa: He's a fraud! Ethereum's Buterin calls out "Fake Satoshi" at Deconomy: https://btcmanager.com/hes-a-fraud-ethereums-buterin-calls-out-fake-satoshi/

126 Jordan Pearson. The Man Who Claimed to Invent Bitcoin Is Being Sued for $10 Billion. https://motherboard.vice.com/en_us/article/3k74qj/craig-wright-is-being-sued-for-10-billion-dave-kleiman

127 Jordan Pearson. The Man Who Claimed to Invent Bitcoin Is Being Sued for $10 Billion. https://motherboard.vice.com/en_us/article/3k74qj/craig-wright-is-being-sued-for-10-billion-dave-kleiman

128 Jordan Pearson. The Man Who Claimed to Invent Bitcoin Is Being Sued for $10 Billion. https://motherboard.vice.com/en_us/article/3k74qj/craig-wright-is-being-sued-for-10-billion-dave-kleiman

129 Andrew Ancheta. Meet Wormhole: The Platform for Bitcoin Cash's First ICOs. https://cryptobriefing.com/meet-wormhole-the-platform-for-bitcoin-cashs-first-icos/

130 Andrew Ancheta. Meet Wormhole: The Platform for Bitcoin Cash's First ICOs. https://cryptobriefing.com/meet-wormhole-the-platform-for-bitcoin-cashs-first-icos/

131 Bitcion Exchange Guide News Team. Omni Layer – Decentralized Bitcoin Blockchain Custom Asset Platform? https://bitcoinexchangeguide.com/omni-layer/

132 Andrew Ancheta. Meet Wormhole: The Platform for Bitcoin Cash's First ICOs. https://cryptobriefing.com/meet-wormhole-the-platform-for-bitcoin-cashs-first-icos/

133 Andrew Ancheta. Meet Wormhole: The Platform for Bitcoin Cash's First ICOs. https://cryptobriefing.com/meet-wormhole-the-platform-for-bitcoin-cashs-first-icos/

134 Bitcoin Exchange Guide News Team. BitcoinToken: Bitcoin Cash (BCH) Based Smart Contract & Token Creator Tool. https://bitcoinexchangeguide.com/bitcointoken-bitcoin-cash-smart-contracts-token-creator/

135 https://bitcointalk.org/index.php?topic=1391350.0

136 https://bitcointalk.org/index.php?topic=1391350.0

137 https://www.bitcoinabc.org/

138 https://bitcoinsv.io/

139 https://www.bitcoinabc.org/2018-08-24-bitcoin-abc-vision/

140 Harsh Agrawal. How & Where To Buy Bitcoin Cash (BCH). https://coinsutra.com/bitcoin-cash-fork/

141 https://www.bitcoinabc.org/2018-08-24-bitcoin-abc-vision/

142 https://twitter.com/satoshilite/status/1060607981664972800

143 Rick D. Bad to Worse for Bitcoin Cash SV: "Satoshi's Vision" Proves Unpopular. https://www.newsbtc.com/2018/12/19/bad-worse-bitcoin-sv/

144 Craig Wright. Satoshi's Vision: The Art of Bitcoin. Howson Books, 2019

145 https://b2x-segwit.io/es/news/article/45

146 Peter McCormack. Why the Futures Market Will Destroy B2X Before It Launches.

https://medium.com/@whatbitcoindid/why-the-futures-market-will-destroy-b2x-before-it-launches-f1e7a2ab317f

147 Peter McCormack. Why the Futures Market Will Destroy B2X Before It Launches. https://medium.com/@whatbitcoindid/why-the-futures-market-will-destroy-b2x-before-it-launches-f1e7a2ab317f

148 https://bitcoingold.org/

149 Peter McCormack. Why the Futures Market Will Destroy B2X Before It Launches. https://medium.com/@whatbitcoindid/why-the-futures-market-will-destroy-b2x-before-it-launches-f1e7a2ab317f

150 Scotch & Ramen Media, Inc. Recapping the May 2018 51% Attacks on Bitcoin Gold https://medium.com/@ScotchAndRamen/recapping-the-may-2018-51-attacks-on-bitcoin-gold-b10e09688a7d

151 https://bitcoingold.org/responding-to-attacks/

152 https://bitcoingold.org/responding-to-attacks/

THE ETHEREUM ECOSYSTEM

153 http://ethdocs.org/en/latest/introduction/what-is-ethereum.html

154 Craig Anthony.How Did Peter Thiel Get Rich. https://www.investopedia.com/articles/insights/082216/how-did-peter-thiel-get-rich-pypl-fb.asp

155 Mark Harris.   How Peter Thiel's Secretive Data Company Pushed Into Policing. https://www.wired.com/story/how-peter-thiels-secretive-data-company-pushed-into-policing/

156 Mark Harris.   How Peter Thiel's Secretive Data Company Pushed Into Policing. https://www.wired.com/story/how-peter-thiels-secretive-data-company-pushed-into-policing/

157 If you want to learn more about Palantir, you can find a very interesting perspective searching for the interviews of Quinn Michaels.

158 Phyro. The DAO is History... or is it? https://medium.com/coinmonks/the-dao-is-history-or-is-it-47a6f457338a

159 Alan T. Norman. Blockchain Technology Explained: The Ultimate Beginner's Guide About Blockchain Wallet, Mining, Bitcoin, Ethereum, Litecoin, Zcash, Monero, Ripple, Dash, IOTA and Smart Contracts. Alan T. Norman, 2017

160 David Siegel. Understanding The DAO Hack for Journalists. https://medium.com/@pull-news/understanding-the-dao-hack-for-journalists-2312dd43e993

161 Max Ganado. Malta: Legal Personality For Blockchains, DAOs And Smart Contracts. http://www.mondaq.com/x/707696/fin+tech/Legal+Personality+For+Blockchains+DAOs+And+Smart+Contracts

162 Marie Huillet. https://cointelegraph.com/news/malta-crypto-exchange-binance-backs-plans-to-create-first-decentralized-tokenized-bank

163 Kyle Wang. Ethereum: Turing-Completeness and Rich Statefulness Explained. https://hackernoon.com/ethereum-turing-completeness-and-rich-statefulness-explained-e650db7fc1fb

164 Altnews.nu via AMBCrypto. Bitcoin (BTC) Is Turing Complete, Says Craig Wright. http://www.altnews.nu/bitcoin-btc-is-turing-complete-says-craig-wright/

165 Marcelo Morgado. RSK: Bitcoin smart contracts (EN). https://medium.com/coinmonks/rsk-bitcoin-smart-contracts-en-5b474ce87cd6

166 https://www.reddit.com/r/Bitcoin/comments/907tn0/bitcoin_can_do_smart_contracts_and_ringct/

167 Lea Nonninger. Intercontinental Exchange, Microsoft and Starbucks Are Launching a Crypto Venture. https://businessinsider.com/ice-microsoft-starbucks-bakkt-crypto-venture-2018-8

168 David Siegel. Understanding The DAO Hack for Journalists. https://medium.com/@pull-news/
understanding-the-dao-hack-for-journalists-2312dd43e993

169 David Siegel. Understanding The DAO Hack for Journalists. https://medium.com/@pull-news/
understanding-the-dao-hack-for-journalists-2312dd43e993

170 Chris Stewart. How hard forks justified the biggest bailout in cryptocurrency history. https://medium.com/@Chris_Stewart_5/how-hard-forks-justified-the-biggest-bailout-in-cryptocurrency-history-62a1daa8430e

171 Chris Stewart. How hard forks justified the biggest bailout in cryptocurrency history. https://medium.com/@Chris_Stewart_5/how-hard-forks-justified-the-biggest-bailout-in-cryptocurrency-history-62a1daa8430e

172 https://ethereumclassic.github.io/

173 Yasmeen Turayhi. An Introduction to Ethereum. https://hackernoon.com/an-introduction-to-ethereum-68fb9b95fc62

174 Daniele Pozzi. ICO Market 2018 vs 2017: Trends, Capitalization, Localization, Industries, Success Rate. https://cointelegraph.com/news/ico-market-2018-vs-2017-trends-capitalization-localization-industries-success-rate

175 https://www.icodata.io/stats/2017 and https://www.icodata.io/stats/2018

176 Yasmeen Turayhi. An Introduction to Ethereum. https://hackernoon.com/an-introduction-to-ethereum-68fb9b95fc62

177 Nikhilesh De. The SEC Just Released Its Long-Awaited Crypto Token Guidance. https://www.coindesk.com/the-sec-just-released-its-crypto-token-guidance

178 Yasmeen Turayhi. An Introduction to Ethereum. https://hackernoon.com/an-introduction-to-ethereum-68fb9b95fc62

179 Robert Devoe.   Ether Miners Are All Losing Money, According to Recent Statistics. https://blockonomi.com/ether-miners-losing-money/

180 Robert Devoe.   Ether Miners Are All Losing Money, According to Recent Statistics. https://blockonomi.com/ether-miners-losing-money/

181 Rachel Rose O'Leary. Ethereum ASICs Are Here: What the New Miners Mean and What's Next? https://www.coindesk.com/ethereum-asics-means-whats-next/

182 Rachel Rose O'Leary. Ethereum ASICs Are Here: What the New Miners Mean and What's Next? https://www.coindesk.com/ethereum-asics-means-whats-next/

183 Rachel Rose O'Leary. Ethereum ASICs Are Here: What the New Miners Mean and What's Next? https://www.coindesk.com/ethereum-asics-means-whats-next/

184 Max Thake. What is Proof of Stake? (PoS). https://medium.com/nakamo-to/what-is-proof-of-stake-pos-479a04581f3a

185 Vlad Zamfir. Introducing Casper "the Friendly Ghost". https://ethereum.github.io/blog/2015/08/01/introducing-casper-friendly-ghost/

186 Max Thake. What is Proof of Stake? (PoS). https://medium.com/nakamo-to/what-is-proof-of-stake-pos-479a04581f3a

187 Vlad Zamfir. Introducing Casper "the Friendly Ghost". https://ethereum.github.io/blog/2015/08/01/introducing-casper-friendly-ghost/

188 Danny Ryan and Chih-Cheng Liang EIP 1011 https://eips.ethereum.org/EIPS/eip-1011

189 Tim Falk. Ethereums Casper Protocol Explained in Simple Terms. https://www.finder.com/pl/ethereum-casper

190 https://ethereum.github.io/blog/2015/08/01/introducing-casper-friendly-ghost/

191 Tim Falk. Ethereums Casper Protocol Explained in Simple Terms. https://www.finder.com/pl/ethereum-casper

192 Andrew Gillick.   Casper, Plama and Sharding: A Light on Etherhttps://bravenew-coin.com/insights/casper-plasma-and-seums Scaling Spectrum. harding-a-light-on-ethereums-scaling-spectrum

193 Andrew Gillick.   Casper, Plama and Sharding: A Light on Etherhttps://bravenew-coin.com/insights/casper-plasma-and-seums Scaling Spectrum. harding-a-light-on-ethereums-scaling-spectrum

194 Julia Magas.   Casper: What Will the Upgrade Bring to the Ethereum's Network? https://cointelegraph.com/news/casper-what-is-known-about-the-new-ethereums-network-upgrade

195 Ben Edgington: State of Ethereum Protocol #2: The Beacon Chain. https://media.consen-sys.net/state-of-ethereum-protocol-2-the-beacon-chain-c6b6a9a69129

196 Hsiao-Wei Wang. What You Can Do for Ethereum 2.0 a.k.a. Sharding. https://docs.google.com/presentation/ d/1G5UZdEL71XAkU5B2v-TC3lmGaRIu2P6QSeF8m3wg6MU/edit#slide=id.p4

197 Amir Rosic. What is Ethereum Gas? [The Most Comprehensive Step-By-Step Guide Ever!] https://blockgeeks.com/guides/ethereum-gas/

198 Anisa Batabyal. Ethereum Constantinople Hard Fork Is Concluded | Read All Updates. https://coinswitch.co/news/ethereum-hard-fork-jan-19-know-everything-about-3-upcoming-eth-hard-forks

199 Ben Edgington: State of Ethereum Protocol #2: The Beacon Chain. https://media.consensys.net/state-of-ethereum-protocol-2-the-beacon-chain-c6b6a9a69129

200 Raul Jordan. Ethereum 2.0 Prysm Demo Release v0.0.0. https://medium.com/prysmatic-labs/ethereum-2-0-prysm-demo-release-v0-0-0-78d33e9cdbdf

201 William M. Peaster. Ethereum "ETH 2.0" Genesis Block May Launch in January 2020. https://blockonomi.com/ethereum-eth-2-0-genesis-block-january-2020/

202 Ben Edgington: State of Ethereum Protocol #2: The Beacon Chain. https://media.consensys.net/state-of-ethereum-protocol-2-the-beacon-chain-c6b6a9a69129

203 Ben Edgington: State of Ethereum Protocol #2: The Beacon Chain. https://media.consensys.net/state-of-ethereum-protocol-2-the-beacon-chain-c6b6a9a69129

204 Runtime Environment RTE. https://www.techopedia.com/definition/5466/runtime-environment-rte

205 Facundo Spagnuolo. Ethereum in Depth, Part 1. https://blog.zeppelin.solutions/ethereum-in-depth-part-1-968981e6f833

206 Daria Rud. Ethereum's Constantinople Hard Fork Might Not Be Possible in 2018. https://www.coinspeaker.com/ethereums-constantinople-hard-fork-might-not-be-possible-in-2018

207 Daria Rud. Ethereum's Constantinople Hard Fork Might Not Be Possible in 2018. https://www.coinspeaker.com/ethereums-constantinople-hard-fork-might-not-be-possible-in-2018

208 Daria Rud. Ethereum's Constantinople Hard Fork Might Not Be Possible in 2018. https://www.coinspeaker.com/ethereums-constantinople-hard-fork-might-not-be-possible-in-2018

209 Nick Chong. Ethereum Hard Fork Test Goes Awry, "No Constantinople in 2018" Developer Says. https://ethereumworldnews.com/ethereum-hard-fork-test-goes-awry-no-constantinople-in-2018-developer-says/

210 Daria Rud. Ethereum's Constantinople Hard Fork Might Not Be Possible in 2018. https://www.coinspeaker.com/ethereums-constantinople-hard-fork-might-not-be-possible-in-2018

211 Nick Chong. Ethereum Hard Fork Test Goes Awry, "No Constantinople n 2018" Developer Says. https://ethereumworldnews.com/ethereum-hard-fork-test-goes-awry-no-constantinople-in-2018-developer-says/

212 Julia Magas. Casper: What Will the Upgrade Bring to the Ethereum's Network? https://cointelegraph.com/news/casper-what-is-known-about-the-new-ethereums-network-upgrade

213 Carolyn Coley. Ethereum (ETH) News: Vitalik Buterin's Proof of Stake Proposal to Increase The Reward of Block Validators. https://smartereum.com/52557/ethereum-eth-news-vitalik-buterins-proof-of-stake-proposal-to-increase-the-reward-of-block-validators/

214 Tim Falk. What is Ethereum's Casper Update? Everything You Need to Know. https://www.finder.com/pl/ethereum-casper

215 Tim Falk. What is Ethereum's Casper Update? Everything You Need to Know. https://www.finder.com/pl/ethereum-casper

216 Johannes Hagemann. Proof of Stake (Casper Ethereum) Explained. https://medium.com/@johanneshage97/proof-of-stake-casper-ethereum-explained-682d663440d5

217 Johannes Hagemann. Proof of Stake (Casper Ethereum) Explained. https://medium.com/@johanneshage97/proof-of-stake-casper-ethereum-explained-682d663440d5

218 Vitalik Buterin. Slasher: A Punitive Proof-of-Stake Algorithm. https://blog.ethereum.org/2014/01/15/slasher-a-punitive-proof-of-stake-algorithm/

219 Julia Magas. Casper: What Will the Upgrade Bring to the Ethereum's Network? https://cointelegraph.com/news/casper-what-is-known-about-the-new-ethereums-network-upgrade

220 Julia Magas. Casper: What Will the Upgrade Bring to the Ethereum's Network? https://cointelegraph.com/news/casper-what-is-known-about-the-new-ethereums-network-upgrade

221 Abishek Sharma. Understanding Proof of Stake through it's Flaws. Part 3— 'Long Range Attacks'. https://medium.com/@abhisharm/understanding-proof-of-stake-through-its-flaws-part-3-long-range-attacks-672a3d413501

222 Abishek Sharma. Understanding Proof of Stake through it's Flaws. Part 3— 'Long Range Attacks'. https://medium.com/@abhisharm/understanding-proof-of-stake-through-its-flaws-part-3-long-range-attacks-672a3d413501

223 Nick Chong. Ethereum Constantinople Delayed, ETH Down 5%. https://ethereumworldnews.com/ethereum-constantinople-potentially-delayed/

224 Rajarshi Mitra. Lightning Protocol & The Raiden Network: A Beginner's Guide. https://blog.springrole.com/lightning-protocol-the-raiden-network-a-beginners-guide-c9d7bc702748

225 Daily Hodl Staff. Vitalik Buterin Says Ethereum Must Reach 100,000 Transactions Per Second, Bitcoin May Remain Solely a Store of Value. https://dailyhodl.com/2019/03/20/vitalik-

buterin-says-ethereum-must-reach-100000-transactions-per-second-bitcoin-may-remain-solely-a-store of-value/

226 Andrew Gillick. Casper, Plasma and Sharding: A Light on Ethereum's Scaling Spectrum. https://bravenewcoin.com/insights/casper-plasma-and-sharding-a-light-on-ethereums-scaling-spectrum

227 Andrew Gillick. Casper, Plasma and Sharding: A Light on Ethereum's Scaling Spectrum. https://bravenewcoin.com/insights/casper-plasma-and-sharding-a-light-on-ethereums-scaling-spectrum

228 John P. Njui. Vitalik: Ethereum (ETH) Can Scale to 500 TPS Using Zcash's ZK-SNARKs. https://ethereumworldnews.com/vitalik-ethereum-eth-can-scale-to-500-tps-using-zcashs-zk-snarks/

229 Laura Shin. Vitalik Buterin, Creator of Ethereum, on the Big Guy Vs. the Little Guy. http://unchained.forbes.libsynpro.com/vitalik-buterin-creator-of-ethereum-on-the-big-guy-vs-the-little-guy

230 Vitalik Buterin. On-Chain Scaling to Potentially ~500 tx/sec Through Mass Tx Validation. https://ethresear.ch/t/on-chain-scaling-to-potentially-500-tx-sec-through-mass-tx-validation/3477

231 John P. Njui. Vitalik: Ethereum (ETH) Can Scale to 500 TPS Using Zcash's ZK-SNARKs. https://ethereumworldnews.com/vitalik-ethereum-eth-can-scale-to-500-tps-using-zcashs-zk-snarks/

232 James Hallaway. The Biggest Myth In Blockchain: Transactions Per Second. hhttps://hackernoon.com/the-biggest-myth-in-blockchain-transactions-per-second-c300ca16d802

233 John P. Njui. Vitalik: Ethereum (ETH) Can Scale to 500 TPS Using Zcash's ZK-SNARKs. https://ethereumworldnews.com/vitalik-ethereum-eth-can-scale-to-500-tps-using-zcashs-zk-snarks/

234 Dr. Arthur Gervais. Raiden, Lightning and Plasma Aren't the Only Contenders in Crypto Speed Battle. https://bravenewcoin.com/insights/raiden-lightning-and-plasma-arent-the-only-contenders-in-crypto-speed-battle

235 https://raiden.network

236 https://brainbot.li

237 Rajashri Mitra. Lightning Protocol & The Raiden Network: A Beginner's Guide. https://blog.springrole.com/lightning-protocol-the-raiden-network-a-beginners-guide-c9d7bc702748

238 Steven White. What is Raiden Network? https://www.investinblockchain.com/what-is-raiden-network/

239 Chris Tsimogiannis. The Proof Lies in Not Sharing Data. https://www.foundery.co.za/blog/the-proof-lies-in-not-sharing-data/

240 Kieran Smith. Mobius to Bring Anonymity of Monero to Ethereum. https://bravenewcoin.com/insights/mobius-to-bring-anonymity-of-monero-to-ethereum

241 Kieran Smith. Mobius to Bring Anonymity of Monero to Ethereum. https://bravenew-coin.com/insights/mobius-to-bring-anonymity-of-monero-to-ethereum

242 https://twitter.com/VitalikButerin/status/993851982296297478

243 https://www.crypto-economy.net/en/ethereum-eth-spanish-banking-giant-banco-santander-issues-20m-bond-on-ethereum-blockchain/

YOUR PRIVACY IS IMPORTANT TO US

244 Cryptoconomy. Dandelions, and a Bright Future for Bitcoin Privacy. https://medium.com/@thecryptoconomy/dandelions-and-a-bright-future-for-bitcoin-privacy-712dbc4b1ec5

245 Cryptoconomy. Dandelions, and a Bright Future for Bitcoin Privacy. https://medium.com/@thecryptoconomy/dandelions-and-a-bright-future-for-bitcoin-privacy-712dbc4b1ec5

246 Cryptoconomy. Dandelions, and a Bright Future for Bitcoin Privacy. https://medium.com/@thecryptoconomy/dandelions-and-a-bright-future-for-bitcoin-privacy-712dbc4b1ec5

247 Anonymous. (Tney may have just wanted their privacy).

248 Frank Chaparro. A Kidnapped Crypto Executive Was Reportedly Released After Paying a $1 Million Bitcoin Ransom. http://uk.businessinsider.com/kidnapped-crypto-exec-released-after-paying-1-million-bitcoin-ransom-2017-12?IR=T

249 Aaron Van Wirdum. Bitcoin As a Privacycoin: This Tech is Making Bitcoin More Private. https://bitcoinmagazine.com/articles/bitcoin-privacycoin-tech-making-bitcoin-more-private/

250 John Carvalho. Bitcoin is Not Fungible, Should It Be? https://medium.com/@BitcoinError-Log/bitcoin-is-not-fungible-should-it-be-620a28f3f8b1

251 John Carvalho. Bitcoin is Not Fungible, Should It Be? https://medium.com/@BitcoinError-Log/bitcoin-is-not-fungible-should-it-be-620a28f3f8b1

252 John Carvalho. Bitcoin is Not Fungible, Should It Be? https://medium.com/@BitcoinError-Log/bitcoin-is-not-fungible-should-it-be-620a28f3f8b1

253 https://bitcoinmagazine.com/articles/confidential-transactions-how-hiding-transaction-amounts-increases-bitcoin-privacy-1464892525/

254 Aaron Van Wirdum. Confidential Transactions: How Hiding Transaction Amounts Increases Bitcoin Privacy. https://medium.com/@BitcoinErrorLog/bitcoin-is-not-fungible-should-it-be-620a28f3f8b1

255 Cryptoconomy. Dandelions, and a Bright Future for Bitcoin Privacy. https://medium.com/@thecryptoconomy/dandelions-and-a-bright-future-for-bitcoin-privacy-712dbc4b1ec5

256 John Carvalho. Bitcoin is Not Fungible, Should It Be? https://medium.com/@BitcoinError-Log/
bitcoin-is-not-fungible-should-it-be-620a28f3f8b1

257 Rachel Rose O'Leary. Will Lightning Help or Hurt Bitcoin Privacy? https://www.coin-desk.com/will-lightning-help-hurt-bitcoin-privacy/

258 John Carvalho. Bitcoin is Not Fungible, Should It Be? https://medium.com/@BitcoinError-Log/
bitcoin-is-not-fungible-should-it-be-620a28f3f8b1

259 Ádám Ficsór. Who Will Steal Satoshi's Bitcoins? https://medium.com/@nopara73/stealing-satoshis-bitcoins-cc4d57919a2b

260 Stifftoshi Nakamoto Youtube channel: Bitcoin SV on Infowars War Room (interview with Derek Moore). https://www.youtube.com/watch?v=scsWB2Tyjfg&t=1016s

261 Stifftoshi Nakamoto Youtube channel: Bitcoin SV on Infowars War Room (interview with Derek Moore). https://www.youtube.com/watch?v=scsWB2Tyjfg&t=1016s

262 Stifftoshi Nakamoto Youtube channel: Bitcoin SV on Infowars War Room (interview with Derek Moore). https://www.youtube.com/watch?v=scsWB2Tyjfg&t=1016s

263 William Suberg. Lightning Network Will Be Highly Centralized: Gavin Andresen. https://-cointelegraph.com/news/lightning-network-will-be-highly-centralized-gavin-andresen

264 Cointelegraph Guides. What Is Lightning Network And How It Works. https://-cointelegraph.com/lightning-network-101/what-is-lightning-network-and-how-it-works#what-is-the-lightning-network

265 Keerthi Nelaturu. Lightning Network. https://medium.com/coinmonks/lightning-network-7fcdf3e7b735

266 Cointelegraph Guides. Altcoins With Lightning Network Support. https://cointele-graph.com/lightning-network-101/altcoins-with-lightning-network-support#monero-and-lightning-network

267 Mitchell Moos. BTC Lightning Network Company Rejects $1.25 Million from Roger Ver to Build on Bitcoin Cash. https://cryptoslate.com/btc-lightning-network-company-rejects-million-roger-ver-bitcoin-cash/

268 Cointelegraph Guides. What Is Lightning Network And How It Works. https://-cointelegraph.com/lightning-network-101/what-is-lightning-network-and-how-it-works#what-is-the-lightning-network

269 https://bitcoinvisuals.com/lightning

270 Pranjal Mahajan. Bitcoin Lightning Network: Why & How It's a Game Changer. https://-coinsutra.com/bitcoin-lightning-network/

271 Pranjal Mahajan. Bitcoin Lightning Network: Why & How It's a Game Changer. https://-coinsutra.com/bitcoin-lightning-network/

272 Pranjal Mahajan. Bitcoin Lightning Network: Why & How It's a Game Changer. https://coinsutra.com/bitcoin-lightning-network/

273 Pranjal Mahajan. Bitcoin Lightning Network: Why & How It's a Game Changer. https://coinsutra.com/bitcoin-lightning-network/

274 https://bitcoinvisuals.com/ln-nodes

275 https://bitcoinvisuals.com/ln-capacity

276 Andrew Ancheta. Litecoin, Not Bitcoin, Will Drive The Lightning Network. https://cryptobriefing.com/litecoin-not-bitcoin-will-drive-the-lightning-network/

277 Wilma Woo. Lightning Network Can't Guarantee Transactions Larger Than 3 Cents...Yet. https://bitcoinist.com/lightning-network-3-cent-transactions/

278 Andrew Ancheta. Litecoin, Not Bitcoin, Will Drive The Lightning Network. https://cryptobriefing.com/litecoin-not-bitcoin-will-drive-the-lightning-network/

279 Andrew Ancheta. Litecoin, Not Bitcoin, Will Drive The Lightning Network. https://cryptobriefing.com/litecoin-not-bitcoin-will-drive-the-lightning-network/

280 Andrew Ancheta. Litecoin, Not Bitcoin, Will Drive The Lightning Network. https://cryptobriefing.com/litecoin-not-bitcoin-will-drive-the-lightning-network/

281 Rachel Rose O'Leary. Will Ligtning Help or Hurt Bitcoin Privacy? https://www.coindesk.com/will-lightning-help-hurt-bitcoin-privacy/

282 Knightrider. Andreas Antonopoulos is a Shitcoin Expert, Says Craig Wright. https://www.altcoinera.com/28928-2/

283 https://www.coindesk.com/will-lightning-help-hurt-bitcoin-privacy/

284 https://en.wikipedia.org/wiki/Onion_routing

285 https://www.torproject.org/docs/faq#WhyCalledTor

286 https://en.wikipedia.org/wiki/Tor_%28anonymity_network%29#Weaknesses

287 https://www.torproject.org/docs/faq#WhatIsTor

288 https://www.torproject.org/docs/faq#AttacksOnOnionRouting

289 https://en.wikipedia.org/wiki/Tor_%28anonymity_network%29#cite_note-torproject-one-cell-91

290 Kristov Atlas. The Inevitability of Privacy in Lightning Networks. https://www.kristovatlas.com/the-inevitability-of-privacy-in-lightning-networks/

291 Racher Rose O'Leary. Will Lightning Help or Hurt Bitcoin Privacy? https://www.coindesk.com/will-lightning-help-hurt-bitcoin-privacy/

292 Racher Rose O'Leary. Will Lightning Help or Hurt Bitcoin Privacy? https://www.coindesk.com/will-lightning-help-hurt-bitcoin-privacy/

293 Racher Rose O'Leary. Will Lightning Help or Hurt Bitcoin Privacy? https://www.coindesk.com/will-lightning-help-hurt-bitcoin-privacy/

294 Racher Rose O'Leary. Will Lightning Help or Hurt Bitcoin Privacy? https://www.coin-desk.com/will-lightning-help-hurt-bitcoin-privacy/

295 Dr. Arthur Gervais. Raiden, Lightning and Plasma Aren't the Only Contenders in Crypto Speed Battle. https://bravenewcoin.com/insights/raiden-lightning-and-plasma-arent-the-only-contenders-in-crypto-speed-battle

296 https://twitter.com/gavinandresen/status/897579813657096192 and William Suber. Lightning Network Will Be Highly Centralized: Gavin Andresen. https://cointele-graph.com/news/lightning-network-will-be-highly-centralized-gavin-andresen

297 Toronex. Increasing Bitcoin-Privacy Using the Lightning Network OR How to Delete the Origin of Your Bitcoins. https://medium.com/@scidexer/increasing-bitcoin-privacy-using-the-lightning-network-or-how-to-delete-the-origin-of-your-bitcoins-3c611d072e40

298 Toronex. Increasing Bitcoin-Privacy Using the Lightning Network OR How to Delete the Origin of Your Bitcoins. https://medium.com/@scidexer/increasing-bitcoin-privacy-using-the-lightning-network-or-how-to-delete-the-origin-of-your-bitcoins-3c611d072e40

299 Prajnal Mahajan. Bitcoin Lightning Network: Why & How It's a Game Changer. https://-coinsutra.com/bitcoin-lightning-network

300 Ian Miers, in: Rachel Rose O'Leary. Will Lightning Help or Hurt Bitcoin Privacy? https://www.coindesk.com/will-lightning-help-hurt-bitcoin-privacy/

301 Christian Decker, in: Rachel Rose O'Leary. Will Lightning Help or Hurt Bitcoin Privacy? https://www.coindesk.com/will-lightning-help-hurt-bitcoin-privacy/

302 Rachel Rose O'Leary. Will Lightning Help or Hurt Bitcoin Privacy? https://www.coin-desk.com/will-lightning-help-hurt-bitcoin-privacy/

303 Crypto Jayson. Atomic Swap – Why Its a Game Changer for Exchanges. https://hacker-noon.com/atomic-swap-why-its-a-game-changer-for-exchanges-fb1380f5cb6c

304 Crypto Jayson. Atomic Swap – Why Its a Game Changer for Exchanges. https://hacker-noon.com/atomic-swap-why-its-a-game-changer-for-exchanges-fb1380f5cb6c

305 Antonio Madeira. What Are Atomic Swaps? https://www.cryptocompare.com/coins/guides/what-are-atomic-swaps/

306 https://en.wikipedia.org/wiki/Ethash

307 World Crypto Network. Bitcoin News #58 - An interview With Andrew DeSantis. https://www.youtube.com/watch?v=EyNWCw3Ak-8

308 World Crypto Network. Bitcoin News #58 - An interview With Andrew DeSantis. https://www.youtube.com/watch?v=EyNWCw3Ak-8

309 World Crypto Network. Bitcoin News #58 - An interview With Andrew DeSantis. https://www.youtube.com/watch?v=EyNWCw3Ak-8

310 Crypto Jayson. Atomic Swap – Why Its a Game Changer for Exchanges. https://hacker-noon.com/atomic-swap-why-its-a-game-changer-for-exchanges-fb1380f5cb6c

311 Antonio Madeira. What Are Atomic Swaps? https://www.cryptocompare.com/coins/guides/

what-are-atomic-swaps/

312 Daniel. Atomic Swaps: Komodo's Ultimate Guide to Atomic Swap Technology. https://komodoplatform.com/atomic-swaps/

313 Daniel. Atomic Swaps: Komodo's Ultimate Guide to Atomic Swap Technology. https://komodoplatform.com/atomic-swaps/

314 Oliver. Komodo Platform Just Out-Performed Visa. https://medium.com/@EthAdvisor/komodo-platform-just-out-performed-visa-9e250dae8b4b

315 WeUseCoins. What Is Komodo? https://bitcoinist.com/lightning-network-3-cent-transactions/

316 Wilma Woo. Lightning Network Cant Guarantee Transactions Larger Than 3 Cents...Yet. https://bitcoinist.com/lightning-network-3-cent-transactions/

317 Kristov Atlas. The Inevitability of Privacy in Lightning Networks. https://www.kristovatlas.com/the-inevitability-of-privacy-in-lightning-networks/

318 Kristov Atlas. The Inevitability of Privacy in Lightning Networks. https://www.kristovatlas.com/the-inevitability-of-privacy-in-lightning-networks/

319 Jonald Fyookball. Lightning Netwok Vs. Bitcoin Cash or the Non-Technical Person. https://medium.com/@jonaldfyookball/lightning-network-vs-bitcoin-cash-for-the-non-technical-person-7ea2b9a657f5

320 Ádám Ficsór. Traditional Bitcoin Mixers. https://medium.com/@nopara73/traditional-bitcoin-mixers-6a092e59d8c2

321 Robert Olsson. Tsunami in Lightning Network and Half of the Network Disabled? https://medium.com/coinmonks/tsunami-in-lightning-network-and-half-of-the-network-soon-disabled-8500625d9916

322 dám Ficsór. Understanding TumbleBit Part 1: Making The Case. https://hackernoon.com/understanding-tumblebit-part-1-making-the-case-823d786113f3

323 Ádám Ficsór. Traditional Bitcoin Mixers. https://medium.com/@nopara73/traditional-bitcoin-mixers-6a092e59d8c2

324 Ethan Heilman. Improving Bitcoin's Privacy and Scalability with TumbleBit. https://freedom-to-tinker.com/2016/09/13/improving-bitcoins-privacy-and-scalability-with-tumblebit/

325 Alex Elliott. Decentralizing Privacy for Bitcoin: The Breeze Wallet, TumbleBit and the Future of Scaling. https://www.investinblockchain.com/stratis-breeze-wallet-tumblebit/

326 Ethan Heilman. Improving Bitcoin's Privacy and Scalability with TumbleBit. https://freedom-to-tinker.com/2016/09/13/improving-bitcoins-privacy-and-scalability-with-tumblebit/

327 Ethan Heilman. Improving Bitcoin's Privacy and Scalability with TumbleBit. https://freedom-to-tinker.com/2016/09/13/improving-bitcoins-privacy-and-scalability-with-tumblebit/

328 Ethan Heilman. Improving Bitcoin's Privacy and Scalability with TumbleBit. https://freedom-to-tinker.com/2016/09/13/improving-bitcoins-privacy-and-scalability-with-tumblebit/

329 Ethan Heilman. Improving Bitcoin's Privacy and Scalability with TumbleBit. https://freedom-to-tinker.com/2016/09/13/improving-bitcoins-privacy-and-scalability-with-tumblebit/

330 Ethan Heilman. Improving Bitcoin's Privacy and Scalability with TumbleBit. https://freedom-to-tinker.com/2016/09/13/improving-bitcoins-privacy-and-scalability-with-tumblebit/

331 Ethan Heilman. Improving Bitcoin's Privacy and Scalability with TumbleBit. https://freedom-to-tinker.com/2016/09/13/improving-bitcoins-privacy-and-scalability-with-tumblebit/

332 Ethan Heilman. Improving Bitcoin's Privacy and Scalability with TumbleBit. https://freedom-to-tinker.com/2016/09/13/improving-bitcoins-privacy-and-scalability-with-tumblebit/

333 Deepak Parmar. Stratis Releases TumbleBit Masternode Beta on the Mainnet. https://www.investinblockchain.com/stratis-tumblebit-masternode-beta-mainnet/

334 Deepak Parmar. Stratis Releases TumbleBit Masternode Beta on the Mainnet. https://www.investinblockchain.com/stratis-tumblebit-masternode-beta-mainnet/

335 Alex Elliott. Decentralizing Privacy for Bitcion: The Breeze Wallet, TumbleBit and the Future of Scaling. https://www.investinblockchain.com/stratis-breeze-wallet-tumblebit/

336 https://privacypatterns.org/patterns/Anonymity-set

337 Bitcoin Lightning News. CoinJoin Looks Towards the Lightning Network for Added Privacy. https://www.bitcoinlightning.com/coinjoin-looks-towards-the-lightning-network-privacy/

338 https://en.bitcoinwiki.org/wiki/CoinJoin

339 Bitcoin Lightning News. CoinJoin Looks Towards the Lightning Network for Added Privacy. https://www.bitcoinlightning.com/coinjoin-looks-towards-the-lightning-network-privacy/

340 https://en.bitcoinwiki.org/wiki/CoinJoin

341 Ádám Ficsór. Wasabi: Privacy Focused Bitcoin Wallet for Desktop. https://medium.com/@nopara73/wasabi-privacy-focused-bitcoin-wallet-for-desktop-3962d567045a

342 https://github.com/zkSNACKs/WalletWasabi

343 Ádám Ficsór. Wasabi: Privacy Focused Bitcoin Wallet for Desktop. https://medium.com/@nopara73/wasabi-privacy-focused-bitcoin-wallet-for-desktop-3962d567045a

344 Ádám Ficsór. Wasabi: Privacy Focused Bitcoin Wallet for Desktop. https://medium.com/@nopara73/wasabi-privacy-focused-bitcoin-wallet-for-desktop-3962d567045a

345 Ádám Ficsór. Wasabi: Privacy Focused Bitcoin Wallet for Desktop. https://medium.com/@nopara73/wasabi-privacy-focused-bitcoin-wallet-for-desktop-3962d567045a

346 Ádám Ficsór. Wasabi: Privacy Focused Bitcoin Wallet for Desktop. https://medium.com/@nopara73/wasabi-privacy-focused-bitcoin-wallet-for-desktop-3962d567045a

347 Ádám Ficsór. Wasabi: Privacy Focused Bitcoin Wallet for Desktop. https://medium.com/@nopara73/wasabi-privacy-focused-bitcoin-wallet-for-desktop-3962d567045a

348 Ádám Ficsór. Wasabi: Privacy Focused Bitcoin Wallet for Desktop. https://medium.com/

@nopara73/wasabi-privacy-focused-bitcoin-wallet-for-desktop-3962d567045a

349 Cryptoconomy. Dandelions, and a Bright Future for Bitcoin Privacy. https://medium.com/
@thecryptoconomy/dandelions-and-a-bright-future-for-bitcoin-privacy-712dbc4b1ec5

350 Cryptoconomy. Dandelions, and a Bright Future for Bitcoin Privacy. https://medium.com/
@thecryptoconomy/dandelions-and-a-bright-future-for-bitcoin-privacy-712dbc4b1ec5

351 Cryptoconomy. Dandelions, and a Bright Future for Bitcoin Privacy. https://medium.com/
@thecryptoconomy/dandelions-and-a-bright-future-for-bitcoin-privacy-712dbc4b1ec5

352 Cryptoconomy. Dandelions, and a Bright Future for Bitcoin Privacy. https://medium.com/
@thecryptoconomy/dandelions-and-a-bright-future-for-bitcoin-privacy-712dbc4b1ec5

353 Colin Harper. The Anatomy of Anonymity: How Dandelion Could Make BitcoinMore Private. https://bitcoinmagazine.com/articles/anatomy-anonymity-how-dandelion-could-make-bitcoin-more-private/

354 Colin Harper. The Anatomy of Anonymity: How Dandelion Could Make BitcoinMore Private. https://bitcoinmagazine.com/articles/anatomy-anonymity-how-dandelion-could-make-bitcoin-more-private/

355 Colin Harper. The Anatomy of Anonymity: How Dandelion Could Make BitcoinMore Private. https://bitcoinmagazine.com/articles/anatomy-anonymity-how-dandelion-could-make-bitcoin-more-private/

356 Cryptoconomy. Dandelions, and a Bright Future for Bitcoin Privacy. https://medium.com/
@thecryptoconomy/dandelions-and-a-bright-future-for-bitcoin-privacy-712dbc4b1ec5

357 Cryptoconomy. Dandelions, and a Bright Future for Bitcoin Privacy. https://medium.com/
@thecryptoconomy/dandelions-and-a-bright-future-for-bitcoin-privacy-712dbc4b1ec5

358 Cryptoconomy. Dandelions, and a Bright Future for Bitcoin Privacy. https://medium.com/
@thecryptoconomy/dandelions-and-a-bright-future-for-bitcoin-privacy-712dbc4b1ec5

359 Cryptoconomy. Dandelions, and a Bright Future for Bitcoin Privacy. https://medium.com/
@thecryptoconomy/dandelions-and-a-bright-future-for-bitcoin-privacy-712dbc4b1ec5

360 Cryptoconomy. Dandelions, and a Bright Future for Bitcoin Privacy. https://medium.com/
@thecryptoconomy/dandelions-and-a-bright-future-for-bitcoin-privacy-712dbc4b1ec5

361 Sebastian Mack. Zcoin Dev Update October 4th. https://zcoin.io/zcoin-dev-update-october-4th/

362 Cryptoconomy. Dandelions, and a Bright Future for Bitcoin Privacy. https://medium.com/
@thecryptoconomy/dandelions-and-a-bright-future-for-bitcoin-privacy-712dbc4b1ec5

363 Cryptoconomy. Dandelions, and a Bright Future for Bitcoin Privacy. https://medium.com/
@thecryptoconomy/dandelions-and-a-bright-future-for-bitcoin-privacy-712dbc4b1ec5

364 SFOX. Investors' Bitcoin Roadmap for 2019: Schnorr, Dandelion, and More.
https://blog.sfox.com/investors-bitcoin-roadmap-for-2019-schnorr-dandelion-and-more-6d6c058d02ab?gi=d8d741ca1f08

365 Europol Press Release. Multi-Million Euro Cryptocurrency Laundering Service Best-mixer.io Taken Down. https://www.europol.europa.eu/newsroom/news/multi-million-euro-cryptocurrency-laundering-service-bestmixerio-taken-down

366 https://bestmixer.io/

367 Aaron Van Wirdum. Chainalysis: Most Mixed Bitcoin Not Used for Illicit Purporses. https://bitcoinmagazine.com/articles/chainalysis-most-mixed-bitcon-not-used-for-illicit-purposes

368 Brett Scott. The Cashless Society Is a Con – And Big Finance Is Behind it. https://www.theguardian.com/commentisfree/2018/jul/19/cashless-society-con-big-finance-banks-closing-atms

369 "Lockheed Martin Corporation is an American global aerospace, defense, security and advanced technologies company with worldwide interests." https://en.wikipedia.org/wiki/Lockheed_Martin

370 Andreas Antonopoulos. Universal Access to Basic Finance. aantonop Youtube channel. https://www.youtube.com/watch?v=Pkg005Hdnfg

371 Leigh Cuen. Microsoft Launches Decentralized Identity Tool on Bitcoin Blockchain. https://www.coindesk.com/microsoft-launches-decentralized-identity-tool-on-bitcoin-blockchain

372 Aaron Wood. Amazon Web Services Launches Managed Blockchain Service. https://cointelegraph.com/news/amazon-web-services-launches-managed-blockchain-service

373 William Suberg. Amazon Patent Casts Light on Plans to Create Proof-of-Work Blockchain Analog. https://cointelegraph.com/news/amazon-patent-casts-light-on-plans-to-create-proof-of-work-blockchain-analog

374 William Suberg. Amazon Patent Casts Light on Plans to Create Proof-of-Work Blockchain Analog. https://cointelegraph.com/news/amazon-patent-casts-light-on-plans-to-create-proof-of-work-blockchain-analog

375 Michael del Castillo. A Technical Breakdown Of Google's New Blockchain Search Tools. https://www.forbes.com/sites/michaeldelcastillo/2019/02/05/google-launches-search-for-bitcoin-ethereum-bitcoin-cash-dash-dogecoin-ethereum-classic-litecoin-and-zcash/#3b8f962dc789

376 NewsBTC. Google Enters Crypto and Blockchain Search Business With New Tools. https://www.newsbtc.com/2019/02/07/google-enters-crypto-and-blockchain-search-business-with-new-tools/

377 Irina Tsumarava. Will Google Ban Blockchain? https://medium.com/@irinatsumarava/will-google-ban-blockchain-d629042c341e

PRIVACY FIRST: PRIVACY COINS

378 Mike Volpi. How Open-Source Software Took Over the World. https://techcrunch.com/2019/01/12/how-open-source-software-took-over-the-world

379 https://en.wikipedia.org/wiki/History_of_Linux

380 Alex Lielacher. Best Privacy Coins, Rated and Reviewed for 2018. https://www.bitcoinmarketjournal.com/best-privacy-coins-rated-and-reviewed-for-2018/

381 Alex Lielacher. Best Privacy Coins, Rated and Reviewed for 2018. https://www.bitcoinmarketjournal.com/best-privacy-coins-rated-and-reviewed-for-2018/

382 Lucas Nuzzi. Monero Becomes Bulletproof. https://medium.com/digitalassetresearch/monero-becomes-bulletproof-f98c6408babf

383 Lucas Nuzzi. Monero Becomes Bulletproof. https://medium.com/digitalassetresearch/monero-becomes-bulletproof-f98c6408babf

384 Concepcion Guzman. 5 Unique Features of Monero (XMR) That Will Increase Your Financial Privacy and Security. https://steemit.com/cryptocurrency/@concepcionguzman/5-unique-features-of-monero-xmr-that-will-increase-your-financial-privacy-and-security

385 Andrew Ancheta. Monero Upgrades to Bulletproof Privacy: XMR Dev News. https://cryptobriefing.com/monero-upgrades-bulletproof-privacy-xmr/

386 Pat Rabbitte. Is Monero Now Bulletproof? https://thebitcoinmag.com/is-monero-now-bulletproof/2819/

387 Pat Rabbitte. Is Monero Now Bulletproof? https://thebitcoinmag.com/is-monero-now-bulletproof/2819/

388 Pat Rabbitte. Is Monero Now Bulletproof? https://thebitcoinmag.com/is-monero-now-bulletproof/2819/

389 Concepcion Guzman. 5 Unique Features of Monero (XMR) That Will Increase Your Financial Privacy and Security. https://steemit.com/cryptocurrency/@concepcionguzman/5-unique-features-of-monero-xmr-that-will-increase-your-financial-privacy-and-security

390 Olga Kharif. Bitcoin Is Being Dropped by Criminals in Favour of Privacy Coins like Monero. https://www.independent.co.uk/news/business/analysis-and-features/bitcoin-latest-updates-price-privacy-coins-cryptocurrency-monero-digital-currency-price-a8137901.html

391 Olga Kharif. Bitcoin Is Being Dropped by Criminals in Favour of Privacy Coins like Monero. https://www.independent.co.uk/news/business/analysis-and-features/bitcoin-latest-updates-price-privacy-coins-cryptocurrency-monero-digital-currency-price-a8137901.html

392 Olga Kharif. Bitcoin Is Being Dropped by Criminals in Favour of Privacy Coins like Monero. https://www.independent.co.uk/news/business/analysis-and-features/bitcoin-latest-updates-price-privacy-coins-cryptocurrency-monero-digital-currency-price-a8137901.html

393 Concepcion Guzman. 5 Unique Features of Monero That Will Increase Financial Privacy and

Security. https://steemit.com/cryptocurrency/@concepcionguzman/5-unique-features-of-monero-xmr-that-will-increase-your-financial-privacy-and-security

394 Monero Stack Exchange. What Advantages Does Monero Offer That Are Not Provided by Other Cryptocurrencies? https://monero.stackexchange.com/questions/2254/what-advantages-does-monero-offer-that-are-not-provided-by-other-cryptocurrencie

395 https://z.cash/team

396 Consensus Systems. What Does Zcash Mean for Ethereum? https://blockgeeks.com/zcash-mean-ethereum/

397 Lukas Schor. On Zero-Knowledge Proofs in Blockchains. https://medium.com/@argongroup/
on-zero-knowledge-proofs-in-blockchains-14c48cfd1dd1

398 Lukas Schor. On Zero-Knowledge Proofs in Blockchains. https://medium.com/@argongroup/
on-zero-knowledge-proofs-in-blockchains-14c48cfd1dd1

399 Peter Yang. Zero-Knowledge Proofs in Blockchain. http://cryptographybuzz.com/zero-knowledge-proofs-in-blockchains/

400 Ben Whittle. The Ultimate Privacy Coin: Monero or Zcash? https://coincentral.com/ultimate-privacy-coin-monero-zcash/

401 Ben Whittle. The Ultimate Privacy Coin: Monero or Zcash? https://coincentral.com/ultimate-privacy-coin-monero-zcash/

402 Alex Lielacher. Best Privacy Coins, Rated and Reviewed for 2018. https://www.bitcoinmarketjournal.com/best-privacy-coins-rated-and-reviewed-for-2018/

403 Chris Wheal. A History of Zcash (ZEC). https://dex.openledger.io/a-history-of-zcash-zec/

404 https://zcoin.io/

405 https://twitter.com/snowden/status/1092827086497239041

406 Alex Lielacher. Best Privacy Coins, Rated and Reviewed for 2018. https://www.bitcoinmarketjournal.com/best-privacy-coins-rated-and-reviewed-for-2018

407 Yogita Khatri. OKEX Korea Delisting All Privacy Coins, Including Monero, Zcash and Dash, as These "Violate" FATF's "Travel Rule". https://www.theblockcrypto.com/post/39724/okex-korea-delisting-all-privacy-coins-including-monero-zcash-and-dash-as-these-violate-fatfs-travel-rule

408 Yogita Khatri. OKEX Korea Delisting All Privacy Coins, Including Monero, Zcash and Dash, as These "Violate" FATF's "Travel Rule". https://www.theblockcrypto.com/post/39724/okex-korea-delisting-all-privacy-coins-including-monero-zcash-and-dash-as-these-violate-fatfs-travel-rule

409 William Foxley. OKEx Korea Reviewing Decision to Delist Privacy Coins Zcash and Dash. https://www.coindesk.com/okex-korea-reviewing-decision-to-delist-privacy-coins-zcash-and-dash

410 Yogita Khatri. OKEX Korea Delisting All Privacy Coins, Including Monero, Zcash and Dash, as These "Violate" FATF's "Travel Rule". https://www.theblockcrypto.com/post/39724/okex-korea-delisting-all-privacy-coins-including-monero-zcash-and-dash-as-these-violate-fatfs-travel-rule

411 Andy Greenberg. The Dark Web's Favorite Currency Is Less Untraceable Than It Seems. https://www.wired.com/story/monero-privacy/

PAGES FROM THE CRYPTO BESTIARIUM

412 Mike Parker. Ripple Is Now Even More Suspicious: Bernanke Aligns with Ripple. https://steemit.com/cryptocurrency/@mikeparker/ripple-is-now-even-more-suspicious-bernanke-aligns-with-ripple

413 Infourminutes.co. White Paper in Four Minutes. https://hackernoon.com/whitepaper-in-four-minutes-ripple-a27103e4d265

414 Mike Orcutt. No, Ripple Isn't the Next Bitcoin. https://www.technologyreview.com/s/609958/no-ripple-isnt-the-next-bitcoin/

415 Mike Orcutt. No, Ripple Isn't the Next Bitcoin. https://www.technologyreview.com/s/609958/no-ripple-isnt-the-next-bitcoin/

416 Stefan Thomas. How We Are Further Decentralizing the XRP Ledger o Bolser Robustness for Enterprise Use. https://ripple.com/insights/how-we-are-further-decentralizing-the-ripple-consensus-ledger-rcl-to-bolster-robustness-for-enterprise-use/

417 Michael Kimani. Ex-Fed Reserve Chair Ben Bernanke Lauds Ripple, Says Bitcoin Will Be Squashed by Governments. https://cryptovest.com/news/ex-fed-reserve-chair-ben-bernanke-lauds-ripple-says-bitcoin-will-be-squashed-by-governments/

418 Jacob J. Former Fed Chairman Ben Bernanke Believes Bitcoin Unlikely to Succeed. https://cointelegraph.com/news/former-fed-chairman-ben-bernanke-believes-bitcoin-unlikely-to-succeed

419 The Analyst Team. What is IOTA? Introduction to MIOTA Token. https://cryptobriefing.com/what-is-iota-introduction-to-miota-token/

420 Victor Lay, Kieran O'Day. Deep Dive Review Into IOTA (August 2018). https://crushcrypto.com/iota-cryptocurrency-deep-dive/

421 TheCoinEconomy. IOTA & the Tangle: The Future Backbone of the IoT. https://hackernoon.com/iota-the-tangle-the-future-backbone-of-the-iot-e7e417d5d86b

422 Markus of Coinmonks. IOTA Expands Industrial Partnerships... https://medium.com/coinmonks/iota-expands-industrial-partnerships-13b6d7145ad0

423 Johann Jungwirth. IOTA & Volkswagen Will Release Blockchain Cars in 2019. https://www.bitguru.co.uk/iota-news/iota-volkswagen-will-release-blockchain-cars-in-2019/

424 Jonnie Emsley. Bosch Doubles Down on IOTA Data Marketplace. https://cryptoslate.com/bosch-doubles-down-on-iota-data-marketplace/

425 https://www.5gspaceappeal.org/the-appeal

426 RFSafe. 5G Network Uses Nearly Same Frequency as Weaponized Crowd Control Systems. https://www.rfsafe.com/5g-network-uses-nearly-same-frequency-as-weaponized-crowd-control-systems/

427 Cabin Talk Youtube channel. Harald Kautz-Vella on 5G and the Wave Salad We Are Exposed To! https://www.youtube.com/watch?v=0r5ofmfHcNI

428 https://www.5gspaceappeal.org/the-appeal The quote refers to the following publication: Hardell L. World Health Organization, radiofrequency radiation and health—a hard nut to crack (review). Int J Oncol. 2017;51:405-413. doi:10.3892/ijo.2017.4046.

429 Dr. Ellis Evans. 5G Telecomm Raidation The Perfect Tool to Mass Modify Human Brain Waves. https://www.wakingtimes.com/2016/09/12/5g-telecomm-radiation-perfect-tool-mass-modify-human-brain-waves/

430 John P. Thomas. 20,000 Satellites for 5G To Be Launched Sending Focused Beams of Intense Microwave Radiation Over Entire Earth. https://www.wakingtimes.com/2019/01/08/20000-satellites-for-5g-to-be-launched-sending-focused-beams-of-intense-microwave-radiation-over-entire-earth/

431 European Space Agency, ESA Youtube channel. Satellite for 5G. https://www.youtube.com/watch?v=30PIO3Keras

432 Michael Alba. 5G In Space? https://www.engineering.com/ElectronicsDesign/Electronics-DesignArticles/ArticleID/17112/5G-in-Space.aspx

433 NASA. Tracers – Clouds and Trails. https://www.nasa.gov/mission_pages/sounding-rockets/tracers/metals.html

434 Zen. NASA Admits Chemtrails. https://www.geoengineeringwatch.org/nasa-admits-chemtrails/

ONE COIN TO RULE THEM ALL?

435 Aaron Hankin. JPM Coin Is Not a Cryptocurrency, Says Crypto Advocacy Group. https://www.marketwatch.com/story/jpm-coin-is-not-a-cryptocurrency-says-crypto-advocacy-group-2019-02-14

436 Aaron Hankin. JPM Coin Is Not a Cryptocurrency, Says Crypto Advocacy Group. https://www.marketwatch.com/story/jpm-coin-is-not-a-cryptocurrency-says-crypto-advocacy-group-2019-02-14

437 Aaron Hankin. JPM Coin Is Not a Cryptocurrency, Says Crypto Advocacy Group. https://www.marketwatch.com/story/jpm-coin-is-not-a-cryptocurrency-says-crypto-advocacy-group-2019-02-14

438 Michael J. de la Merced, Nathaniel Popper. JPMorgan Chase Moves To Be First Big U.S. Bank With Its Own Cryptocurrency. https://www.nytimes.com/2019/02/14/business/dealbook/jpmorgan-cryptocurrency-bitcoin.html

439 Chris Isidore. JPMorgan Is Creating Its Own Cryptocurrency. https://edition.cnn.com/2019/02/14/investing/jpmorgan-jpm-coin-cryptocurrency/index.html

440 Hugh Son. JP Morgan Is Rolling Out the First US Bank-Based Cryptocurrency to Transform Payments Business. https://www.cnbc.com/2019/02/13/jp-morgan-is-rolling-out-the-first-us-bank-backed-cryptocurrency-to-transform-payments-.html

441 Jed Graham. JPM Coin, New JPMorgan Cryptocurrency, Is No Bitcoin. https://www.investors.com/news/jpm-coin-new-jpmorgan-cryptocurrency-blockchain-bitcoin/

442 Marie Huillet. Fed Chairmain: "No One Uses It" - Bitcoin a Speculative Asset Like Gold. https://cointelegraph.com/news/fed-chairman-no-one-uses-it-bitcoin-a-speculative-asset-like-gold

443 Leigh Cuen. Venezuela Isn't the Crypto Use You Want It to Be. https://www.coindesk.com/venezuela-isnt-the-crypto-use-case-you-want-it-to-be

444 Priyeshu Garg. Venezuela Could Set New Precedent for Bitcoin as a Medium of Exchange. https://cryptoslate.com/venezuela-precedent-bitcoin/

445 Genny Díaz. Banco Central de España Afirma que Bitoin No Es Eficiente Como Sistema de Pago. https://www.criptonoticias.com/regulacion/banco-espana-bitcoin-sistema-pago/

446 OMFIF and IBM Blockchain World Wire collaboration. Central Bank Digital Currencies. https://www.omfif.org/media/5415789/ibm-central-bank-digital-currencies.pdf and Genny Díaz. Informe: Bancos Centrales Están Adoptando el Concepto de Monedas Digitales. https://www.criptonoticias.com/banca-seguros/informe-bancos-centrales-estan-adoptando-concepto-monedas-digitales/

447 Craig Wright. Satoshi's Vision: The Art of Bitcoin. Howson Books, 2019

448 Jeremy Wall. Binance: Latest Major Crypto Exchange To Launch OTC Trading. https://www.investinblockchain.com/binance-major-crypto-exchange-launch-otc-trading/

449 Nick Chong. OTC Volume of Bitcoin is Rising: Are Institutions Buying? https://www.newsbtc.com/2019/01/11/otc-volume-of-bitcoin-is-rising-are-institutions-buying/

450 SFOX. 14 Bitcoin OTC brokers you need to know. https://blog.sfox.com/13-bitcoin-otc-brokers-you-need-to-know-67755a1d4ccc

451 Daily Hodl Staff. Vitalik Buterin Sas Ethereum Must Reach 100,000 Transactions Per Second, Bitcoin May Remain Solely a Store of Value. https://dailyhodl.com/2019/03/20/vitalik-buterin-says-ethereum-must-reach-100000-transactions-per-second-bitcoin-may-remain-solely-a-store of-value/

452 World Crypto Network. The Bitcoin News Show #79 – Interview with Andrew DeSantis. https://www.youtube.com/watch?v=YMvI73jJ6uc

453 Craig Wright. Satoshi's Vision. The Art of Bitcoin. Howson Books, 2019

LIBRA HITS THE FAN

454 Aantonop Youtube channel. Andreas Antonopoulos. Libre Not Libra: Facebook's Blockchain Project. https://www.youtube.com/watch?v=7S6506vkth4&t=271s

455 Aantonop Youtube channel. Andreas Antonopoulos. Libre Not Libra: Facebook's Blockchain Project. https://www.youtube.com/watch?v=7S6506vkth4&t=271s

456 Aantonop Youtube channel. Andreas Antonopoulos. Libre Not Libra: Facebook's Blockchain Project. https://www.youtube.com/watch?v=7S6506vkth4&t=271s

457 Josh Constine. Highlights From Facebook's Libra Senate Hearing. https://techcrunch.com/2019/07/16/libra-in-messenger-whatsapp/

458 Ian Shorr. Facebook Libra Cryptocurrency Hearings With Congress Day 2: Watch Here. https://www.cnet.com/news/facebook-libra-cryptocurrency-hearings-with-congress-day-2-watch-here-live/

459 Aantonop Youtube channel. Andreas Antonopoulos. Libre Not Libra: Facebook's Blockchain Project. https://www.youtube.com/watch?v=7S6506vkth4&t=271s

460 Aantonop Youtube channel. Andreas Antonopoulos. Libre Not Libra: Facebook's Blockchain Project. https://www.youtube.com/watch?v=7S6506vkth4&t=271s

461 Aantonop Youtube channel. Andreas Antonopoulos. Libre Not Libra: Facebook's Blockchain Project. https://www.youtube.com/watch?v=7S6506vkth4&t=271s

462 Aantonop Youtube channel. Andreas Antonopoulos. Libre Not Libra: Facebook's Blockchain Project. https://www.youtube.com/watch?v=7S6506vkth4&t=271s

463 Lauren Feiner. Facebook's Libra Cryptocurrency Coalition is Falling Apart as eBay, Visa, Mastercard and Stripe Jump Ship. https://www.cnbc.com/2019/10/11/ebay-drops-out-of-facebook-libra-cryptocurrency-one-week-after-paypal.html

464 Kyle Torpey. Bitcoin's Use In Online Payments Faces A Serious Regulatory Hurdle. https://www.forbes.com/sites/ktorpey/2019/08/06/bitcoins-use-in-online-payments-faces-a-serious-regulatory-hurdle/

465 Kyle Torpey. Bitcoin's Use In Online Payments Faces A Serious Regulatory Hurdle. https://www.forbes.com/sites/ktorpey/2019/08/06/bitcoins-use-in-online-payments-faces-a-serious-regulatory-hurdle/

466 Kyle Torpey. Bitcoin's Use In Online Payments Faces A Serious Regulatory Hurdle. https://www.forbes.com/sites/ktorpey/2019/08/06/bitcoins-use-in-online-payments-faces-a-serious-regulatory-hurdle/

467 PYMNTS. France and Germany Call For Public Crypto, Oppose Libra. https://www.pymnts.com/cryptocurrency/2019/france-germany-oppose-libra-support-public-crypto/

468 E.B. Tucker. Surviving Fedcoin. https://www.caseyresearch.com/daily-dispatch/surviving-fedcoin-2/

469 William M. Peaster. Chinese Central Bank Ramps Up Digital Currency Hires. https://blockonomi.com/chinese-central-bank-ramps-up-digital-currency-hires/

470 William M. Peaster. Chinese Central Bank Ramps Up Digital Currency Hires. https://block-onomi.com/chinese-central-bank-ramps-up-digital-currency-hires/

471 David Pan. China's Congress Passes Cryptography Law, Effective Jan. 1, 2020. https://www.coindesk.com/chinas-congress-passes-cryptography-law-effective-jan-1-2020

472 Daily Hodl Staff. US Banker Calls Digital Currency From US Federal Reserve Bank 'Inevitable'. https://dailyhodl.com/2019/10/03/us-banker-calls-digital-currency-from-us-federal-reserve-bank-inevitable/

473 Wendy McElroy. Fedcoin: The U.S. Will Issue E-Currency That You Will Use. https://news.bitcoin.com/fedcoin-u-s-issue-e-currency/

474 Arnab Shome. Line Launches Its Crypto Exchange in Japan. https://www.financemag-nates.com/cryptocurrency/news/line-launches-its-crypto-exchange-in-japan/

475 Jeff Berwick. The Dollar Vigilante YouTube channel. Facebook Libra Collapsing... Advice for Mark Zuckerberg on Competing With the Monetary Cartel. https://youtu.be/LZRezf_odbk

THE FINANCIAL LEECHING OF THE BITCOIN POWER

476 Sarah Rothrie. A Brief History of Bitcoin Futures and What Comes Next. https://coincen-tral.com/bitcoin-futures/

477 Stephen O'Neal. SEC Postpones VanEck Bitcoin ETF, Yet Again. Should We Expect an Approval in 2019? https://cointelegraph.com/news/sec-postpones-vaneck-bitcoin-etf-yet-again-should-we-expect-an-approval-in-2019

478 Daniel Palmer. VanEck, SolidX to Offer Bitcoin ETF-Like Product to Institutions. https://www.coindesk.com/van-eck-solidx-to-offer-bitcoin-etf-to-institutions-via-sec-exemption-report

479 Daniel Palmer. VanEck, SolidX to Offer Bitcoin ETF-Like Product to Institutions. https://www.coindesk.com/van-eck-solidx-to-offer-bitcoin-etf-to-institutions-via-sec-exemption-report

480 https://www.vaneck.com/institutional/bitcoin-144a/overview

481 Stephen O'Neal. VanEck, SolidX Drop Bitcoin ETF Race, SEC Approval Until 2020 Unlikely. https://cointelegraph.com/news/ vaneck-solidx-drop-bitcoin-etf-sec-race-approval-until-2020-unlikely

482 Nikhilesh De. Bakkt is Finally Launching Its Bitcoin Futures Today. Here's What To Expect. https://www.coindesk.com/bakkt-is-finally-launching-its-bitcoin-futures-today-heres-what-to-expect

483 Jonnie Emsley. Bakkt Bitcoin Futures Launch Volumes 75 Times Smaller Than CME's First Day. https://cryptoslate.com/bakkt-bitcoin-futures-launch-volumes-75-times-smaller-than-cmes-first-day/

484 Jonnie Emsley. Bakkt Bitcoin Futures Launch Volumes 75 Times Smaller Than CME's First

Day. https://cryptoslate.com/bakkt-bitcoin-futures-launch-volumes-75-times-smaller-than-cmes-first-day/

485 Mr_Kristóf. Bakkt Bitcoin Trading Volume Is Horrible! Institutional Investors Don't Care About Bitcoin! https://youtu.be/MtVgRYaxDOY

486 Allen Scott. CME Chairman Admits Bitcoin's Finite Amount Is a Problem. https://bitcoin-ist.com/cme-chairman-admits-bitcoins-finite-amount-is-a-problem/

487 Mr_Kristof YouTube channel. Bakkt Bitcoin Trading Volume Is Horrible! Institutional Investors Don't Care About Bitcoin! https://youtu.be/MtVgRYaxDOY

488 John Boyle's comment on Mr_Kristof's video titled Bakkt Bitcoin Trading Volume Is Horrible! Institutional Investors Don't Care About Bitcoin! https://youtu.be/MtVgRYaxDOY

489 Mr_Kristof YouTube channel. Bakkt Bitcoin Trading Volume Is Horrible! Institutional Investors Don't Care About Bitcoin! https://youtu.be/MtVgRYaxDOY

490 David Pan. Fidelity Digital Assets Opens to All Qualified Investors. https://www.coin-desk.com/fidelity-digital-assets-opens-to-all-qualified-imvestors

491 Alex Lielacher. Bitcoin Options: Where To Trade Them. https://www.bitcoinmarketjour-nal.com/bitcoin-options-trading/

492 CryptoNinja.net. Bakkt Launching New Bitcoin (BTC) Options Contract. https://www.cryptoninjas.net/2019/10/24/bakkt-laumching-new-bitcoin-btc-options-contract/

493 The Crypto Lark YouTube channel. Shock Move by Fed Reveals Crisis...Time to Buy Bitcoin! https://youtu.be/4S1S2s81j3w

494 Joeri Cant. Venezuelan Central Bank is Considering Holding Bitcoin and Ether. https://cointelegraph.com/news/venezuelan-central-bank-is-considering-holding-bitcoin-and-ether

495 Caitlin Long. The Real Story of the Repo Market Meltdown, and What It Means for Bitcoin. https://www.forbes.com/sites/caitlinlong/2019/09/25/the-real-story-of-the-repo-market-meltdown-and-what-it-means-for-bitcoin/

496 Caitlin Long. The Real Story of the Repo Market Meltdown, and What It Means for Bitcoin. https://www.forbes.com/sites/caitlinlong/2019/09/25/the-real-story-of-the-repo-market-meltdown-and-what-it-means-for-bitcoin/

497 Mr_Kristof. IRS knows Bitcoin Will Destroy the USD! I Believe Bitcoin Will Win Regardless. https://youtu.be/kFiiaam3wzA

498 Anna Baydakova. The IRS Just Issued Its First Cryptocurrency Tax Guidance in 5 Years. https://www.coimdesk.com/the-irs-just-issued-its-first-cryptocurrency-tax-guidance-in-5-years

499 Anna Baydakova. The IRS Just Issued Its First Cryptocurrency Tax Guidance in 5 Years. https://www.coimdesk.com/the-irs-just-issued-its-first-cryptocurrency-tax-guidance-in-5-years

500 Brady Dale. Trump Admimistration Popped 2017 Bitcoin Bubble, Ex-CFTC Chair Says. https://www.coindesk.com/trump-admimistration-popped-2017-bitcoin-bubble-ex-cftc-chair-says

501 Brady Dale. Trump Admimistration Popped 2017 Bitcoin Bubble, Ex-CFTC Chair Says. https://www.coindesk.com/trump-admimistration-popped-2017-bitcoin-bubble-ex-cftc-chair-says

502 J. Christopher Giancarlo and Daniel Gorfine. We Sent a Man to the Moon. We Can Send the Dollar to Cyberspace. https://www.wsj.com/articles/we-sent-a-man-to-the-moon-we-can-send-the-dollar-to-cyberspace-11571179923

503 William Suberg. US Congressman Warns: Crypto May 'Displace or Imterfere with Dollar'. https://cointelegraph.com/news/us-congressman-warns-crypto-may-displace-or-interfere-with-dollar

READY OR NOT, TRUTH GOES DIGITAL

504 Leemon Baird. The Swirlds Hashgraph Consensus Algorithm: Fair, Fast, Byzantine Fault Tolerance. http://www.leemon.com/papers/2016b.pdf

505 Project Veritas Staff Report. Current Sr. Google Engineer Goes Public on Camera: Tech Is "Dangerous", "Taking Sides". https://www.projectveritas.com/2019/07/24/current-sr-google-engineer-goes-public-on-camera-tech-is-dangerous-taking-sides/

506 Project Veritas Staff Report. UPDATE: Google Engineer Who Went Public Placed on Administrative Leave. https://www.projectveritas.com/2019/07/25/update-google-engineer-who-went-public-placed-on-administrative-leave/

GRAB 'EM BY THE BITCOINS

507 https://bitcointalk.org/index.php?topic=4430055.0

508 Jasper Hamill. The NSA May Have Helped to Invent Bitcoin, Founder of World's Second Largest Cryptocurrency Ethereum Claims. https://metro.co.uk/2018/06/15/nsa-helped-invent-bitcoin-founder-worlds-second-largest-cryptocurrency-ethereum-claims-7631719/

509 Paddy Baker. Snowden Talks Up Monero and Zcash, but Is Privacy Still Possible? https://cryptobriefing.com/snowdens-crypto-privacy/

510 Faia Youtube channel. BSV Singapore Meetup Ft. Craig Wright & Brendan Lee. https://www.youtube.com/watch?v=rn6HtnrM3tQ

511 Faia Youtube channel. BSV Singapore Meetup Ft. Craig Wright & Brendan Lee. https://www.youtube.com/watch?v=rn6HtnrM3tQ

512 CoinGeek Youtube channel. Craig Wright: Bitcoin Is Not A Cryptocurrency. https://www.youtube.com/watch?v=26LDWnM7qe4

513 CoinGeek Youtube channel. Craig Wright: Bitcoin Is Not A Cryptocurrency.

https://www.youtube.com/watch?v=26LDWnM7qe4

514 CoinGeek Youtube channel. Craig Wright: Bitcoin Is Not A Cryptocurrency.
https://www.youtube.com/watch?v=26LDWnM7qe4

515 Binance. Binance Announces Open Blockchain Project "Venus". https://www.bi-
nance.com/en/support/articles/360032604131

516 Michael K. Spencer. The Fall of Ethereum. https://medium.com/futuresin/the-fall-of-
ethereum-15c4b64467d8

About the Author

Bernadett Keczer is a Hungarian born writer, Quantum Sphere Healing practitioner and Transformational Catalyst. She also writes music for gothic harp.

She studied English and Hungarian linguistics and literature, environmental engineering and politology. Besides, she is a qualified Alternative Movement and Massage Therapist and even had received certification as an aerobics instructor.

Bernadett lives with her telepathic dog.

To get in touch with her and find out what she is up to next, or to be notified when a new book of her is published, please subscribe to her mailing list.

You can connect with me on:

🌐 https://www.createfromyourcore.com

🔗 https://medium.com/renaissance-is-now

🔗 https://discord.gg/5wYkv9H

Subscribe to my newsletter:

✉ https://www.createfromyourcore.com/signup

Printed in Great Britain
by Amazon

33198139R00196